THE ETHICAL SOUNDSCAPE

CULTURES OF HISTORY

CULTURES OF HISTORY

Nicholas Dirks, Series Editor

The death of history, reported at the end of the twentieth century, was clearly premature. It has become a hotly contested battleground in struggles over identity, citizenship, and claims of recognition and rights. Each new national history proclaims itself as ancient and universal, while the contingent character of its focus raises questions about the universality and objectivity of any historical tradition. Globalization and the American hegemony have created cultural, social, local, and national backlashes. Cultures of History is a new series of books that investigates the forms, understandings, genres, and histories of history, taking history as the primary text of modern life and the foundational basis for state, society, and nation.

Shail Mayaram, *Against History, Against State: Counterperspectives from the Margins*

Tapati Guha-Thakurta, *Monuments, Objects, Histories: Institutions of Art in Colonial and Postcolonial India*

THE ETHICAL SOUNDSCAPE

{ *Cassette Sermons and Islamic Counterpublics* }

CHARLES HIRSCHKIND

COLUMBIA UNIVERSITY PRESS   NEW YORK

Columbia University Press
Publishers Since 1893
New York   Chichester, West Sussex
Copyright © 2006 Columbia University Press
All rights reserved

Library of Congress Cataloging-in-Publication Data

Hirschkind, Charles.   The ethical soundscape :
cassette sermons and Islamic counterpublics / Charles Hirschkind.
p. cm.—(Cultures of history)
Includes bibliographical references (p.   ) and index.
ISBN 0–231–13818–0 (cloth : alk. paper)—ISBN 0–231–51088–8 (electronic)
1. Daʿwah (Islam) 2. Religious awakening—Islam. 3. Islamic sermons, Arabic.
4. Communication—Religious aspects—Islam. 5. Audiocassettes
6. Islamic fundamentalism—Egypt. 7. Islam and politics—Egypt.
I. Title. II. Series. BP170.85.H57 2006
297.7′4—dc22   2006007599

Columbia University Press books are printed on permanent
and durable acid-free paper.

To Nameer and Dominic

CONTENTS

ACKNOWLEDGMENTS

THIS BOOK, from its inception to its current form, bears the imprint of a number of interlocutors, friends, and colleagues whose generous support I want to acknowledge briefly. I wish to express my deepest gratitude to Talal Asad, under whose care and intellectual guidance this book has made its way in the world. His intellectual rigor, philosophical erudition, and searing critiques of normative modes of thinking in anthropology present a formidable model of scholarship that has nourished me intellectually ever since I first embarked on this academic journey. The doors his scholarship and way of thinking have opened for me will most certainly guide me in any future project that I undertake; here I can only gesture to the immense debt I owe to Talal.

The research project animating this book was initially conceived at the New School for Social Research in New York and developed further while I was writing my dissertation at Johns Hopkins University in Baltimore. I would like to thank Steve Caton, Kirstie McClure, Gyan Prakash, and Donald Scott for their comments and engagements at various stages of this project—all of which informed the final form this book has taken. I am particularly grateful to Hussein Agrama and Armando Salvatore who, in their engagement with this work over the years, have helped me clarify and articulate a number of crucial themes at the center of this book. While I was a postdoctoral fellow at the University of Toronto (Canada), Janice Boddy, Michael Lambek, and Anne Meneley not only commented on various chapters of this book but also provided a model for how a community of scholars might challenge one to think beyond the confines of one's own thought. I remain deeply grateful to them for this gift. My gratitude also extends to my colleagues at the University of Wisconsin-Madison, particularly Charles Cohen, Ken George, Sharon Hutchinson, and Kirin Narayan, all of whom offered me their collegiality, friendship, and intellectual support while I was teaching in the Department of Anthropology and the Religious Studies Program.

My discussion of the contested place accorded to the subject of hearing in modernist accounts benefited from the comments of Veit Erlmann, Penelope Gouk, and Hillel Schwartz at the Wenner-Gren workshop organized on the topic of "Hearing Culture" in Oaxaca, Mexico, in April 2001. Similarly my extended participation (during fall 2002) in the working group on the study of religion and media at the University of Amsterdam proved to be a crucial time to think through many of the arguments about listening presented in this book. My gratitude extends to Birgit Meyer (the convener of this working group), Rafael Sanchez, and Patricia Spyer for their inspiring interlocutions. Finally, another institutional forum where my work was presented and discussed, from which I learned enormously, was the Late Liberalism Project at the University of Chicago; my thanks to Lauren Berlant, Patchen Markell, Elizabeth Povinelli, and Candace Vogler for their critical reading of the chapter on counterpublics.

Numerous friends and colleagues have extended me generosity and critical support over the years, and I wish to acknowledge them here. Thanks to Marlene Hidalgo, William Glover, Ted Swedenberg, Hatem al-Atai, Donald Moore, Zahir al-Ghafiri, David Scott, Stefania Pandolfo, Farina Mir, Walter Armbrust, Lawrence Cohen, Tanya Baker, Gregory Starrett, Martina Rieker, John Bowen, Bruce Lincoln, and Webb Keane. I am also grateful to Noah Salomon, Navid Fozi-Abivard, Ruth Mas, and Sylvia Sellers-Garcia for the research assistance they provided in the preparation of this monograph. No book is ever complete without the critical roles played by a competent editor and copy editor: for this I owe a special debt of gratitude to Peter Dimock and Michael Haskell at Columbia University Press and Krista Faries for her careful editing of the manuscript.

This book rests on research conducted under the generous support provided by the Social Science Research Council and the Wenner-Gren Foundation for Anthropological Research. In the initial formulation of this project, I was supported by the Woodrow Wilson Foundation's Charlotte Newcombe Dissertation Write-up Fellowship and later the Rockefeller Foundation Postdoctoral Fellowship at the University of Toronto. A grant from the American Council of Learned Societies (during the academic year 2002–03) made it possible to take time off from teaching so as to expand the book to its current form. I also received support from the Sultan Program of the Center for Middle Eastern Studies at the University of California, Berkeley.

Finally, last but not the least, I wish to express my deep gratitude to the people I worked with in Cairo, Egypt, over two stints of fieldwork between 1994 and 1997. Foremost among them are all those individuals who will remain unnamed (due to reasons of confidentiality) but who were crucial to my ability to think through the thicket of assumptions and reductionisms that haunt any engagement with the subject of sermons and their role in crafting a political community. Without their insights and incisive observations, this book would never have been possible. Then there are a number of friends in Egypt (whose names I *can* mention) who made my intellectual and personal journey through Cairo a pleasurable one. In this regard, I wish to thank Ayman Bakr, Said Samir, Saif Hamdan, Ashraf Ibrahim, Abdel Wahab al-Messiri, and Warda Yusuf.

The person who has taught me the most about listening with the heart is Saba Mahmood. This book has blossomed under her critical insight and tender care, and whatever fruit it has born belongs as much to her as me. Her love and companionship over these years have been the most wonderful of gifts.

NOTE ON TRANSCRIPTION

I N ACCORDANCE with the guidelines of Columbia University Press, I have adopted a highly simplified system for transcribing words and phrases in Modern Standard and colloquial Arabic. All diacritical marks have been omitted except for the ayn and hamza. In the case of proper names, honorific titles, and Arabic words that are found in an unabridged English dictionary, I have also avoided the use of diacritical marks. I have deferred to transcriptions that have been used in standard bibliographic reference texts and to the styles that have been chosen by authors for their own names when these have appeared in English-language publications. English-language titles that incorporate Arabic words retain the original style of transcription.

THE ETHICAL SOUNDSCAPE

{ 1 }

INTRODUCTION

---

*I climb into a taxi cab just outside of the Ramses Mosque in the city center. The driver steers onto the busy thoroughfare of Ramses Street, and listens. A sermon struggles out through the frayed speakers and dust-encrusted electronics of a tape player bolted under the taxi's dashboard, just beneath a velvet-covered box holding a small Quran. The voice careens and crescendos along its rhetorical pathways, accompanied by the accumulated vibration, static, hiss, and squeak inherited from the multiple copies that have preceded the one now in the machine. Street noise picked up by the microphone continually rises up to engulf the speaking voice, redoubling the sonic jumble of horns, shouts, the rattles and pops of rusted exhaust pipes now buffeting the car. In the back seat, two friends joke and laugh together, their bodies pushed and pulled as the car proceeds through the congested alleyways, jerking, braking, jumping forward. Billboards advertising computer parts, soft drinks, and the latest films loom above the storefronts and crowded sidewalks. The driver hits the horn at a car attempting to cut in front of him, as the voice on the tape intones a Quranic verse on the inescapability of death: "Every soul tastes death . . ." (*kullu nafs dha'iqa al-mawt). *A wave of cries from the mosque assembly pierce through the background noise and the thick layer of reverb, the driver's lips lightly and inaudibly tracing the contours of the words "There is no God but the one God," as he accelerates ahead of the car seeking to pass him. One of the men in the back stops his conversation to comment: "That preacher must be Saudi. They're the ones who really know how to scare you." The recorded voice begins a series of supplications as the cab passengers go back to their previous conversation and* *the driver adjusts the volume knob: "May God lessen the death throes for us. May God light our graves. May God protect us on Judgment Day." The speakers rattle as the crowd roars "Amin" after each supplication. The taxi stops at the entrance to the 26th of July Bridge, named in celebration of Egypt's 1973 war with Israel, and the two passengers pay the driver and get out. Merging back into traffic, the driver heads for the onramp to the bridge that will take him to the upper-middle-class suburb of Muhandesin. As he approaches the ramp, the voice on the tape is asking, "How will you feel when the grave closes tightly around you from all of the evil deeds you have done?" The bass line to a Michael Jackson hit sweeps in from the open window of a passing car and quickly fades away. "C'mon shaykh, get to the three questions," the driver implores as he accelerates, anxious for the scene of divine interrogation that he knows from experience will soon arrive. Heading over the bridge, he is still listening.*

THIS BOOK is a study of a popular Islamic media form that has had a profound effect on the configuration of religion, politics, and community in the Middle East. As a key element in the technological scaffolding of what is called the Islamic Revival (*al-Sahwa al-Islamiyya*), the cassette sermon has become an omnipresent background of daily urban life in most Middle Eastern cities, accompanying and punctuating the mundane toils of men and women like the taxi driver whose journey through Cairo and the hereafter I began with above. As I will argue, the contribution of this aural media to shaping the contemporary moral and political landscape of the Middle East lies not simply in its capacity to disseminate ideas or instill religious ideologies but in its effect on the human sensorium, on the affects, sensibilities, and perceptual habits of its vast audience. The soundscape produced through the circulation of this medium animates and sustains the substrate of sensory knowledges and embodied aptitudes undergirding a broad revival movement within contemporary Islam. From its inception in the twentieth century, this movement has centered on a critique of the existing structures of religious and secular authority. For those who participate in the movement, the moral and political direction of contemporary Muslim societies cannot be left to politicians, religious scholars, or militant activists but must be decided upon and enacted collectively by ordinary Muslims in the course of their normal daily activities. The notions of individual and collective responsibility that this movement has given rise to have come to be embodied in a wide array of institutions, media forms, and practices of public sociability. In doing so, they have changed the political geography of the Middle East in ways that have vast implications for the future of the region. This book examines the contribution of the cassette-recorded sermon to the revival movement and to the transformations it has engendered. Although the listening practices I explore inhabit a counter-history—counter to the modernist formations of politics and religion and the ideologies that sustain and legitimate them—this history nonetheless exerts forcible claims on the contemporary, and thus on the futures imaginable from its shores.

Islamic cassette sermons are commonly associated with the underworld of militants and radical preachers, a world quite distinct from one centered in the popular quarters of Cairo that I will describe in this book. Turn to any recent news item about a violent attack undertaken by Muslim radicals and chances are that there among the artifacts left behind by the perpetrators lies a taped sermon, inciting, propagandizing, working its insidious causality. "Bin Laden's Low-Tech Weapon," as a recent *New York Times* article dubs this media form, "well suited to underground political communication . . . easy to use and virtually impossible for governments to control" (Nunberg 2004). This menacing image of the cassette sermon as a symbol of Islamic fanaticism goes back to the 1979 Iranian Revolution, when the circulation of Ayatollah Khomeini's recorded missives played a key role in the mobilizations leading up to the overthrow of the Shah (Mohammedi and Mohammedi 1994).[1] The Islamic cassette resurfaced again in 1993 at the trial of Shaykh Omar Abdul Rahman, the Egyptian cleric convicted of inciting and conspiring with the Muslim radicals who undertook the first attack on the World Trade Center. The prosecution relied heavily on Abdul Rahman's recorded sermons in making its case.[2] Since then, cassette sermons have appeared again and again among the personal effects of Muslim militants gathered up by investigators in the wake of an arrest or attack. "The cassette tapes tossed casually in a cardboard box would normally not arouse too much suspicion," an Australian journalist reports, "It was these recordings which the suicide bomber who detonated a massive car bomb outside the Australian Embassy last month and the members of his group listened to and learned from in the past year" (Wockner 2004). At once a tool of ideological indoctrination and a vehicle for the transmission of militant directives, cassettes, it would seem, are to fundamentalist Islam what the press was to the bourgeois public sphere of the European Enlightenment—its media form par excellence.

Scholars of contemporary Islam have also alerted us to the central role of the cassette sermon within fundamentalist or radical Islam. The following comment by a well-known investigator of Islamic militancy echoes popular journalistic accounts:

> Since Ayatollah Khomeini's movement in Iran in the mid-1970s, the cassette has played a crucial role in the spread, survival, and success of fundamentalist Islamic movements. Tapes have such an important role because in the absence of a Comintern-style hierarchical structure, they constitute a resilient web that holds together a plethora of local movements and groups, operating mostly within national borders. The constant flow of tapes in the area from Afghanistan to Morocco knits like-minded Muslims into a larger whole. Indeed, tapes even flow into Europe and North America.
>
> (SIVAN 1995:13)

In this view, it is the cassette's capillary motion, its ability to proliferate beneath the radar of law enforcement, that has rendered this media form so useful to the task of international Islamic insurgency. The ominous web that cassette technology weaves—able to "flow," as this author warns, even across the borders of Europe and North America—recalls the hydra-headed image of al-Qaeda described by Western security agencies, with its loose network of hate-filled conspirators.

In this book I take issue with many of the assumptions and judgments through which the image of the militant or, to use more recent vocabulary, "the terrorist," has come to be sutured with the phenomenon of Islamic media and especially with the cassette sermon. Apart from the fact that the vast majority of these tapes do not espouse a militant message, listening to cassette sermons is a common and valued activity for millions of ordinary Muslims around the world, men and women who hold regular jobs, study at the university, send their kids to public schools, and worry about the future of their communities. As I will describe in the chapters that follow, for almost all of those who listen to them, these tapes are not part of a program of radical mobilization but, instead, part of a complex ethical and political project whose scope and importance cannot be contained within the neat figure of the militant or terrorist. Islamic sermon tapes have helped craft and give expression to a religious sensibility moored in a set of ethical and social problems whose rationale deserves a serious engagement by anyone concerned with the future of Muslim societies or, for that matter, with the much-espoused goal of "promoting democracy" in the Middle East. To read the cassette sermon primarily as a technology of fundamentalism and militancy reduces the enormous complexity of the lifeworld enabled by this medium, forcing it to fit into the narrow confines of a language of threat, fear, rejection, and irrationality.

This should not be taken to mean, of course, that these popular cassette media are devoid of political content. On the contrary, cassette sermons frequently articulate a fierce critique of the nationalist project, with its attendant lack of democracy and accountability among the ruling elites of the Muslim world. The form of public discourse within which this critique takes place, however, is not oriented toward militant political action or the overthrow of the state. Rather, such political commentary gives direction to a normative ethical project centered upon questions of social responsibility, pious comportment, and devotional practice. In addition, the styles of use that characterize this media form also bear the imprint of popular entertainment media and some listeners intersperse sermon and music tapes in their listening habits. These diverse strands that are conjoined in Islamic cassette media—the political, the ethical, and the aesthetic—at times sit in some tension with one another, provoking intense debate and contestation among their consumers about issues ranging from the appropriate use of such media to broader questions about the ethical and political bases upon which the future of the community should be established.

Much of the scholarly literature on contemporary Islam centers on the question, "Is the Islamic Revival movement compatible with democracy?" While I do discuss forms of public reason and critique that show a clear debt to democratic thinking and its institutional norms, my interest in these forms extends beyond the question of their relationship to that particular tradition of political thought. The line of investigation I pursue, in this regard, reflects my conviction that the analytical standpoint afforded by the notion of democracy is inadequate for grasping the articulations of politics, ethics, and religion in postcolonial contexts like Egypt, and for assessing the possibilities of social and political justice they may enfold. As scholars of postcolonialism have increasingly brought to our attention, the abstract principle of popular sovereignty stands in a complex and often contradictory relation to the norms and regulatory institutions of the modern nation-state—to the moral and political disciplines that Foucault refers to as technologies of governmentality.[3] Practices of democratic political participation cannot be understood solely by reference to the formal rights enjoyed by legally defined citizens, nor by reference to the democratic culture that such rights are understood to engender. The conditions of citizenship that allow for the development and exercise of democratic prerogatives also depend upon the techniques of social disciplines—the institutional networks of welfare, education, health, religion, and so on—through which the actual capacities of citizens are fashioned.[4] In this light, even to begin to think about what a democratic *practice* might look like in a context such as postcolonial Egypt requires careful attention to the complex and contingent linkages between discourses of collective agency and the specific forms of associational life, community, and authority within which those discourses are deployed.

THE POLITICS OF SOUND

From the inception of the practice in the late 1960s and early 1970s, cassette-sermon audition has been an important and integral part of the Islamic Revival. While this movement encompasses a wide variety of phenomena, from political parties to underground militant organizations, in Egypt its broadest section has always remained grounded in grassroots efforts to revitalize Islamic forms of knowledge, pedagogy, comportment, and sociability.[5] As a result of this movement, many in Egypt from across the class spectrum, and particularly younger people, have increasingly found it important to deepen their knowledge of the Quran and the multiple disciplines it mediates, to participate in mosque study groups, to acquire competence in preaching and recitation techniques, and, more generally, to abide by the dictates of what they consider to be virtuous Muslim conduct in both their religious and nonreligious activities.

The effects of this movement are evident throughout Egypt but most strikingly and pervasively in the popular quarters of Cairo's lower-middle and lower classes, where a renewed concern with Islam is visible in everything from dress styles to mosque attendance to the prevalence of Islamic welfare organizations.[6] Indeed, networks of Islamic charitable, service, educational, and medical associations, many of them directly affiliated with local mosques, have increasingly proliferated in such popular quarters and have further enhanced the function of mosques as centers of neighborhood life (see chapter 2). These developments have been accompanied by the creation of what might be called Islamic soundscapes, ways of reconfiguring urban space acoustically through the use of Islamic media forms. Rooted in this amalgam of forms of association, practice, learning, and sensibility, the Islamic Revival has exerted a profound effect on Egypt as well as other Middle Eastern societies over the last few decades. Its paradigmatic media form is the cassette sermon.

In Cairo, where I spent a year and a half exploring this common media practice, cassette-recorded sermons of popular Muslim preachers, or *khutaba'* (sing. *khatib*), have become a ubiquitous part of the contemporary social landscape. The sermons of well-known orators spill into the street from loudspeakers in cafes, the shops of tailors and butchers, the workshops of mechanics and TV repairmen; they accompany passengers in taxis, minibuses, and most forms of public transportation; they resonate from behind the walls of apartment complexes, where men and women listen alone in the privacy of their homes after returning home from the factory, while doing housework, or together with acquaintances from school or office, invited to hear the latest sermon from a favorite preacher. Outside most of the larger mosques, following Friday prayer, thriving tape markets are crowded with people looking for the latest sermon from one of Egypt's well-known *khutaba'* or a hard-to-find tape from one of Jordan's prominent mosque leaders. The popularity of sermon tapes has given public prominence to these orators that the Egyptian state, despite its attempts to silence such figures through rigid censorship policies, has been able to do little about.

During my stay in Egypt, I spent much of my time meeting both with the *khutaba'* who produced sermon tapes and with young people who listened to them on a regular basis. Ibrahim was one of the men who would often take time to listen to sermon tapes with me and explain their significance. A recent graduate of Cairo University now working for a small publishing company, Ibrahim had first become an enthusiast of sermon tapes while he was a student. He would often listen to them when he came home from work, either alone in his room or together with his younger sister and his parents. His sister, Huda, a university student herself at the time, also greatly appreciated cassette sermons and would frequently bring home new tapes she had borrowed from friends at school. As her brother had when he was a student, Huda participated in a study group at the university in which she and other students would sit and discuss current issues and events they considered germane to their lives as Muslim men and women. Like many of the young Egyptians who make up the backbone of the Islamic Revival, the siblings both condemned the violent tactics of Egypt's militant Islamic groups while agreeing with many of their social and political critiques. For both brother and sister, and many others like them, cassette sermons were at once entertaining, politically informative, educational, and ethically nourishing, a media form consonant with the challenge of living as a Muslim in today's world.

This book explores the practice of listening to such taped sermons and the forms of public life this practice serves to uphold in contemporary Egypt. In the popular neighborhoods of Cairo, sermon tapes are part of the acoustic architecture of a distinct moral vision, animating and sustaining the ethical sensibilities that enable ordinary Muslims to live in accord with what they consider to be God's will. Recorded and rerecorded, passing through worn-out electronics, bustling crowds, and noisy streets, the vocal performances resonate both within the sensorium of sensitive listeners and outside, around them and between them. In doing so, they create the sensory conditions of an emergent ethical and political lifeworld, with its specific patterns of behavior, sensibility, and practical reasoning. To call this lifeworld "fundamentalist," to chalk it up to the contortions of the religious mind in a secular age, misses the point of this ethicopolitical project. The reduction enacted by such terms blinds us to a variety of ambitions, goals, and aspirations, foremost among them the desire on the part of ordinary Muslims to live in accord with the demands of Islamic piety within a context of rapidly changing social, political, and technological conditions. As I show in chapter 4, this attempt entails the creation of new discursive forms for collectively arguing about and acting upon the conditions of social and political life. The emergent public arena articulated by the circulation of cassette-recorded sermons connects Islamic traditions of ethical discipline to practices of deliberation about the common good, the duties of Muslims in their status as national citizens, and the future of the greater Islamic community (the *umma*). These deliberative practices are not oriented toward *politics* as it is conventionally understood: their purpose is not to influence the formation of state policy or to mobilize voting blocs behind party platforms. Rather, the activities that constitute the public arena I describe are political in a way close to the sense Hannah Arendt (1958) gives to the term: the activities of ordinary citizens who, through the exercise of their agency in contexts of public interaction, shape the conditions of their collective existence. As conceived by its participants, this arena constitutes that space of communal reflexivity and action understood as necessary for perfecting and sustaining the totality of practices upon which an Islamic society depends.

To explore this lifeworld requires that we confront the inadequacies of such binaries as moral/political, disciplinary/deliberative, and emotion/

reason, that have shaped our normative understandings of both political life and the public sphere wherein aspects of that life are explicitly thematized and worked upon. Indeed, one of the central arguments of this book is that the affects and sensibilities honed through popular media practices such as listening to cassette sermons are as infrastructural to politics and public reason as are markets, associations, formal institutions, and information networks.[7] My analysis, in this sense, follows upon a growing recognition by scholars that the forms of thinking and reasoning that constitute our political discourses are profoundly indebted to evaluative dispositions outside the purview of consciousness, to what political theorist William Connolly refers to as "visceral modes of appraisal" (Connolly 1999). This book is a study of the contribution of a popular media practice to the fashioning of such modes of appraisal, and of the religious and political constellations this practice sustains within Egypt today.

THE VIRTUE OF SERMONS

The practice of listening to sermons that I will explore over the following chapters is grounded first and foremost in a recognition and elaboration of the ethical and therapeutic virtues of the ear. From early in the development of Islam, sermon audition has been identified as essential to the cultivation of the sensitive heart that allows one to hear and embody in practice the ethical sensibilities undergirding moral action. Beyond the cognitive task of learning rules and procedures, listeners hone those affective-volitional dispositions, ways of the heart, that both attune the heart to God's word and incline the body toward moral conduct. Although sermons retain this ethical function within contemporary Muslim societies, listening to them now takes place in a social and political context increasingly shaped by modern structures of secular governance, on the one hand, and by styles of consumption and culture linked to a mass media of global extension, on the other. As I explore in chapter 2, modern styles of political oratory and popular media entertainment have redefined the discursive conditions of sermon practice and thus the sermon's relationship both to the institutions of national life and to transnational forms of Islamic association and community.

The ear of today's sermon-tape listener is one in tune with the instruments of modernity: an ear accustomed to the cacophony of Cairo's urban soundscape; an ear that requires background noise, the murmur of electronically produced sound, even in moments of private repose or reflection. According to the sermon listeners I lived and worked with, tapes allow a relaxed attentiveness from which one can nonetheless expect an ethical therapeutics, a cathartic and purifying operation on the soul, a strengthening of the will, and the ability to resist what in some traditions of Islam are called "the devil's whispers." As opposed to television, through which one falls into the "animality of instincts," tapes provide a sonorous environment where the nourishing, transformative power of ethical speech works to improve the conditions of one's heart, fortifying the moral sensibilities that, in accord with Islamic ethical traditions, incline toward right actions. Tapes may be listened to alone in the relative silence of one's bedroom or in the aurally saturated environment of Cairo's congested streets. Both of these moments of audition are understood to contribute, if in qualitatively distinct ways, to the honing of an ethically responsive sensorium: the requisite sensibilities that many of those engaging in cassette-sermon listening see as enabling them to live as devout Muslims in a world increasingly ordered by secular rationalities. I explore the affective and sensory dimension of this style of modern ethical listening in chapter 3.

Insomuch as the cassette sermon conjoins an ethical exercise with political debate and popular entertainment, it is an exemplary form of modern mass communication and social discipline.[8] Traditionally, the Friday sermon occurs within a highly structured spatial and temporal frame, as a duty upon the Muslim community as established in the exemplary practices of the Prophet.[9] As an obligatory component of Muslim weekly routine, the *khatib*'s performance anchors its authority in its location and timing, in the *khatib*'s competent enactment of a tradition-required role as established within the instituted practices of Muslim societies. During the initial years of their use during the late 1960s and early 1970s, taped sermons permitted an extension and replication of this performance but remained beholden to it, a mere supplement to a long-standing Islamic oratorical form. Sermon speech was now displaced outside its assigned locus in the mosque but only as a re-presentation of an original founding performance to which it referred. However, with the increasing popularity of such tapes, the development of tape markets, and new practices of listening, association, and commentary, taped sermons have become increasingly independent from the mosque performances that they reproduce: they now constitute a new signifying practice, one oriented to the emergent forms of ethical and political community being forged by the Islamic Revival.

Even before the use of cassettes, the sermon's capacity to serve as a vehicle of political contestation had already been exploited by Muslim activists in Egypt from early in the twentieth century, a trend that only increased following independence in 1952. As in other postcolonial states, in Egypt the process of recruiting citizens into the structures of national political life produced expectations and participatory demands before the administrative, ideological, and security apparatuses that could accommodate these demands had been fully developed. Given the state's complete monopoly on all television and radio broadcasting in postcolonial Egypt,[10] and strict censorship policies that severely limit unofficial viewpoints in the press, sermons became one of the critical sites for the expression of those demands engendered by political modernization, especially among those ill-versed in the literacy of newsprint (see chapter 4 for a more expansive discussion of this point).

Since the 1970s, as challenges to the Egyptian state increasingly came to be articulated in the languages and concepts of Islam and circulated in popular media forms, the *khutaba'* of the revival movement began to experiment with styles of sermon oratory more flexible to the modes of attention and styles of consumption characteristic of a modern listener. These rhetorical innovations, which I analyze in chapter 5, combine classical sermon elements with languages and narrative forms rooted in such diverse genres as modern political oratory, television dramas, radio news broadcasts, and cinematic montage. The resulting synthesis (or rather syntheses, as no single form has ever entirely eclipsed the others) ushered in a new authoritative Islamic discourse grounded in the sensibilities and habits of concentration and attention of the modern Egyptian individual: one nurtured on popular media, trained in the linguistic competencies of the secular national school system, and incorporated into the bureaucracies of a state fashioned in the image of a liberal-pluralist democracy.

Sermon tapes have provided one of the means by which Islamic ethical traditions have been recalibrated to a new political and technological order, to its rhythms, noise, its forms of pleasure and boredom, but also to its political incitements, its call to citizenly participation. These tapes now play a key mediatory role within an expanding arena of popular Islamic argumentation and deliberation among ordinary Egyptian Muslims, what I describe in chapter 4 as an "Islamic counterpublic." The sensibilities and affects cultivated by sermon listeners contribute to and find expression within this form of public life and its associated styles of speech, gesture, and sociability. From the 1970s onward, this public arena has increasingly defined and shaped the attitudes, interests, and modes of appraisal of an Egyptian Muslim citizen.

One of the people who shaped my understanding of this practice of ethical listening and its contribution to contemporary Islam in Egypt was Muhammad Subhi, a *khatib* from whom I took lessons in the art of preaching during most of the year and a half I spent in Cairo. Muhammad worked part-time for the Ministry of Religious Affairs and often spent his Fridays delivering sermons at government mosques in the small towns outside of Cairo. He had long had the ambition of writing a manual for preachers, and when he heard I was looking for someone who might guide me in studying the rhetorical styles of some of Egypt's more popular *khutaba'*, he suggested that the two projects might be combined. He would analyze aspects of sermon rhetoric with me, on the one hand, while culling from those analyses a set of guidelines that would be useful to other preachers, on the other. Having agreed upon this arrangement, we began a program of listening to the recorded sermons of Egypt's most well known Islamic orators, unpacking and comparing them in many of their rhetorical, doctrinal, social, and political dimensions. These discussions often took us beyond sermon practice itself into such issues as the role of media in the contemporary Islamic Revival, the key points of intersection and divergence among the various currents that were shaping this movement, or the reconfiguration of Islamic authority in modern Egypt and its effect on traditions of Islamic practice.

One of the things that struck me during our listening sessions was the particular emphasis Muhammad placed on the rhetorical and stylistic elements of the taped performances, such as tonal qualities of voice, modulations of affect, rhythmic structure, and so on. Contrary to my expectations, Muhammad's concern for these features of sermon oratory did not stem from their instrumentality in relation to the act of persuasion, their ability to sway an audience in favor of a *khatib*'s argument. Indeed, as I noted early on during our meetings, many of the cassette sermons we listened to did not conform to a syllogistic model, the positing of an argument followed by the reasons warranting its acceptance. Rather, Muhammad's ear focused on the way the *khatib*'s passional rhetoric might move a listener not only to give his or her assent to a proposition but also to enact the ethical attitudes and sensibilities given expression in the sermon speech. For example, at times Muhammad would find fault with the argument of a *khatib* on doctrinal or political grounds but would judge the tape valuable on the basis of the quality of the sincerity, humility, and pious fear given vocal embodiment by the speaker. Moreover, Muhammad's own appreciation of and response to these qualities were not purely intellectual or cognitive: in the course of listening to a sermon, he would continuously give expression to the sermon's ethical movements through facial expressions, postural shifts, subtle gestures of the hand, even his breathing. The more I worked with Muhammad, the more I came to appreciate the unique musicality of sermon discourse, with its crescendos, andantes, and sotto voce passages, performed not only by the *khatib* but by the listener as well. As I argue in this book, this musicality is not an aesthetic gloss applied to a discursive content but a necessary condition for sermonic speech and for ethical action more generally, as the expressive repertoires learned through repeatedly listening to such tapes were integral to the forms of sociability and practical reasoning of many Egyptian Muslims.

LISTENING AND MODERNITY

There are a variety of obstacles that one must confront when analyzing an object as overdetermined as the Islamic cassette sermon. I alluded earlier to the trope of fundamentalism, and the series of reductionisms it enables, as one such impediment. While the association of Islamic sermons with militancy and fundamentalism is a more recent invention, a far more pervasive and longstanding obstacle to the analysis of homiletic speech owes to the way listening, as a perceptual mode, has been valorized and positioned within modernity's regime of the senses. While historians have become increasingly cautious about accounts of modernity that posit a fundamental shift from the dominance of the ear to that of the eye, it is widely recognized that the politics, ethics, and epistemologies that defined the Enlightenment project were deeply entwined with a set of assumptions regarding the relative value of the senses.[11] As a vast scholarship has documented, primary among these assumptions was a judgment concerning the superiority of vision over hearing. In contrast to the distance maintained between the eye and its objects of perception, listening was seen by its Enlightenment critics to involve the self's immersion within a sound from without, an engulfment that threatens the independence and integrity that grounds the masculine spectatorial consciousness. As evident in one of it meanings, that of *heeding*, listening was understood to require a certain passivity on the part of the subject as a condition of receptivity, an act of self-subordination to another of the kind that Immanuel Kant condemned as immaturity (Kant 1998). While poetry for Kant escapes this condemnation due to its uselessness, its complete detachment from any purpose exterior to it that would necessarily corrupt its purity, oratory—enmeshed in the world of interests, desires, motives and power—can only distort and is thus deserving only of derision:

> I must confess to the pure delight which I have ever been afforded by a beautiful poem; whereas the reading of the best speech of a Roman forensic orator, a modern parliamentary debater, or a preacher, has invariably been mingled with an unpleasant sense of disapproval of an insidious art that knows how, in matters of moment, to move men like machines to a judgment that must lose all its weight with them upon calm reflection.
>
> (KANT 1955:I.II.53)

For Enlightenment critics of the ear such as Kant, the very phenomenological structure of the act of listening came to be seen as a danger to the autonomy of the enlightened liberal subject, and therefore both politically and epistemologically suspect. For such critics, it is only the withering away of "the spiritual sense," as hearing has often been described, that ensured the disenchantment of the universe, thereby securing the possibility of reason's ascendancy (see de Certeau 1982; Schmidt 2000).

Anthropologists have also contributed to this modernist narrative on the pitfalls of the ear. Early practitioners of the discipline, for example, charted the passage southward from Europe to the Middle East and beyond as a journey from the rationality of vision to the mechanics of sonority, descending—further south—to the animality of the lower senses, taste, smell, and touch, in this order.[12] For nineteenth-century European explorers and anthropologists, Egypt, mired in sound and ears, was a privileged site for examining the weaknesses of the auditory sense. Among the observations made by European visitors to the Middle East in this period, one of the more common concerned a perceived excess of sound, gesture, and bodily movement within Muslim intellectual and spiritual practices. Islamic pedagogical techniques of listening, recitation, and memorization and the devotional repertoires of patterned gesture all displayed a sensuality and a mechanical, automatic character incongruous with practices of erudition and pious contemplation. As one nineteenth-century British visitor to Alexandria noted upon observing study at a Quran school,

> While studying, or rather learning to repeat, their lessons, each boy declaims his portion of the Quran aloud at the same time, rocking his body to and fro, in order, according to their theory, to assist the memory; and as everyone

seems desirous of drowning the voices of his companions, the din produced
by so many shrill discordant notes reminds one of the "labourers of Babel."

(ST. JOHN 1845:31–32)

For the Europeans who came to the Middle East in the nineteenth century, Muslims seemed too involved with surfaces and externalities—the
sound of reciting voices, the prescribed movements of the body at prayers,
rules of fasting and ablutions, and so on—all of which defined a kind of life
incompatible with more refined and developed modes of reason, understanding, and religious devotion.[13] This assessment of the superficiality of
Muslim mental and spiritual life was also elaborated in regard to genres of
Muslim speech and writing, in what Europeans took to be a privileging of
formal and aesthetic criteria over content or meaning. Europeans, speaking a language that for them was free from embellishment except that demanded by its own content, found the Arabic of their colonial subjects too
ceremonial, too closely bound to classical religious texts, too restricted by
the emphasis placed on grammar and syntax. A language of chanting, ritual, and grammatical obsession, in short, of mechanics, Arabic further confirmed the opinion that Muslim existence was shallow, mere ostentation.[14]
The fact that Muslim historical writing, or even bureaucratic manuals, were
sometimes written using rhyming verse (*saj‘*), that much of daily life was
punctuated by the utterance of Quranic verses, or that scholars continued
to rely on an ancient and highly elaborate set of grammatical rules—all provided evidence for the Europeans that Muslims were concerned with external forms over inner meanings, surfaces rather than depths, a trait colonial
observers saw as characteristic of a petrified, stagnant civilization.

Many scholars today, of course, are skeptical of such modernist judgments and the sensory hierarchies they assume. It is all the more striking, therefore, to find that the contemporary critique of Islamic activism
mobilizes many of the same assumptions that guided colonial observers a
century before, especially in regard to the susceptibility of the untutored ear
to the voice of religious fanaticism. This susceptibility, it is claimed today,
is a product of the practices of recitation, audition, and memorization at
the heart of traditional Islamic pedagogy: in foregrounding the sonic qualities of language and an attitude of reverence for the sheer words over and
above their signifying content such practices instill credulity rather than
critical reason. A good deal of the analysis following the events of September 11, 2001, suggests that it is the rote education of the Islamic *madrasa*

that produces the mental equipment of the Islamic terrorist. Instead of becoming freethinking individuals, madrasa students are transformed into automatons who, in their mentally and psychologically impoverished state, mechanically enact the dictates of their militant instructors. The following comment echoes what has become a widely shared view: "In the madrasas, the Muslim religious schools in Pakistan and Afghanistan, students are strictly forbidden from learning anything except the Koran, that is, anything except mythos. When zealots talk about bombing Afghanistan back to the Stone Age, it is futile not only because the Taliban are already there physically but because they are also there epistemologically" (Gabler 2001). A similar critique is frequently echoed in Egypt as well. As an editorial in al-Ahram, the Egyptian ruling party's primary newspaper, comments: "We must base our educational system on the promotion of research, the cultivation of talents and a team spirit and not on memorization, and dictation which nullify the mind and inculcate terrorist thought" (al-Ahram 1993, my translation).[15] Such comments suggest that many of the assumptions about the articulation of reason, knowledge, and sensory experience have remained relatively stable since the nineteenth century when it comes to assessing Islamic oratorical practices and their injurious role in crafting the Muslim subject.[16]

These assumptions gain particular salience and force when the object of analysis is cassette-sermon listening. Already suspect by their association with the lower classes, their low-tech status, their religious content, and their contestatory stance, sermon tapes elicit modernist worries about the epistemological trustworthiness of the ear with particular intensity. The cassette partakes of the repetitive, droning quality of the madrasa's dangerous educational technique and exploits the ear's vulnerability to manipulation by nonrational means. As an Egyptian commentator observes in regard to the Islamic cassette phenomenon in Cairo, "Written works allow one to reread, to check sources in order to confirm the validity of assertions. They usually rely upon the logical organization of ideas, the flow of language, and the cogency of argument . As for the cassette tape, it depends on vocal and auditory effects, and gives great place to the workings of the imagination, and to the impression made by the speakers style of delivery" (Diyab 1996:21). This innate susceptibility of the ear to the irrational is even more pronounced when it is the popular classes who are listening, a segment of the national population whose capacities of reasoning and reflection are already considered to be questionable.

As I suggested earlier, the suspicion surrounding the pitfalls of the ear becomes particularly acute when combined with the longstanding Orientalist judgment that the sonority and grammatical rigidity of the Arabic language threaten its comprehension and propositional content. Consider, for example, the following comments made by the prominent journalist Chris Hedges in the *New York Times*:

> For the ways in which both the Arabic language and Arab societies have evolved make the language of the poor an exquisite tool with which to corrupt the Koran into an instrument of class hatred and tribal warfare. . . . The poor often cannot grasp the subtle rationalizations put forward by the educated. And the elite, isolated and besieged, are perplexed by the string of slogans and rote scriptural quotations, which they dismiss as an incoherent babble even as they fail to comprehend the anger beneath. . . . [But] theological nuance is beside the point for the zealots. It is enough for unexamined quotations to be injected into the everyday flow of street Arabic, which often uses clichés or slogans in every third or fourth sentence anyway.
>
> (HEDGES 1995)

Here, we see that in the postcolonial period, the opacity and unintelligibility of Arabic speech gets read through class rather than just nation or civilization: a language of clichés and slogans, as one of "the Middle East's leading linguists" cited by Hedges notes in a comment on contemporary vernacular Arabic, "valued by the poor as much as their television sets, or other electronic devices, that they own but do not understand and cannot devise or manufacture themselves" (Badawi, cited in Hedges 1995). The cassette sermon takes this mechanical and incomprehensible din of Arabic to its apogee: a machinic language reproduced by a machine. The sound of metal on metal. A medium of the poor, one they "do not understand and cannot devise or manufacture themselves," the cassette sermon in this view twists listening into ideological indoctrination, moral action into religious violence.

I met many people in Cairo during the period of my fieldwork, both Egyptians and foreigners, who upon hearing the voice of a *khatib* coming from the loudspeaker of a neighborhood mosque or from a cassette recorder at a local store experienced a certain physical or emotional discomfort. Indeed, many expressed sympathy toward me for working on a subject that necessarily involved many hours of listening to sermons. The following comment by an American researcher was not uncommon in this regard: "It's scary walking by a mosque on Friday when the preacher is raging away, filling the minds of those people with wild fears about the tortures of hell, or the perversity of sex-obsessed Westerners. All of these bearded men crying and shouting 'Allah'—I'm always half-expecting them to jump up and come running after me." This visceral discomfort felt by many people suggests that the reasonableness or interpretation of a speech form is not something decided abstractly, at a purely theoretical level. Beyond what is customarily designated as "content" (and religious content always remains suspect for the "cultured" ear), reason has a feel to it, a tone and volume, a social and structural architecture of reception, and particular modes of response.

The point I wish to emphasize here is the immense force that a modernist occularcentric epistemology continues to exercise within contemporary analyses of Muslim oratorical practices. Recall, for example, the urban scene depicted at the opening of this chapter and note the direction our analytical instincts take us. What mode of attentiveness could possibly be redeemed here that would be worthy, not simply of "hearing," of "playing the tape," but of the morally and aesthetically freighted notion of *listening*? Instead of the stillness and depth of the listening subject, we see an ear calibrated and subordinated to the circuits of capital and technology, a functionally integrated component of the media of distraction. What about the object? Even the religious content, a natural home for the listening ear, fails to provide an anchor: What religious meaning might survive the passage through the channels of commoditization, the technological mediations, the cluttered and deafening soundscapes, the urban geographies of visual and kinesthetic displacement, to then offer itself to a waiting ear? What could an ear "gather up and preserve [*legein*],"[17] besides decay, static, and noise, the debris of a tradition transformed into popular distraction by the force of modernity's disintegrating embrace? Certainly, a listening proportionate to the demands of indoctrination, but beyond this, any reflection on substantive issues—such as ethics, reason, or epistemology—would seem entirely incongruous with the scene.[18]

SUBTERRANEAN SOUNDS

Within the modernist discourse on the ear, movements such as the one I discuss in this book—grounded in sensory practices unrepresentable and imperceptible within regnant constructions of public memory—constitute the noncontemporary within the contemporaneous. It is not surprising, therefore, that the dominant analysis of the Islamist movement either views it as a nostalgic gesture in the face of the psychological disorientation brought by modernization or as an attempt to give historical authenticity to a form of life without actual historical roots. When Muslims argue for the traditional Islamic status of the headscarf, Islamic conceptions of political pluralism, or the idea of an Islamic state, for example, the objective historian unmasks such claims as strategic moves within a modern politics of cultural authenticity, and thus as not really—historically—authentic (see, for example, Kepel 1993; al-Azmeh 1996; Roy 1996).[19] One paradoxical aspect of this argument, it might be noted, is that while cultural authenticity is often criticized as a reactionary form of modern politics, it is assumed that there is an *authentic* relation to the past (not nostalgic, invented, or mythological), and that Islamists are in some sense living falsely not to acknowledge it and adjust to its demands.[20]

One of the key difficulties encountered in complicating such a picture lies in what I consider to be an inadequate theorization of the senses within modernity and the extent to which our notion of tradition derives from a particular encoding and hierarchization of the senses that structures our experience of the past in accord with the precepts of secular historical consciousness. Can one speak of the ethical sensibilities cultivated by contemporary consumers of aural media without anachronistically resurrecting the nostalgic figure of the monastic listener? For the modern observer, one trained to be skeptical of the epistemological claims of the ear, such practices and the forms of life they inhabit must be recoded through the temporal figure of nostalgia and therefore interpreted as evidence of an alienated consciousness, a reactive gesture by those struggling to secure identity in a disenchanted and unstable world. Indeed, nostalgia is one of the terms by which secular forms of memory secure their privilege: in recoding nonsecular forms of memory as romantic sentimentality, the term secures the transparency and authority of secular historical practice. As the anthropologist Nadia Seremetakis notes, "Nostalgia, in the American sense, freezes the past in such a manner as to preclude it from any capacity for social transformation in the present, preventing the present from establishing a dynamic perceptual relationship to its history" (1994:4). Where such a dynamic relationship to the past is asserted, the skeptical analyst uncovers invention and fabrication.[21]

The historian Dipesh Chakrabarty describes how the methods of the discipline of history function to relegate certain forms of memory to the margins of modern historical consciousness:

> Some constructions and experiences of the past stay "minor" in the sense that their very incorporation into historical narratives converts them into pasts "of lesser importance" vis-à-vis dominant understandings of what constitutes fact and evidence (and hence vis-à-vis the underlying principle of rationality itself) in the practices of professional history. Such "minor" pasts are those experiences of the past that always have to be assigned to an "inferior" or "marginal" position as they are translated into the academic historian's language. These are pasts that are treated, to use an expression of Kant's, as instances of human "immaturity," pasts that do not prepare us for either democracy or citizenly practices because they are not based on the deployment of reason in public life.
>
> (2000:100–101)

The recoding and marginalization of these subjugated (or what Chakrabarty calls "minority") histories marks the historical discipline's insertion within modern juridical and bureaucratic modes of reason and the positivist epistemologies they deploy.[22] In writing against this evaluative stance, Chakrabarty argues that the historian's ability to historicize in this manner is, paradoxically, enabled by her own participation in nonmodern relationships to the past; it is the fact that much of her daily experience—generally relegated to the sphere of private life—does not accord with the protocols of secular historical consciousness that allows the historian to recognize nonmodern forms of life as such, even though such experience must be effaced in the moment of historicizing (2000:101). Chakrabarty's point may be read, I want to suggest, to imply that the historical time of the senses is not the same as that valorized by the social scientific criteria of the historian or the anthropologist. The senses are not a stable foundation upon which a singular and unassailable truth can be erected, as an empiricist epistemology would claim, but rather a space of indeterminacy, heterogeneity, and possibility. Both perceived objects and perceiving subjects are sensorially plural, enfolding a set of possibilities that take on a determinant but not final form in a moment of perceptual completion (Seremetakis 1994; see also Benjamin 1969; Buck-Morss 1989). Modernity itself encompasses "plural ways of being in the world," forms of reason, memory, and experience grounded in histories other than those authorized by dominant secular rationalities. Modernity is not a functionally integrated totality governed by a singular overarching logic but rather a constellation of practices and technologies contingently connected within discontinuous formations of power.[23]

Scholars attentive to the heterogeneous temporalities of modernity have begun to chart an alternative history of the senses, one in which, not surprisingly, listening emerges as an important site of inquiry, pervading the modern in both overt and unacknowledged ways.[24] I want to briefly trace three moments in this account of listening that are of particular relevance to my analysis of cassette sermons and the forms of self, sociability, and politics they have helped create in contemporary Egypt. The first concerns the prevalence of "subterranean" listening practices within modern sensory landscapes: entwinings of sound and subject that are often ignored or misrecognized within modern spaces due to our dominant sensory epistemologies. Steven Connor, one of the most original scholars working on the topic of the modern sensorium, argues that within modern cities, often understood as spaces of intense visuality, we rely on a vocal-auditory consciousness to orient ourselves and find our way around. In his reading of such modernist classics as Joyce's *Ulysses* and Woolf's *Mrs. Dalloway*, Connor notes: "The unsteadiness of the ways of looking and seeing characteristic of city life—the glance or the glimpse rather than the sustained gaze—goes along with a sense of shifting and saturated space of which the plural, permeable ear can evidently make more sense than the eye" (1997:210; on this point, also see Jay 1994). Connor's work throws into question the assumption that listening cannot find a place for itself within the cacophony of the urban soundscape. Much of our capacity, he argues, to navigate the city, to enjoy its pleasures and be attentive to its dangers, relies crucially on subterranean forms of auditory knowledge and skill frequently ignored by analysts of urban life. This work alerts us to the way traditions of sound and listening have been articulated in changing and unpredictable ways with the constellation of sensory aptitudes and practices inhabiting contemporary cultural-historical formations, as an often unrecognized undercurrent emerging into and out of perceptual experience.

The epigraph to this chapter highlights the aurally saturated urban environment within which the practice of cassette-sermon listening takes place. If the solitary listener ensconced in the relative silence of his home represents one end of the spectrum of contexts within which this practice takes place, then the taxi driver struggling through the roar of downtown Cairo represents the other. In chapter 4, I address listening as it is practiced in such conditions of sonic intensity. Played in public transport, in shops, garages, and cafes, sermon tapes reconfigure the urban soundscape, imbuing it with an aural unconscious from which ethical reasoning and action draw sustenance. In other words, beyond their utility as a distraction from toil, such media create the intensifying sensory background for the forms of social and political life that the Islamic Revival has sought to promote and extend. Sermon tapes enable their listeners to orient themselves within the modern city *as a space of moral action*, with its characteristic challenges, threats, and daily problems. The style of listening that tape consumers bring to the practice render this media form something very different from a popular distraction or an instrument of religious propaganda, a difference, I argue, that has profound implications for collective life within contemporary Egypt.

A second key moment in this counterhistory (aimed at displacing an ocularcentric account of modernity) concerns the place of auditory practices within techniques of self-fashioning, most notably psychoanalysis. In the elaboration of Freud's call for a "calm, quiet attentiveness—of 'evenly hovering attention'" on the part of the analyst (Freud [1912] 1958:118), listening, with its therapeutic and transformative capacities, acquires its modern disciplinary function. Listening establishes the conditions of intersubjectivity, of the transference, of affect and unconscious, enabling the reorganization of psychic elements by the analysand (see Stein 1999).[25] For these reasons, the practice has remained a subject of inquiry and experimentation within the broader field of psychology. The philosopher and psychologist Peter Wilberg, for example, elaborates a notion of therapeutic audition—what he terms "maieutic listening"—on the model of musical sensibilities:

The medium of maieutic listening is not the airy medium of words but the fluid medium of feeling tone—the tones of silence that communicate "through the word," radiate from the listener and underlie all verbal communication. These may or may not be echoed in the tone of a person's language or their tone of voice. Rather, speech itself may be regarded as a type of song, one that provides a more "tuned in" expression of the silent music of the soul—the music of feeling tone.

(2004:8)

Not unlike psychoanalysis, as I will show, cassette-sermon audition is also a technique of self-fashioning predicated on the therapeutic capacities of listening, albeit one elaborated in ethical (rather than psychological) terms and in relation to a theologically based form of reasoning. Wilberg's attention to the affective and intersubjective dimensions of listening, as captured in his notion of "feeling tone," bears a distinct resemblance to the agentival and sensorially rich form of listening practiced by those I worked with in Cairo. Of particular relevance is his understanding of communication not as the transmission of thought from the speaker to the listener through the medium of words but as a collective performance, founded upon an affective dynamic for which both the speaker and the listener are responsible. In chapter 2, I will flesh this out by exploring the structure of affect relevant to sermon audition and to the forms of public speech and sociability promoted by the Islamic Revival.

The last aspect of the modern ear that I want to address concerns the important role that technologies of listening—the gramophone, the telephone, the radio, and the tape recorder among them—have played in the fashioning of modern subjectivity.[26] As the religious historian Leigh Eric Schmidt has recently shown, auditory technologies were essential to the formation of the sensory dispositions and aptitudes characteristic of a modern secular subject (2000). Schmidt's book provides an account of the attenuation of what, up through the seventeenth and eighteenth centuries, had been the commonplace Christian experience of hearing God's direct speech, an account centered not on the familiar tropes of disenchantment and the triumph of reason but on auditory discipline. The silencing of God's voice was achieved, Schmidt argues, through a retraining of the ear, one part of a broader disciplinary undertaking aimed at educating the senses in the service of polite sociability, civic virtue, and scientific knowledge.

Emerging in the seventeenth century, the field of acoustics invented by Francis Bacon and his contemporaries was profoundly influenced by pursuits in natural magic and the hermetic traditions revived during the Renaissance. The development of auditory technologies was therefore often driven by an interest in the illusionist effects of natural magic, such as talking statues, speaking trumpets, and the arts of ventriloquism. By the eighteenth century, demonstrations of the technological means by which voices could be projected across distances and located within inanimate objects were increasingly used to undermine claims to divine communication: oracular voices, the whispering of demons, the ringing of invisible bells—all long a part of Christian experience—were unmasked as the effects of artificial contrivances cunningly deployed by priests to deceive and control their followers (Schmidt 2000:78–134). As Schmidt shows, the revealing of priestly power in acoustic illusionism provided the basis for a natural history of religion. Importantly, such demonstrations, performed by natural philosophers, magicians, and ventriloquists, rapidly became a popular form of entertainment, one that served to cultivate the pleasure of auditory suspicion. Reproduced in spectacles, carnivals, and exhibits throughout Europe and North America, these events were meant to educate audiences in the "deceits of the senses" and the dangers to which the unrefined ear remained an heir (Schmidt 2000:101–24).

Schmidt's work emphasizes the important relationship between technologies of auditory discipline and the historical redefinition and repositioning of religion central to the emergence of secular modernity. As he persuasively demonstrates, the technological extension and attunement of the ear have provided the conditions for modernity's unique forms of reason and experience. In this book, I extend Schmidt's analytic to the Egyptian context by exploring the way new media practices have helped bring about the discursive relocation of Islamic traditions within Egyptian social, political, and religious life. Schmidt's historical work provides more than just a useful point of comparison for such an inquiry: the techniques and technologies of modern aurality whose development Schmidt traces in the early-modern American context have been a key component within the nationalist project in postcolonial societies like Egypt. As I describe in chapter 2, radio—an important precursor of the cassette and one that powerfully shaped its context of reception—was perhaps the single most important technology in the effort to mold a national citizenry throughout much of the twentieth century. The impact of sermon tapes on the perceptual habits of their vast audience, I argue, has produced a unique religiopolitical configuration that simultaneously compliments and challenges both the secular-bureaucratic rationalities of the state and Egypt's longstanding institutions of religious authority. My discussion of styles of cassette use in chapter 3 centers on how the functional possibilities peculiar to the cassette medium (such as rewind, pause, and home duplication) affect the sensory habits acquired in the course of listening practices.

Another aspect of Schmidt's account that carries great relevance for my own analysis lies in his exploration of religious responses to the secular retraining of the ear. As Schmidt relates, the Enlightenment assault on the ear did not result in a complete victory by any means. Swedenborgians, Methodists, Shakers, Mormons, and others sought to counter the charge of ocular deception in various ways—scientifically, theologically, as well as practically—through an ongoing emphasis on the disciplines of prayer, meditation, and spiritual listening that attuned the ear to divine sound. Even though the claim to hear voices from beyond, from the early nineteenth century on, would never free itself from the threat posed by the Enlightenment judgment of the ear's propensity for illusion, voices continue to be heard. One of the critical interventions of the Islamic Revival movement, in this regard, has been precisely an attempt to sustain certain virtues of the ear in the face of their threatened dissolution or obsolescence, an attempt carried out, in part, through the creation of new forms of social and political engagement consonant with the practice of such auditory virtues. Through these efforts, forms of sensory memory and experience pushed to the margins of daily life by the dominant perceptual regime have been renewed and redirected to meet a set of present challenges.

THE FLESH OF THE EAR

We are accustomed to think of listening as a cognitive act and often tend to ignore its practical and sensory dimensions.[27] The attentive reader will recognize, however, that the images of listening I have sketched so far exhibit few of the qualities we customarily associate with the act, a certain quiescence, attentiveness, silence: the physiognomy of aural comprehension and aural aesthetics. The style of listening I am specifically concerned with in this book—sermon listening—recruits the body in its entirety, requiring one to pay attention to the ways in which repertoires of bodily responsiveness articulate with the narrative forms of contemporary sermon rhetoric.

To elaborate an approach to practices of cassette listening sensitive to its plurisensory dimensions, I want to draw on an unlikely source, Walter Benjamin's essay *The Storyteller* (1969). Like most of Benjamin's other writings, *The Storyteller* is less an empirical history than a proverb, one that simplifies and schematizes what is undoubtedly a much more complex, partial, and incomplete set of historical transformations. Indeed, the essay rehearses precisely the modernist story of the ear's decline that I have sought to challenge in my discussion here. For my purpose, however, the value of the essay is that it helps us to trace the outline of the problem space where the activity of listening has become situated in modernity, and it also opens up certain avenues of inquiry that lead beyond this space. Specifically, it is precisely Benjamin's ability to make us recognize the embodied dimensions of listening and the shifting perceptual conditions that bear on its performance that make his work so relevant to the analysis of modern media practices such as the Islamic cassette. My use of this piece, in other words, is to exploit the materials it provides for thinking beyond a cognitivist conception of hearing.

According to Benjamin, prior to the expansion of markets in fifteenth- and sixteenth-century Europe, storytelling was one of the principle activities through which the accumulated wisdom of a people was passed from one generation to the next. Adept at the "particular co-ordination of the soul, the eye, and the hand" that constituted his craft, the storyteller fashioned his own experience, as well as that of others, into a useful and communicable form. The practical and perceptual conditions that made it possible for the narrator's account to take root in the listener's experience were found in the slow rhythms associated with artisanal labor. Indeed, the labor process itself in some sense constituted the auditory membrane, the receptive medium that enabled the storyteller's speech and gesture to sink into the worker's experience, much as the techniques of manufacture would sink into his bodily habits and modes of expression. Listening in this context is a process of sedimentation: a narrative reveals its secret depths only in its multiple retellings, by the accumulation of layer upon layer within the soul of the listener, like coats of lacquer applied to a wooden box that becomes clearer with each new layer. For this process to occur, the listener must assume "a naïve relationship to the storyteller," a state of passivity that facilitates memorization, understood as the habitus that makes possible what Benjamin calls tradition.

> The process of assimilation, which takes place in depth, requires a state of relaxation which is becoming rarer and rarer. If sleep is the apogee of physical relaxation, boredom is the apogee of mental relaxation. Boredom is the dreambird that hatches the egg of experience. A rustling in the leaves drives him away. His nesting places—the activities that are intimately associated with boredom—are already extinct in the cities and declining in the country as well. With this the gift for listening is lost and the community of listeners disappears.
>
> (1969:91)

Benjamin correlates the decline of the storyteller and the community of listeners with a shift in the conditions of knowledge and the rise of a new form of communication that he calls "information." Information is distinguished by the requirement that it be "understandable in itself," and subject to "prompt verifiability" (1969:89). No longer vouchsafed by the authority of tradition or grounded in accumulated experience or lengthy apprenticeship, information is fundamentally rootless and has the effect of under-mining the forms of knowledge and practice that depended on processes of gradual sedimentation and embodiment. The acceleration of temporal rhythms under capitalism, particularly in its technoindustrial phase, brings about a steady downgrading of the value of experience and hence of the practices by which experience is communicated.[28] The time of the ear dooms it to obsolescence.

This essay has the virtue of condensing a complex set of transformations into a concrete image, one presented with the same "chaste compactness" by which the storyteller's narrative, according to Benjamin, "preserves and concentrates its strength and is capable of releasing it even after a long time" (1969:90) While this account of listening's demise is overstated for a variety of reasons, it highlights certain aspects of an auditory context to which I want to draw attention. First, effective audition, an act that enables the integration of the narrative into the listener's own experience, requires a subordination to the authority of the storyteller and thus, in some sense, a heeding to the story itself. This is Benjamin's point about the "naïve rela-tionship" between speaker and listener. This is not simply a cognitive rec-ognition of the storyteller's authority but the adoption of the dispositions—sensory as much as mental—that allow the absorptive process to unfold. The entire sensorimotor apparatus, with its mnemonic layers of kinesthetic and visceral experience, will form the auditory membrane. In other words, within the model of absorptive listening figured in *The Storyteller*, it is in some sense the body in its entirety that constitutes both the medium of expression and the organ of audition.

How might we now return to Cairo, to the taxi driver caught in traf-fic and listening to the divine interrogation unfolding from his rusted speakers? Benjamin suggests that the accelerated pace of such modern conditions renders the body inadequate to the task of learning. But ac-celeration also generates its opposite, slowness, modern monotony with its distinct qualities of repetition, syncopation, dullness. The body as me-dium of experience is not transcended here but congeals to a specific rhythm, thickness, and density, a sensory substance that now mediates the listener's relation to the voice on the tape. If boredom is what Benja-min calls "the songbird of experience" for its ability to anchor the slow, sedimentary process of listening, what forms of experience might nest within the rhythms and textures of urban monotony? As I explore in this book, it is precisely within the sensorium of taxi drivers, shopkeepers, university students, and state bureaucrats that an ethics of listening has found its home.

Second, note also that listening for Benjamin is not simply a mode of concentration; it is, rather, something close to a practice in the Aristotelian sense.[29] The ability to both recognize and take delight in small differences in the telling of a story one has heard many times before, to grasp the workings of providence or the effects of sin in the actions of characters, to register with appropriate awe and surprise the appearance of the miraculous: these define the outline of a practice, one that requires honed sensory skills and the criteria for their assessment, namely, the ability of listeners to reproduce the story in all of its expressive modalities of gesture, attitude, intonation, and affect. As I show in this book, cassette-sermon listening should also be thought of as a practice in this sense, one that necessitates a responsiveness that crosses many sensory registers on the part of those who undertake it, including the affective, kinesthetic, and gestural. Much like Benjamin's storytelling audience, the taxi drivers and shop owners in Cairo who listen to recorded sermons also engage in a listening practice organized around rhythm and repetition, one that exploits moments of boredom and labor as a means to shape a self through a process of ethical sedimentation. For these listeners as well, the organ of audition is the human sensorium in its entirety, not the narrow passageway of the ear and its cognitive functioning. The patterns of sensory attunement configured through continuous practice of such a listening constitute an intensifying perceptual background for the distinct forms of ethical agency and public reason that I explore in chapter 4.

THE ANTHROPOLOGY OF SENSUAL REASON

The discipline of anthropology has much to contribute to our understanding of the modes of sensory appraisal that underlie modern political rationalities of the sort I am concerned with in this book. A growing body of anthropological literature focusing on the patterning of perception and sensory experience across different cultural and historical contexts offers many resources for such an inquiry.[30] One of the more fruitful ideas to emerge from this literature has been to move away from a notion of the senses as capacities of subjective experience and, instead, to approach sensory perception as a relationship between a perceiving subject and a world of sensible, material objects. As Seremetakis has eloquently noted:

> The sensory is not only encapsulated within the body as an internal capacity of power, but is also dispersed out there on the surface of things as the

latter's autonomous characteristics, which then can invade the body as perceptual experience. Here sensory interiors and exteriors constantly pass into each other in the creation of extra-personal experience.

(1994:6)

An inquiry into the senses, in this light, directs us beyond the faculties of a subject to the transfers, exchanges, and attachments that hinge the body to its environment. Objects are endowed with histories of sensory experience, stratified with a plurality of perceptual possibilities: those that become available to consciousness or integral to human actions will depend on the capacities the subject brings to bear, and thus on the perceptual regimes that work to organize attention and inattention. Seremetakis suggests that we interrogate this relation between cultural practice and sensory experience through a notion of "perceptual completion": "The surround of material culture is neither stable nor fixed, but inherently transitive, demanding connection and completion by the receiver" (1994:7). Perception is not a moment of passivity but an act, a performance that links the sensory sedimentations of the past to the horizon of present actions. Fashioned outside explicit awareness, in the interval between subject and object worlds, such linkages occur in the encounter between what Bergson refers to as virtual memory—residues of past actions installed in the motor mechanisms of the body—and a sensory surround (Bergson [1896] 1990; see chapter 3). Such an approach moves us away from a mentalist understanding that locates experience in a silent interior toward one that places it in a body practically engaged with the world.

Any inquiry into the sensorium as historical artifact must begin with the historically specific categories and symbols that organize experience, that shape the perceptual skills by which culturally sanctioned modes of discrimination are learned and practiced. In chapter 3, I give considerable attention to the concepts of affective and somatic responsiveness that inform Islamic traditions of ethical cultivation. My study, in this regard, follows avenues of inquiry opened up by scholars such as Robert Desjarlais who, in his study of Yolmo trance, examines the "aesthetics of experience" as it is articulated within Yolmo epistemologies (1992).[31] Thomas Csordas's work on Charismatic Christian notions of healing and bodily experience (1999) has also sharpened my attention to the kinesthetic and synesthetic dimensions of Islamic moral psychology. His explorations into how a preobjective relation to the world orchestrates the culturally specific

objectifications produced through reflexive practice have given anthropologists an ethnographically rich demonstration of the value of phenomenological analysis.[32] The anthropologist whose work bears most directly on my
own study of listening practices in Cairo is Steven Feld (1982, 1996). Feld's
sensitive analysis of the relation between structures of meaning in Kaluli
myth and modalities of sensory experience and expression has provided an
invaluable template for my own inquiry into the plurisensory dimensions
of a number of Islamic ethical concepts. His insightful interrogation of the
auditory practices through which Kaluli hone the substrate of sensory skills
requisite to the performance of culturally valued styles of expression and
behavior is particularly germane to my own study, as is his careful tracking
of the way modes of perception developed in one domain of social action
structure the performative skills brought to other domains.[33]

Feld's work on the auditory finds an interesting compliment in historian
Michael Baxandall's rich study of fifteenth-century Italian painting (1988). In
this work, Baxandall demonstrates how the perceptual skills that fifteenth-
century viewers brought to acts of viewing works of art were grounded in
habits developed in other arenas of common practice: in common uses of
certain mathematical procedures; commercial practices involving geom-
etry and the gauging of volumes and proportions; conventions of gestural
expression practiced in preaching; and habits of allegorical interpretation
associated with piety and religious knowledge. One of the central questions guiding my own study is: How do affects and sensibilities cultivated
by contemporary Egyptian Muslims through popular practices of media
audition shape the modes of appraisal that listeners bring to daily contexts
of sociability and labor?

In this book, I seek to extend this rich tradition of anthropological inquiry
into the senses in an explicitly political direction through an interrogation
of the sensorium as both a condition for and object of an emergent form of
ethical-political reasoning. It is increasingly difficult to sustain an image of
political life that does not include recognition of the role of embodied sensibilities and prereflexive habits in shaping our commitments and reasons.
Political judgments are not the product of rational argumentation alone
but also of the way we come to care deeply about certain issues, feel passionately attached to certain positions, as well as the traditions of practice
through which such attachments and commitments have been sedimented
into our emotional-volitional equipment. As Talal Asad has succinctly put
it: "The public sphere is not an empty place for carrying out debates. It
is constituted by the sensibilities—memories and aspirations, fears and

hopes—of speakers and listeners. And also by the manner in which they exist (and are made to exist) for each other, and by the propensity to act and react in distinctive ways" (T. Asad 2003:185). Within modern society, popular media play an essential role in the crafting of such public sensibilities, hence their importance to modern political method.

For some liberal scholars, the power of contemporary mass media to mold affects and desires represents an immense threat to democratic practices of political deliberation (see, most notably, Habermas 1989). By introducing nonrational elements into political discourse, the argument goes, popular media practices undermine the rational-critical character of public debate necessary to deliberative democracy. This claim, of course, also undergirds the secular judgment that religion should be confined to the sphere of private life, as the passionate attachments that are said to characterize religious belief corrupt the rationality of political discourse.

As should be clear from what I stated above, the vision of disembodied reason that undergirds these normative judgments in my view provides an inadequate standpoint from which to think about political practice *as sensible activity*. Moral and political judgments always owe part of their force and reasonableness to evaluative dispositions outside the purview of consciousness, to orientations grounded in affective and visceral registers of human existence. There is, of course, a long tradition of philosophical and political reflection that gives explicit recognition to the pervasive role of such nonreflexive registers in shaping thought and action, a tradition that scholars like Talal Asad (1993, 2003) William Connolly (1999, 2002), Brian Massumi (2002), and Gilles Deleuze (1988, 19995) have sought to recuperate and extend in different ways.

This book shares many of the questions and concerns that these scholars have pursued. The public arena articulated by the practices of media, speech, and listening that I explore in the following chapters is founded on a tradition that emphasizes the epistemic and ethical value of religious sensibilities and affects for social and political life. My own view is that the forms of memory, thought, and practice shaping this arena of Islamic ethicopolitical life have something important to teach us, especially in light of the new constellations of religion and politics emerging in the world today and the inadequacy of our secular political vocabularies for thinking about these formations.

{ 2 }

ISLAM, NATIONALISM, AND AUDITION

There is nothing but Speech and listening. There can be nothing else. Were it not for Speech we would not know what the Desirer desires from us. Were it not for hearing, we would not reach the point of gaining what is said to us. Through Speech we move about, and as a result of Speech, we move about in listening.

—IBN AL-ARABI

FOR RELIGIOUS and secular reformers from the late nineteenth century through the present, the sermon has provided a favored problem space for reassessing the virtues and dangers of the ear and for attempting to establish the conditions enabling its reeducation. The innovations these reformers brought about cannot be understood in terms of the replacement of a premodern listener by a modern one, an attentive and pious ear by a distracted and secular one. While modernization changed the terrain upon which acts of listening take place, its very partial and incomplete character also opened up new spaces of possibility for alternative articulations of sound and subject and new ways of animating and embodying historical experience. Today, within Egypt's institutions of Islamic authority and the forms of public life these institutions articulate, we find practices, languages, and techniques of ethical listening entwined with, but also counterpoised to, a set of forms linked to the nationalist effort to construct a modern public sphere. Indeed, as I explore in both this chapter and the next, the arena of public life in Egypt has been profoundly marked by contrasting projects for recruiting and attuning the ear. While the state has sought to harness the sermon to the juggernaut of modernity, its efforts have continued to be stymied and overshadowed by a vigorous renewal of the preaching tradition taking place outside (and often in direct opposition to) the state's own religious bureaucracies. Appropriated and transformed by the Sahwa al-Islamiyya, the sermon has found new uses beyond the context of Friday worship, as a popular media form for political critique, on one hand, and as a vehicle for the cultivation of those affects and attitudes underlying an emergent form of Islamic public engagement, on the other. The tensions between such statist and nonstatist projects and the regimes of discourse and sensibility they have made possible constitute a key axis of Egypt's political geography today. What forms of politics and dialogue can be imagined that may navigate the conceptual and sensory divide that separates the different ethical subjects within contemporary Egypt? Such is the daunting question that contemporary Egyptians confront and that this chapter—tracing the ethics and politics of the ear in Egypt as they developed in the twentieth century—seeks to elucidate.

THE RHETORIC OF THE LISTENER

I want to start by discussing a certain tradition of thinking about listening in relation to language and human agency, one that has played a decisive role in determining how Muslim scholars and nonscholars alike have understood the act of listening to sermons. Until the early twentieth century, Muslim scholars—in print, at least—were relatively unconcerned with elaborating an art of sermon rhetoric or devising techniques to ensure the persuasiveness of a preacher's discourse, as, for example, is found in Christianity. The scholarly tradition of *'ilm al-balagha* (the Islamic discipline frequently glossed in English as either "rhetoric" or "the art of eloquence") did not take oratorical practices such as the Friday sermon either as its object of analysis or as its point of practical application. Rather, as formulated by the grammarian Abd al-Qahir al-Jurjani (d. 1018), *'ilm al-balagha* explored Arabic semantics, taking the particular eloquence of the Quran as its central topic of investigation.[1] One of the doctrines through which earlier scholars had sought to identify and substantiate the uniqueness of the Quranic revelation was that of *i'jaz al-qur'an*, an expression often translated as "the miraculousness of the Quran," but whose literal meaning refers to the idea that the Quran's sublime beauty rendered humans "incapable" (*'ajiz*) of producing anything of equal value.[2] This doctrine took on a fundamental importance in the development of *al-balagha* by al-Jurjani and his successors. While their investigations frequently drew examples from poetry, the basic framework of the field revolved around an analysis of the linguistic devices through which the Quran achieves its aesthetic excellence. A concern for the civic function of speech, for the techniques by which an orator might move an audience to action as had been elaborated by Roman and medieval Christian rhetors, was never rigorously pursued by Muslim scholars of language.[3] Instead of elaborating formal rules of speaking, Muslim scholars gave priority to the task of listening, a fact reflecting the particular status ascribed to the revealed text over the course of the development of Islam (Smyth 1992). In this sense, *'ilm al-balagha* can be considered one branch of Islamic hermeneutics: whereas the discipline of *fiqh* (jurisprudence) sought to derive the principles of divinely sanctioned human action from the text, *'ilm al-balagha* indicated how the text should be listened to, read, and appreciated in what we might call its poetic aspects.[4]

The fact that Muslim scholars have been relatively uninterested in elaborating an art of persuasive speaking owes in part to how revelation affected their conceptions of the efficacy of speech. As the miraculous word of God, the divine message convinces not through an artifice of persuasion, the rhetorical labors of skillful human speakers, but by its own perfect unification of beauty and truth. When humans fail to be convinced by this message, the fault lies not in the words but in the organ of reception, the human heart. The message itself has been articulated in the most perfect of possible forms, the Quran. This is made evident in many parts of the Quran where the failure to heed the words of God is attributed to a person's or community's inability or refusal to hear (*sam'*). Indeed, an incapacity to hear the words of God is one of the distinguishing traits of those humans and demons (*jinn*) destined for hell: "They have hearts wherewith they understand not, eyes wherewith they see not, and ears wherewith they hear not [*la yasma'una biha*]" (Quran 7:179).[5] When humans in the Quran do respond in an ethically positive manner, either to the speech of other humans or to that of God, the agency is largely attributed to the hearer.[6] *Sam'*, in other words, is not a spontaneous and passive receptivity but a particular kind of action itself, a listening that is a doing. For this reason, what the divine message requires within this tradition is not so much a rhetor as a listener, one who can correctly hear what is already stated in its most perfect, inimitable, and untranslatable form; not a speaker's persuasiveness, but the instrumentality of God acting through his words on the heart of a listener.

One might say, in other words, that within this interpretive tradition the rhetorical act is accomplished by the hearer and not the speaker.[7]

MUSIC AND MYSTICISM

One finds a similar privileging of the listener in the extensive theological and mystical writings on music that Islamic scholars have produced from the ninth century onward. Fueled by concerns about music's ability to by-pass the faculty of rational judgment and directly affect the senses of the listener, debates over the admissibility of listening to music have engaged many leading Muslim scholars up to the present day.[8]

In general, those who have opposed the audition of music point to its dangerous ability to arouse unruly passions, stimulate sensual pleasures, and distract one from thoughts of God, while those who have advocated the practice—frequently those writers favorably disposed toward mystical currents within Islam—have seen in it a means to move the heart to greater piety and closeness to God. For scholars adopting this latter argument (including A. H. al-Ghazali [d. 1111], al-Darani [d. 830], and Ibn al-Rajub [d. 1392]), it was wrong to view music as intrinsically dangerous. In the words of the ninth-century mystic al-Darani, "Music does not provoke in the heart that which is not there." The agency of music to either corrupt or edify, to distract from moral duty or incline the soul toward its performance lies not in the sound itself but in the moral disposition of the heart of the listener. If the listener brings to the act the proper intentions, goals, and ethical attitude, then he or she will benefit from the audition. In short, as with the Quran, musical performance remains intertwined with and dependent upon the agency of the listener.

The impact of this concern for the moral and emotional state of the listener is evident in the fact that many key musical concepts in the Arabo-Islamic tradition simultaneously indicate both the responsiveness of the listener and the qualities of the performance (see During 1997; Racy 2003; Shannon 2003). Within this tradition, listener and performer form an interdependent dyad in which the former is often seen to precede and make possible the performance of the latter, as we see in the following remarks by the contemporary Syrian musician Sabah Fakhri:

> In order to deliver something you must have it in yourself first and then reflect it, as the moon shines by reflecting the light it receives from the sun. In a large measure, this state emanates from the audience, particularly the

sammi'ah (talented and sensitive listeners), although the singer must also be endowed with *ruh* (soul) and *ihsas* (feeling).

(CITED IN RACY 1998:96)

I might also note that within the mystical currents that contributed much to the tradition of reflection on the powers of music that Fakhri is heir to, *sam'* refers not only to the act of audition, but also to the ritual dance that may accompany it and the music or cantillation that provides its occasion (During 1997:129–33). *Sam'*, in other words, dissolves the distinction between subject and object while enabling their aesthetic or ethical reconstitution and realignment.

A similar conceptual structure appears in the musical-aesthetic term "*tarab*." As described by Egyptians today, *tarab* indicates a relation of harmony (*insijam*) between listener and performer, an intersubjective form enabling an exchange of feeling (*tabadul al-shu'ur*) or an affective melding (*dhawb*) of one with the other (see Frishkopf 2001). Like *sam'* in the mystical tradition, *tarab* connotes both a form of intersubjective experience and the musical traditions and styles that have historically produced it.[9] The fusion of horizons that *tarab* engenders demands from the performer specific skills of musical and poetic expression, as well as a certain talent and sensitivity from the audience. Listeners perform a range of affective responses involving facial, gestural, and postural elements, accompanied by vocal exclamations such as "ah!" and "*ya salam!*" [how marvelous!]." In doing so, the listeners both "inspire the performer and enhance the effectiveness of the musical performance" (Racy 1982:392). While *tarab* is frequently associated with Sufi performances, the term is also applied to a much wider range of musical expression: for example, popular twentieth-century singer–film stars like Abd al-Wahhab and Umm Kulthum (whom I discuss later in the chapter) have been celebrated for the *tarab* qualities of their music (Racy 2003; Stokes in press). Importantly, as a mode of emotional expression founded upon a unique "orchestral" coordination between performer and audience, *tarab* was not immune to the institutional changes that occurred within the field of popular and commercial music during the twentieth century, changes that tended to widen the gulf between stage and public. I will return to this later in the chapter.

Islamic practices of preaching are heir to the same tradition of reflection on agency and audition that I have identified in relation to Arabo-Islamic musical theory, Sufism, and the scholarly tradition of *'ilm al-balagha*.

As I discuss in chapter 5, many of the rhetorical techniques deployed by preachers today are borrowed directly from Sufi traditions, especially the repetitive chanting of the names of God, the practice of extending vowels (*madd*) so as to more deeply move the listener, and breathing techniques. And while sermon listeners do not seek to achieve the experience of *fana';* (the dissolution of the self in the face of God described by mystics), the goal of honing one's moral sensibilities so as to be able to draw near to God is common to both practices.[10] Moreover, much like the talented and sensitive listeners of *tarab*-endowed music, the sermon listener realizes the performance through her own ethical-aesthetic response and, in doing so, hones and deepens the sensibilities that incline her to act morally across the domains of daily life.

AURAL THERAPY

As suggested in the comment by Ibn al-Arabi (d. 1240) cited at the beginning of this chapter, within the tradition I have been discussing, all moral action is in some sense a listening, the reverberation of the words of God within human souls and actions. Sermons provide a powerful instrument for honing this reverberatory faculty and, thus, for attuning and orienting the senses to a divinely ordered world. While the human heart, known only to God and oneself, can never be made the object of a science of persuasion, its capacity to hear can be impaired, particularly through the repeated performance of sinful acts.[11] A verse from the Quran tells us, "God seals the hearts of those who refuse to hear" (Quran 7:100). While this verse has often been taken as evidence in support of the doctrine of predestination, the sealing of the heart is more correctly understood to refer to a gradual process whereby, through the repeated performance of sinful acts, one loses the ability to hear the truth.[12] Sermons are a means to its recovery. Within Islamic societies, sermons have historically served as an instrument of ethical therapy, both in the context of Friday worship at the mosque and outside it, in various formal and informal assemblies where preachers have been called on to enliven an audience's sense of pious fear through a hortatory on such topics as death, the grave, or the coming of the Antichrist (*masih al-dajjal*).[13]

While preaching practices have been significantly transformed over the course of the twentieth century, as I discuss below, a recognition of their capacity to serve as a vehicle of ethical improvement has not been lost. As one of the most prolific contemporary Egyptian writers on the sermon notes, in commenting on the Quranic verse mentioned in the previous paragraph:

> From acts [of sins and disobedience] come the sicknesses of the heart and their causes. God said: "By no means! But on their hearts is the stain of the ill which they do." It covers them like rust, until they are overcome. And they continue sinning and postpone repentance until [their acts] become imprinted on the heart such that it will neither accept good nor incline toward it. There is no medicine for this except the ointment of the *shari'a*, in the form of a precise scientific, chemical compound composed of sermons [*khutab*; sing. *khutba*], exhortations [*mawa'iz*; sing. *maw'iza*], and religious counseling (*nasiha*), all drawn from the Quran and *sunna* [the Prophet's exemplary speech or action]. Without this treatment, hearts cannot be corrected.
>
> (MAHFUZ 1979:63)

Sin corrodes the heart, the organ of both audition and moral comportment.[14] Listening to the godly speech of sermons and exhortations, if done repeatedly and with proper intention, can remove this corrosion.

Another author, writing in *al-Tawhid*, a popular religious digest often read and exchanged by the sermon listeners I worked with in Cairo, likens impaired hearing to a short circuit in wiring that prevents an electrical current from reaching the lamp it is supposed to illuminate. Drawing out the metaphor, he suggests:

> The Quran is effective in itself, just as the electrical current. If the Quran is present [to your ears], and it has lost its effect, then it is you yourself that you must blame. Maybe the conductive element is defective: your heart is damaged or flawed. Maybe a mist covers your heart, preventing it from benefiting from the Quran and being affected by it. Or maybe you are not listening well, or your heart is occupied with problems of money, and thinking about how to acquire and increase it.
>
> (BADAWI 1996A:13)

For the possessor of such a defective heart, the only solution, according to the author, lies in cleansing (*tahir*) the heart, both by giving up the sinful acts that led to such a state and by repeatedly listening, with intention and concentration, to sermons, exhortations, and Quranic verses.

To summarize, within the Islamic homiletic tradition I describe here, listening is privileged as the sensory activity most essential to moral conduct. Once revelation had brought the most powerful and sublime form of speech into the world, the problem of persuasion was shifted onto the listener and the clarity of the listener's heart. An orator within this tradition requires not knowledge of audience psychology, so central to Greek rhetorical study, but rather a complete performative grasp of the true word, revealed in the Quran and exemplified in the *sunna*.[15] Even more, he requires a *listener*, one whose acts of discrimination—at once moral and aesthetic—embody, extend, and enhance his discourse. This is not to suggest that a skillful *khatib* is not appreciated for the excellence of his sermon. Rather, I am simply pointing out how a specific view of the means by which words convince has undergirded a certain depersonalization of the utterance, its agency located more in God and in the disciplined ears and hearts of listeners and less in the speaker.

The sermon grounds a collective discipline but also provides what Foucault terms a "technology of the self" (see Foucault 1983, 1988, 1990, 1997), a set of procedures by means of which individuals can work on their souls and bodies to achieve a distinct ethical or aesthetic form, in this case, one conducive to a proper relationship with God. Through their own efforts, sermon listeners attempt to fashion themselves as auditory receptacles of divine speech. A *khatib*, in accordance with this tradition, does not shape his audience at will but serves as a mediator, providing the linguistic and gestural resources through which the listener can undertake the ethical labor involved in properly attuning his or her faculties to the word of God. Preachers, in other words, have a mediatory function and are not ultimately responsible for the creation of moral subjects. This task lies with God and the individuals themselves. Within the context of this tradition, the institutions and practices wherein moral action occurs and is assessed presuppose such an aural subject, whose particular sensory capacities, honed through auditory disciplines, give rise to ethical performances.[16] While it is the responsibility of *khutaba'* (preachers) to prevent corruption and the spread of erroneous behavior, they are not, properly speaking, assigned the task of enforcing a normative morality, as each individual is ultimately answerable to God on the Day of Judgment. Indeed, it is not surprising that the narration of this event, one in which moral responsibility is radically individualized, has always been a staple of ethical preaching within Islam.

The tradition I have discussed shares certain features with Augustinian rhetoric that I might briefly note. Augustine transformed Greek rhetorical theory into a kind of hermeneutic discipline, one not entirely unlike the *'ilm al-balagha* tradition fashioned by Muslim scholars. Rhetoric taught the Christian scholar how to uncover deeper layers of biblical meaning. "[Christ] did not hide [truths] in order to prevent them from being communicated," Augustine claims, "but in order to provoke desire for them by this very concealment" (cited in Todorov 1982:76).[17] Yet rhetoric was also envisioned by Augustine as the primary weapon of the orator. In his *De doctrina Christiana*, Augustine opens the section that most explicitly deals with preaching with a defense of the art of rhetoric:

> Now, the art of rhetoric being available for the enforcing of either truth or falsehood, who will dare say that truth in the person of its defenders is to take its stand unarmed against falsehood? . . . Since, then, the faculty of eloquence is available for both sides, and is of very great service in the enforcing either of wrong or right, why do not good men study to engage it on the side of truth, when bad men use it to obtain the triumph of wicked and worthless causes, and to further injustice and error?
>
> (1973:494)

For Augustine here, rhetoric is a tool of persuasion bearing a purely instrumental relation to moral truth: no intrinsic connection exists between the eloquence of statements and their veracity. For classical Muslim scholars, on the other hand, the Quran represented the highest form of truthful discourse as well as the model from which the criteria of aesthetic excellence were derived. Placing divine speech at the core of their inquiries, Muslim linguists and philosophers have tended to base their analyses of beautiful elocution on the fundamental unity of the aesthetic and the true. One consequence of this, as suggested earlier, is that the figure of the listener has taken on a paradigmatic status within the field of moral inquiry and practice, including the tradition of Islamic homiletics.

A SENSE OF NATION

The relationships among agency, ethics, and authority inhering in the tradition of active listening I have traced so far were significantly transformed by the processes of modernization and rationalization propelled by anticolonial and nationalist movements in nineteenth- and twentieth-century Egypt. The set of transformations I describe in this section not only affected the organization of law, politics, and economics in Egypt but also introduced new sensory epistemologies that directly challenged the ear's ethical function.[18] The task of creating a modern national auditory—an ear resonant with the tonalities of reason and progress while deaf to the outmoded noises of religious authority—required a concerted intervention into sites of aural discipline. The call to prayer (*adhan*), the pedagogies of Quranic recitation and memorization, and the sermon (with its new mediatic forms) thus became objects of a new political concern. As I explore below, the affects and sensibilities of the ethical listener shaped by such practices have repeatedly chafed against the new political order, a friction that has given rise to new contestatory articulations of ethics, religion, and politics.

One key aspect of the policies undertaken by Egyptian reformists and nationalists from the late nineteenth century to the present has involved the legal and administrative intervention by the state into the domain of religion, so as to render it consonant with the secular-liberal and technocratic discourses central to the state's own legitimacy, functioning, and reformist goals.[19] Nationalism introduced the categories of secular-liberal governance through which Islamic practices could be grasped and reinscribed into the new projects of social and political development. Thus, beginning in the early nineteenth century under the rule of Muhammad Ali, and continuing under his khedival successors, Ottoman Egypt undertook major projects aimed at modernizing and industrializing, one component of which was a gradual undermining of religious institutions though the appropriation of their revenues, now redirected toward the task of state building (Crecelius 1966; Marsot 1968). For the khedival regimes as well as for many of the nationalist reformers who became prominent later in the century, the weakness of Islamic nations before an economically and militarily powerful Europe could be overcome only through the rapid importation of European technology and science. For many, religious institutions had little to contribute to this enterprise, their knowledges and practices inadequate when not outright detrimental to the demands of modern nation building. The solution to this eventually adopted by the state was to incorporate these institutions within its own apparatuses, a process that accelerated greatly in the twentieth century under Nasser and his successors. As a result, today there are few aspects of religious life in Egypt that have remained entirely outside the managerial purview of the state (Hirschkind 1997; Marsot 1968; Skovgaard-Petersen 1997; Zeghal 1996).

Notably, within the new bureaucratic discourses of religion, listening was to be increasingly divested of its agentive dimensions and its complex sensory entanglements with sound and, instead, whittled down to a simply passive receptivity, a narrow channel through which the operations of social discipline might pass. Nineteenth-century Egyptian reformers, both secular and religious, argued that the sermon had a pedagogical role in society and that that role was not being performed, especially among the illiterate masses who constituted the largest section of the audience. Not surprisingly, the model for the new sermon was to be found in the press, the primary political instrument for the articulation and dissemination of the new cultural standards upon which a reformed Egyptian nation was to be founded. Like the press, a revitalized sermon was to serve as an engine of moral progress, inculcating nationalist sentiments while providing useful (in other words, modern) information. The prominent Muslim reformer Jamal al-Din al-Afghani, speaking in 1879, outlined the complementary functions of these institutions: "We cannot arrive at the goal of happiness without them [oratory and the press]; and the only difference between them is that oratory moves the blood though the movement of the speaker and the power of voice, while newspapers serve to fix the issues in peoples' minds" (cited in al-Kumi 1992:137).[20]

Al-Afghani and his followers complained that, in their ignorance, most *khutaba'* only served to spread falsehoods and superstitions. The practice of preaching had deteriorated, they argued, because *khutab'* continued to rely on material gleaned from classical texts and sermon collections that had little relevance to present realities and social needs. Like many within today's Islamist political parties, they found particularly deleterious the promulgation of an ascetic attitude of worldly rejection and complacency, what they saw as an un-Islamic accretion destructive of the industriousness and sense of social responsibility upon which the improvement of Islamic society depended. *Khutaba'* should not focus on "obscurantist" topics, such as the imminent arrival of the Antichrist or the tortures of hell, but should rather use the opportunity to disseminate "useful information," such as news of current events in Egypt and abroad, and to instill in their listeners pride of country and the desire to work for the benefit of the nation. The eschatological themes of death, judgment, and suffering that had always been central in shaping the ethical sensibilities or virtues that underlay correct conduct—such as humility (*khushu'*), fear of God (*taqwa*), and modesty (*tawadu'*)—now became subject to the charge of irrelevance and obscurantism. Thus, Abdullah Nadim, a well-known orator and student of al-Afghani, complains:

> Sermon oratory [al-khataba] was not limited to recalling death, asceticism, to warnings against worldly pleasures and luxuries; rather, oratory during the time of the Prophet and the early caliphs included current events and news of the community [umma]; it did not focus on the promise of heaven [wa'd] or the threat of hell [wa'id] except when the week had produced no new events or important affairs.
>
> (NADIM 1881:237)

In other words, the afterlife, for Nadim, while not to be entirely forgotten, no longer has implications in shaping how the self might understand and respond to "new events or important affairs," topics worthy of the modern citizen's attention. Rather, the structure of knowledge and sentiment invoked by Nadim that was cultivated within the public sphere of the emerging nationalist bourgeoisie and articulated through such forms of discourse as newsprint, political meetings and speeches, and privates clubs.[21] While the rationalist models of knowledge governing these new discursive sites still left scope for the passions—increasingly nationalist ones—the poetic and affective qualities specific to the tradition of ethical listening were to be detached from the structures of public life and circumscribed to the domain of private worship.

The first major attempt to rationalize the practice of preaching in Egypt under a central administrative authority was initiated by the prominent Islamic reformer Muhammad Abduh during his rectorship at al-Azhar University (1895–1905) (Gaffney 1991:35–37). Abduh commissioned a statistical study of those mosques in Cairo administered by the Ministry of Religious Affairs (Wizarat al-Awqaf). In the proposal that resulted from this study, he laid out what was to become a model for the professional activity of preaching (Abduh 1972). The position of khatib was now given a precise bureaucratic definition in terms of educational requirements, a set of specific duties to be performed at the mosque, and a salary scale graded according to educational achievements.[22] While Abduh's recommendations were not put into effect until after his death, his proposal laid the groundwork for the professionalization of the field and the reorientation of the sermon toward a new set of national priorities and goals. Admittedly, within the models of nationhood adopted by Abduh and the *salafi* movement he pioneered, the nation was conceived less as a good in itself and more as a condition for the resurrection of a vital and vigorous Islamic community, or "*umma*."[23] This latter, however, was at the time coming increasingly to be assessed and regulated on the basis of criteria provided by the former. The goal of listening to sermons was still to "move the blood," but now in a decidedly modern and rational direction.

THE OFFICIAL PREACHER

The extension of state control over the institutions of religious authority in Egypt accelerated sharply following independence in 1952. Like al-Afghani, Abduh, and other *salafi* leaders earlier in the century, the nationalists who eventually came to dominate in the wake of the Nasserite revolution emphasized the central role of the mosque in the dissemination of modern attitudes and knowledges, though the ideas of moral improvement they invoked were solidly grounded in European (secular) discourses of citizenship and governance. The project that Nasser inaugurated and that subsequent regimes have continued to pursue to varying degrees has involved both the further incorporation of religious authority under the state and the creation of various educational and bureaucratic institutions to train, certify, and supervise *khutaba'* and other religious specialists. Thus, a series of legislative steps intended to bring all mosques under the direct administrative purview of the Ministry of Religious Affairs was begun in 1960 and subsequently extended, most recently in 1993 and 1996. In regard to training, a Department of Preaching and Guidance (*qism al-wa'z wa al-irshad*) had been established as far back as 1918 at al-Azhar, and was later replaced, in 1961, by the Department of Missionary Activity and Islamic Culture (*qism al-da'wa wa al-thaqafa al-islamiyya*). Finally, in 1978, an independent College of Proselytization Activity (*kulliyyat al-da'wa*) was set up to respond to the rising problem of Islamic militancy through the training and deployment of a corps of state-aligned *khutaba'*.[24] This was also the impetus behind the creation of a number of preaching institutes (*ma'ahid al-da'wa*) set up by the Ministry of Religious Affairs in the 1970s.[25]

For *khutaba'* to play their role in the construction of "national culture" and the dissemination of modern orientations and desires, their training and organization could not be left solely in the hands of religious authorities but had to be placed under the purview of a new class of bureaucrats with expertise in such secular fields as "culture," "media," "psychology," and "security." Indeed, in state planning documents from the 1950s and 1960s, as well as in some of the preaching manuals published at the time, sermons were often assimilated to the category of "mass media" and understood according to the behaviorist models that dominated the field at the time. Preachers were seen to offer the state a preestablished channel of direct communication between itself and the population under its management. Sermons would now provide both useful information and an oratorical form geared to the moral improvement of an Egyptian population still seen to be bound by the ideological constraints of a deep-rooted traditionalism. Informed by an Orientalist critique linking the backwardness of Muslim societies to an Islamic, and particularly Sufi, fatalism, said to be evident in a general denigration of practical, this-worldly concerns in favor of other-worldly ones, sermons could be used to encourage modern virtues of hard work, individual initiative, self-improvement, cooperation, and obedience to state authority.

For example, *khutaba'* within the Ministry of Religious Affairs are now required to attend supplementary training courses set up by the Institute for Criminological and Sociological Investigation, a state-run research center. According to one official statement:

> The aim [of this course] is to move the *khatib* beyond the traditional knowl-edge [*al-fikr al-taqlidi*] which has limited his activities to the religious con-cerns of inciting desire [*targhib*] and fear [*tarhib*], and reward and punish-ment, in isolation from contemporary life with its changes.... Our goal is to furnish the prayer leaders and *khutaba'* with a strong background in culture, economics, sociology, politics and history necessary to their min-isterial function.
>
> (*'AQIDATI* 1995)

Over the last few decades, the Egyptian state has continually devised new courses of this kind, often modifying the curriculum and emphasis as con-cerns shift between national pedagogy and national security.

Although *khutaba'* had always been recruited by Muslim rulers to pro-vide support for their policies and give legitimacy to their rule, the kind of political project into which religious orators were now incorporated was without precedent. Instead of an acclamatory function—the public recog-nition of the legitimacy of the regime—the sermon was now to be rendered an instrument of state-guided social and individual discipline, a pedagogical

technique for the dissemination of the attitudes and orientations appropriate to a modern national citizenry. Needless to say, this attempt to harness
the sermon to the task of nation building has run into numerous obstacles,
many of which I will discuss later. It will suffice here to note that many of
these obstacles stemmed from the fact that popular preaching has always
been grounded less in institutions of formal study (that is, those more easily placed under direct state control) than in social knowledges reproduced
more informally within the structures of local community.

Before the incorporation of Egypt's religious institutions into the bureaucracies of the state, the role of *khatib* was generally performed by a
respected figure from within the local community.[26] Up through the first
half of the twentieth century, *khutaba'* were, for the most part, residents of
the local neighborhood who, having studied and memorized some of the
Quran and a few *hadiths*[27] at a local religious school (*kuttab*), and being
respected in their community, were either asked by fellow residents of the
neighborhood or offered themselves to fulfill that duty, often without monetary compensation.[28] In other words, although the validity of the *khatib*'s
utterance was grounded in traditional Islamic knowledges, he often had no
direct tie to the higher institutions of Islamic learning and authority, his
religious training and social role taking place within the local community.
Preacher and listener were bound together within a common web of social
hierarchy, acquaintance, and learning.

With the incorporation of Egypt's religious institutions into the state,
many *khutaba'* became functionaries of the religious bureaucracy, serving in mosques by appointment from the Ministry of Religious Affairs but
without any deeper ties to the communities they addressed. The knowledge and authority of such state-appointed orators no longer emerged from
within the social fabric of the collective they addressed, but devolved from
their status as representatives of the state.[29] Their words now became *official*, the address of a sovereign state to its subjects. The organization of
authority that undergirded the rhetorical structure of preaching and the
practice of ethical audition—the marginality of the preacher in relation
to both religious and secular authority, the lack of a sharp status distinction between preacher and audience, the embeddedness of the preacher's
learning and authority within local institutions—this edifice collapses (or
at least begins to crack) with the emergence of the "official *khatib*." The listener is now interpellated by the state, at times as the subject of the modern knowledges of the national citizen, though increasingly as the Muslim
believer whose religious commitments and actions must be monitored and

circumscribed to the domain of private devotion. Even when confined to moments of private worship, however, the passional rhetoric of ethical preaching had to remain in check, as they risked opening up sensibilities that increasingly found articulation within the contestatory politics of the Islamic Revival movement.

Although the official *khatib* now bears the authorizing imprimatur of the state, his ability to mediate religious authority is thrown into question. The truthfulness of his discourse now comes to be subject to scrutiny to a far greater extent than had previously been the case. Prior to the incorporation of the institutions of preaching within the apparatuses of the Egyptian state, the authority of the *khatib*'s discourse was grounded in the mastery with which he performed the required elements of the sermon, weaving the common cultural stock of Quranic verses, *hadiths*, invocatory phrases, and stories in a way that demonstrated his competence in performing this traditional role. Once his art was recruited by the state, the *khatib*'s ability to establish the validity of his oratory on the basis of the authority inhering in his religious and communal role diminished. It was in this context that a new figure makes its appearance: the *da'iya* (from "*da'a*," to call, summon), the one who calls on fellow Muslims to live in conformity with God's will. Before I address this character, however, let me expand a little more on the ideas of speech and agency that made official preachers official, by turning to some of the new training manuals used in state religious institutions.

The professionalization of preaching in Egypt that began around the turn of the century was accompanied by the development of a pedagogical literature on the art of oratory (*al-khataba*), one quite distinct from the investigations into poetics and semantics found in the classical field of *'ilm al-balagha* I discussed earlier in this chapter. Before the emergence of these writings, most *khutaba'* relied on a number of classical exhortatory works and collections of prophetic traditions for their material. The preaching manuals that did exist focused primarily on the virtues the *khatib* must possess in order to perform his role and often concluded with a sample of exemplary sermons on common topics. As for the composition of the sermon itself, little was offered beyond a list of doctrinally specified requirements, usually limited to the following: the sermon (*khutba*) was to be divided into two sections, with the *khatib* sitting down briefly between the two; the opening should include the customary locutions of praise to God (the *hamdala*), prayers to the Prophet (*salat 'ala al-nabi*), and the *shahada*, the testimony to the unity of God and the status of Muhammad as his messenger; the *khatib* was instructed to recite verses from the Quran during the first section, and during both sections he should exhort the listeners to greater piety, ending with an invocation to God (*du'a'*). He should be in a state of ritual purity, and, according to some, should lean on a staff or sword during the *khutba*. Only men are allowed to perform the role of *khatib*.[30] Few manuals went beyond this.

From the end of the nineteenth century onward, a new genre of manual came to compete with this earlier ethics-based literature.[31] Within these new writings (and particularly in those published after the 1950s), the whole question of the virtues that had been central to preaching as an ethical practice was largely dropped, as sermons, increasingly modeled on the press, were reoriented around the task of providing and inculcating "useful information." The emphasis on individual ethics was gradually superseded by an amalgam of Aristotelian rhetoric and findings from the field of American communication studies. Thus, a manual entitled "The Art of Rhetoric and the Preparation of the Preacher," used to train *khutaba'* at the government-administered School of Guidance and Preaching at al-Azhar University, defines its subject matter as "that set of laws by which one is able to convince others in regard to whatever topic one desires, by causing the listener to surrender to the correctness of an argument or action" (Mahfuz 1984:13). Rather than serving as a catalyst for the ritual act and ethical exercise of drawing near to God, the *khatib* was now to deploy a morally neutral art of rhetorical manipulation, instilling in his audience the opinions and attitudes that would constitute modern Egyptians. Importantly, what is signaled by this innovation is not simply the adoption of new rhetorical methods or styles of argumentation but also a new conceptual framework for the relation of the *khatib* to his audience: the latter is stripped of its agency, which now lies entirely in the techniques of opinion manipulation exercised by the *khatib* as representative of the state. This is evident in the following comment from another popular sermon manual, written during the Nasser period:

[A *khatib*] with the eloquence and persuasiveness of his speech can incline his listeners toward *whatever good he wishes*, impart to them moral qualities and lead them away from wrongdoing, and rectify their characters; and plant in their souls [the importance of] practical work [*a'mal al-dunya*] as well as good work [*al- a'mal al-saliha*]. He can also be a support for the government in issues of state order and security.

(MUHAMMAD 1972:6, EMPHASIS ADDED)

The new set of assumptions is clear in this comment: by adopting the proper rhetorical style, a *khatib* can mold his audience like clay, transforming them into the sort of people that he, and the government he represents, seek to create. Guided by the state, as the agent responsible for the progressive development of the nation's people and resources, the sermon is to become a device for working on and improving the raw human material that is to be the national citizenry.[32] This shift can be highlighted by comparing the comment quoted above with one from a preaching textbook exemplifying the ethical tradition I discussed. Importantly, the fact that the textbook I cite is of recent publication should not be read as evidence of anachronism but, as I explore below, owes much to the contemporary rearticulation and revival of an auditory ethics within a new social, political, and technological matrix. Writing on the subject of vocal technique, the author of the manual notes:

> Thus, the *khatib*'s voice must embody [*yujassim*] the ideas of his sermon and give form to their meanings; he must perfect his ability to enunciate each letter in its natural way, such that the inflection of his voice gives each expression its due [*haqqihi*]. . . . A good voice and a correct pronunciation [*sidq al-lahja*] accompanied by sincerity [*al-ikhlas*] produces the words that come from the heart of the speaker.
>
> (ABU SAMAK 1995:95)

Notably, the *khatib* in this conception does not make his discourse persuasive by embellishing it; nor is his relation to his speech purely instrumental. Instead, he submits to its discipline, fashioning his voice in accord with the demands of the words he recites, giving them their "due" (*haqqihi*), their "natural" pronunciation. This achieved, his task ends, while that of the listener begins.

With the rising prominence of both reformist and militant Islamic oppositional movements, the pedagogical role of the sermon has been increasingly backgrounded by the Egyptian state in favor of an emphasis on security concerns. A variety of legislative and administrative measures have been adopted since the 1980s in order to extend state control over mosques, among them an acceleration of the process of nationalizing all local neighborhood mosques (*al-masajid al-ahaliyya*); attempts to control the content of sermons at state mosques by stipulating the topics to be discussed each week;[33] stationing government censors (*mufattishun*) in all mosques to monitor sermon content; and, most recently, passing a law that makes it illegal for anyone not licensed by the Ministry of Religious Affairs to give a sermon (*al-Hayat* 1997a, 1997b).[34] During the Sadat era (1970–1981), it was assumed that all mosques could be staffed by preachers appointed directly by the Ministry of Religious Affairs, so as to solve the problem of militant preaching. As it became obvious that this plan was well beyond the state's actual financial and administrative capacity, the focus shifted to the figure of the *khatib* alone, with a program that sought to place a state *khatib* in all mosques: this was the goal behind the foundation of the College of Prosleytization Activity (*kulliyyat al-da'wa*) and other state programs for the training of the *khutaba'* and other religious professionals. Forced to scale down the plan once again, 1996 legislation simply required that all *khutaba'* obtain licenses from the state.[35] The temporary solution to this ongoing problem, however, has been the stationing of censors and police monitors in most mosques. This shift in strategy has also been accompanied by a growing pessimism among many within the state regarding the potential of sermon oratory to serve as a vehicle of enlightenment. With oratory's power to reform increasingly in doubt, the utility of mosques has been redefined, to some extent, in panoptic terms, as structures for the localization, control, and supervision of bodies. In a dramatic shift, mosques have become sites where the *state* now *listens* to the audience for the incipient rumblings of contestation and militancy.

VOICES LOST AND FOUND

While I have discussed a shift in the model and status of the listener that is tied to the incorporation of the institutions of preaching within the state, there are other important transformations that, while not directly involving religious institutions, nonetheless have had an impact on the sensibilities that cassette-sermon listeners today bring to acts of audition. Although the modernizing state in Egypt has sought to impose its own rationalities on traditions of Islamic practice, reason, and sensibility, some of the political and mediatic practices it has promoted have had the unintended consequence of giving new impulse and direction to Islamic ethical traditions, including the tradition of agentive listening. Two media events were particularly key both in introducing a nationalist sensibility to the pious ear and in linking its cultivation to media technology: the radio broadcasts of Gamel Abd al-Nasser's speeches during the 1950s and 1960s, and the weekly concerts of the singer Umm Kulthum during the same period.

Enabled by both the vast proliferation of radios during the decades of the 1950s and 1960s and by a populist political movement centered on the personality of the president himself, Nasser's rousing speeches provided Egyptians with their first experience of a collective national audition (see Gordon 1992). Many contemporary *khutaba'* associated with the oppositional Islamist currents cite Nasser as among those speakers whose oratorical prowess had the greatest influence in shaping sermon oratory during the twentieth century. Far from being bombastic, Nasser's rhetorical style relied on subtle modulations of tone and vocal affect (see Stokes in press:16). By means of such vocal qualities, Nasser was able to mediate, in unparalleled fashion, between contrasting structures of sensibility and affect, between ethics and politics, creating a space of acoustic intimacy between himself and his audience. Notably, as Nasser's successors were unable to match his unique rhetorical skills or rely upon the revolutionary enthusiasm that accompanied Egypt's socialist experiment, they gradually forfeited the ability to enlist the ear as the sense organ of a national imaginary. Instead, hearing and the human voice were rapidly recuperated by an opposition movement grounded in Islamic institutions and the traditions of oratory and ethical audition these institutions embedded. A modern political discourse was, in this way, increasingly incorporated within practices of ethical listening linked to the sermon.

Egypt's definitive moments of collective audition, however, came with the weekly radio concerts of the singer Umm Kulthum during the 1950s and 1960s (Danielson 1997). No performer in Europe or the United States has ever come close to garnering the sort of universal adulation that she commanded among Egyptians and the broader Arab world. Trained in the art of Quranic recitation and the genres of Islamic folk performance popular throughout the Egyptian countryside, Umm Kulthum's music embodied the sensibilities of Egyptians in a way that other contemporary performers, lacking experience in the Islamic traditions of vocal performance, could not. In many ways, her vocal style, particularly in the early part of her career, foregrounded the same affective dynamics that underlay the tradition of ethical-sermon audition. As I mentioned earlier in this chapter, Umm Kulthum was one of the last popular Egyptian singers whose music was said to possess the quality of *tarab*, the "enchantment" produced by the affective synthesis of listener and performer. As noted, the transsubjective dynamism characteristic of *tarab* depends on the skills and knowledge of both performer and audience and on the social and technological forms that mediate their relationship. Umm Kulthum demonstrated, among other things, that these conditions could be created and sustained across the transition from live performance to studio recording to media commodity, a lesson that, as I explore below, preachers took to heart.

In a recent article, Martin Stokes draws an interesting contrast between Umm Kulthum and the singer Abd al-Halim Hafiz, a contemporary of Kulthum's who also garnered great popularity in Egypt and beyond. Although Abd al-Halim's musical prowess was widely celebrated, he was rarely viewed as a performer capable of *tarab*. His unique style was instead described as "'*atafiyya*," a term generally translated as "emotional" but glossed by Stokes as "sentimental." This designation, Stokes suggests, registered a certain ambivalence toward Abd al-Halim regarding what might be called his "authoritarian style," one evident in his approach to his own music, his relations with his fellow performers, and his engagement with the audience. Stokes frames the contrast between Umm Kulthum's *tarab* and Abd al-Halim's sentimentalism in a political register:

> On the one hand is tarab: a democratic art, in which everyone listens to everyone else, and everybody contributes equally in their own particular way. The audience participates (encouraging the singer and the musicians by their commentary and expressions of appreciation as they play). The singer carries the text, and thus assumes a leadership role, but one always understood as being qualified and tempered by the other musicians. On the other hand is sentimentalism, a genre produced by a division of labor in which audiences have no voice, give and take between musicians is not possible, and the singer assumes an authoritarian and undemocratic role.
>
> (STOKES IN PRESS:11)

The anxiety Stokes identifies in regard to Abd al-Halim came in part from the perception of a monologic control but also from a style of emotionality that addressed individuals—and particularly women—in an intensely private and personal manner, an address "simultaneously interiorized and elusive, but also highly public" (Stokes in press:15). Detached from the conventions of expressivity governing *tarab*, proliferating from the singer's microphone to the radios and tape players of women in the intimacy and invisibility of their homes, such *'atafiyya* music reinforced a set of apprehensions tied to the new mobility and consumerist practices of bourgeois women.

Popular music has not been the only arena in which Egyptians have encountered new forms of emotional expression during the twentieth century. Television, a state monopoly until the rise of satellite stations over the last few years, has also played a key role in the politics and aesthetics of affect within contemporary Egypt. In her recent book *Dramas of Nationhood* (2005), Lila Abu-Lughod explores the pedagogical function of popular television serials in training (largely female) audiences in the protocols of expressivity and modes of self-understanding of modern bourgeois individuals. By foregrounding interpersonal relationships and scenes of characters poised in silent contemplation, their passional depths plumbed through close-ups of facial expression accompanied by emotively appropriate musical scores, these television dramas educate their audiences in the affective codes of a modern psychological subject, and a particularly sentimental one at that (Abu-Lughod 2005:123). For this subject, the conventions of passional expression found in the Islamic poetic and folk genres popular throughout the Egyptian countryside are inadequate to the demands of modern selfhood.

What I want to draw attention to here is how tensions accompanying social and political modernization in postindependence Egypt have resonated with contrasting structures of affect and sensibility and within the religious and aesthetic practices wherein such forms of expression and experience have been cultivated. The contemporary configuration of political debate in Egypt owes much to these contrasting structures of affect and appraisal. Just as the death of Nasser marked the end of a national audition in the political arena, Umm Kulthum's death in 1972 coincided with the dissolution of the music industry in Egypt that had made such national superstars possible (see Armbrust 1996). The entire structure that had raised Umm Kulthum and a few other musicians to such prominence, one grounded in a highly centralized control and coordination of film, record, and radio production, was in the process of crumbling, a condition indebted in no small way to the weakening of copyright protections in the face of the possibility of infinite duplication afforded by the cassette. Nasser and Umm Kulthum had, in different ways, helped to define a modern national auditory practice that connected traditions of ethical listening with emerging media practices of political discourse and musical entertainment. However, as neither of the two had a successor in his respective field, the sole inheritors of their legacy were the media-based popular preachers associated with the rising Islamist trend that has progressively gained ascendance since the 1970s.

The social and ethical edifice of *tarab* and its actor/listener have, over the last thirty years, broken away from the national public sphere articulated by the voices of Umm Kulthum and Nasser and instead taken root within the Islamic Revival movement and the forms of public sociability and political critique it has engendered.

As sermons moved outside the mosque to become a popular media practice, one competing with other forms of media entertainment, listeners came to expect some of the same pleasure and cathartic experience that Umm Kulthum's music had previously made available. Moreover, in their capacity to circulate outside the regulatory purview of the state, cassettes became the privileged media form for a contestatory Islamic discourse on state and society. Many of the young men I worked with explicitly identified cassette sermons as an alternative to the televisual and press media promoted by the state. Attempts to produce and distribute cassette sermons featuring state-approved *khutaba'*—including Shaykh Sha'rawi (d. 1998), a *khatib* heavily promoted by the Egyptian government in both print and televisual media—have met with little success. Not surprisingly, the immense attraction of Sha'rawi has always centered on his avuncular grimaces and gestures, that is, on his televisual image and not his vocal performance.

Once hearing lost its privileged relationship to the version of Egyptian national culture promoted by the state, the ear and the institutions that previously organized its cultivation became suspect from the point of view of the modernizing state. Associated with religious customs and knowledges that were now seen as obstacles to modernization, the aural traditions came to be viewed as morally and epistemologically untrustworthy, if not directly responsible for the rise of a violent militant movement carried out in the name of Islam. Today, articles in the government-controlled national press frequently bemoan the ongoing practice of traditions that cultivate a "reverence for the sacred word" and an attention to the sonic and affective qualities of language over and above the symbolic. Hearing bypasses the rational faculties, it is claimed, penetrating directly to the vulnerable emotional core of the untutored Egyptian peasant. Reading, in contrast, encourages reasoned reflection and reasoned assent. The nineteenth-century European critique of the superficiality and artificiality of Muslim practices has found a new purchase in this context: tradition-bound Muslims, it is said, are too involved with the surfaces and externalities of language, speech, and bodily performance, a concern incompatible with more refined and developed modes of reason, understanding, and piety.

ISLAMIC REVIVAL

The centripetal consolidation of religious authority and knowledge by the Egyptian state from the 1950s onward occurred simultaneously with a vast centrifugal countermovement, what both observers and participants often refer to as the Islamic Revival movement, al-Sahwa al-Islamiyya. The revival has had the net effect of dispersing the loci of religious authority across a variety of new locations, media, and associational forms. Because the protagonists of this movement have adopted modes of organization, communication, and technology ushered in by political modernization, they hastened those processes of transformation promoted by the state that aimed at developing a modern public sphere. The emergent networks of politics, media, and religious authority that the Islamic Revival gave rise to, however, also made possible new and unanticipated articulations of Islamic scholarly and practical traditions, including the tradition of ethical listening I described earlier.

It is in this context that the cassette sermon found its calling. As one of the few media forms able to circulate beneath the radar of state sur-veillance and regulation, sermon tapes emerged as the privileged me-dium of an Islamic oppositional discourse. Within the new practices of learning and organization promulgated by the revival movement, listen-ing—an act largely ignored within the discourses on society, politics, and religion that underlay Egypt's modernizing efforts in the first half of the century—now came to be assigned considerable agency in relation to the goal of moral transformation. Through the medium of the cassette tape, acts of individual audition—properly performed—could compen-sate for the limitations the state had imposed on public discourse. Si-lence the speaker, but his words would still proliferate and acquire agency through the actions of listeners within the electronic network. The in-terpretive conventions and forms of aesthetic appraisal central to ethical listening were carried over to the cassette context, where they were revised in accordance with what were understood to be the functional capacities and modes of circulation of the media form. While the mosque—as a space of collective discipline—remained central to the Sahwa movement, it now came to be supplemented by cassette-based techniques of individ-ual self-fashioning. From such new practices, and across the soundscapes they fashioned, other histories of affect and ethical reasoning began to draw breath.

AN INFRASTRUCTURE EMERGES

The preachers who pioneered the cassette sermon in the 1970s emerged from an institutional infrastructure composed, on the one hand, of a number of Islamic reform movements fashioned in the image of political parties (the Muslim Brotherhood being the largest and most influential) and, on the other, the nongovernmental Islamic welfare organizations (*jam'iyyat*), many of which center their activities on preaching and the training of preachers.[36] Founded in 1928 under the leadership of Hassan al-Banna, the Muslim Brotherhood (al-Ikhwan al-Muslimun) articulated a modern political vision responsive to both the demands of Muslim piety and the facts of Western domination, a vision that permanently changed the political landscape throughout the Middle East and well beyond. From its inception as a grassroots piety movement aimed at encouraging Egyptians to abide by Islamic moral standards, through its transformation into a national and international political force, the Ikhwan consistently sought to counter secularizing trends that they claimed had confined Islam to the mosque. While mass media was a key part of this effort, the sermon provided its paradigmatic rhetorical form. Many of the outstanding *khutaba'* of the 1970s and 1980s, including those who pioneered the cassette sermon, were members of the Ikhwan,[37] and even those who were not were deeply influenced by the approach and style of Hassan al-Banna's sermons, and even more so by the writings of Sayyid Qutb, one of the Ikhwan's most influential intellectuals.

Hassan al-Banna marks the appearance of a type of Islamic public figure that, over the course of the century, would play an ever more important role in shaping popular religious expression. As with many of the leaders of the revival who would follow him, al-Banna never received instruction at al-Azhar, historically the site of religious training and authority, but rather at Cairo University's Dar al-Ulum, a secular institution founded in the 1890s to train Egyptians in the forms of knowledge required within the emerging bureaucracies of the modernizing state.[38] Indeed, many of the leading figures of the Islamic Revival have degrees in such nonreligious subjects as medicine, engineering, and law, having acquired their religious knowledge through self-guided study or through informal apprenticeships with shaykhs at local mosques. While many of those who have acquired their training through such nontraditional avenues are recognized by their audiences for their scholarly expertise, they are not considered part of the class of religious scholars, or *'ulama'*. Within the Sahwa they are less bearers of established religious authority than exemplary figures of a form of modern piety and activism. Thus, instead of being assigned the appellation ʿalim, the term traditionally used to designate a recognized religious scholar, the leaders of this movement have increasingly come to be referred to by the term daʿiya (pl. duʿat)—one who "summons" others (from daʿa, to summon or call) to act in accord with norms of divinely sanctioned behavior. While I will discuss daʿwa (from which the nominative daʿiya is derived) at some length in the chapter 4, I simply want to note here that the term marks a shift within the field of religious authority: the agency and authority of the daʿiya derives not from the state-administered religious bureaucracies but from the alternative institutional matrix for the reproduction of religious knowledge that has grown in tandem with the Islamic Revival. The term registers a distinction between the ethical motivation understood to underlie the revival movement, on the one hand, and reasons of the modern state on the other. Although the men and women who practice daʿwa—who take on themselves the moral guidance and improvement of the umma—may have personal and institutional links to the traditional centers of religious learning and authority now under the umbrella of the state, in their capacity as duʿat, they act on behalf of a project understood to be in tension with official policy.

In addition to the Ikhwan, a large number of what might be called Islamic charitable associations offering various forms of social assistance have been founded in Egypt, particularly since the 1970s, many explicitly concerned with upholding and reinvigorating the traditions of Islamic sociability gradually being effaced by the forces of the secular-modern. Some of the largest of these, such as the Jamaʿat Ansar al-Sunna al-Muhammadiyya (Association of the followers of Muhammad's acts and deeds) and al-Jamʿiyya al-Sharʿiyya (The association for moral rectitude), have concentrated their activities on the building of mosques and the training of educators and khutabaʾ to give lessons and sermons.[39] In the vision of these groups, the reform of Egyptian society is to be secured not through the agency of national politics but by means of local-level pedagogical work focused on individual ethics and centered around the mosque and its affiliated welfare institutions.[40] Ethical preaching in general, and the Friday sermon in particular, have been central to this effort.

The distinction between government-administered and independent preaching currents finds a correlate in two varieties of mosques: those under the administration of the Ministry of Religious Affairs and those known as al-masajid al-ahaliyya that are either run by nongovernmental associations (jamʿiyyat) (such as Jamaʿat Ansar al-Sunna al-Muhammadiyya) or by neighborhood committees. As I noted earlier in this chapter, there is now a widespread opinion in Egypt that the *khutaba'* under the ministry umbrella are little more than bureaucratic functionaries (*muwazzafun*) of the state, professionals without any personal commitment to the Islamic institutions they represent. Indeed, most *khatib* positions at government mosques today are filled by graduates from al-Azhar University who fail to obtain more lucrative assignments as teachers in the public school system. In contrast, *khutaba'* who are not government appointees, whether linked to the Ikhwan or to Islamic charitable associations, are widely considered to be acting from a personal commitment to Islamic moral tenets. This difference is also reflected in the term of self-attribution used by the respective types of *khutaba'*: while government employees are referred to by the official designations "*khatib*" or "*imam*," those who are not associated with the government tend to refer to themselves as "*da'iya*."

It is in the context of this shifting and fractured field of Islamic institutional authority that the cassette sermon emerges. While sermons had been recorded on tape in Egypt since recording machines first became available early in the twentieth century, the emergence of the cassette sermon as a popular cultural form dates from the beginning of the 1970s. During those years, it began to be common for people to bring tape recorders to the mosques where popular *khutaba'* were preaching and to record their sermons so as to be able to hear them again at home. This practice grew in tandem with, and was largely fueled by, the rising popularity of Shaykh Abd al-Hamid Kishk (d. 1996), whose reputation for passionate and critical oratory was beginning to draw audiences of an unprecedented size to his mosque in the Cairene district of al-Hada'iq al-Qubba. A coterie of Kishk's followers had, by the early 1970s, begun to record, copy, and distribute his sermons at the mosque on Fridays. Within a few years, the immense popularity of these tapes had led a few modest-sized companies to become involved in recording and distributing sermon tapes, both through their own small stores and on the sidewalks outside of the larger mosques.[41] Small advertisements from these years in the magazine of the Muslim Brotherhood, *al-I'tisam* (1975–1980), announced the sale of sermon tapes from Abd al-Hamid Kishk, Muhammad al-Ghazali, Hassan Ayub, Ibrahim Ezzat, and other *khutaba'* who were well known at that time, many of them with links to the Muslim Brotherhood. In addition, as labor migration between Egypt and the Gulf states intensified during this period, many Egyptians returning home began bringing with them sermon tapes of Saudi and Kuwaiti *khutaba'*, as well as tape recorders purchased with money saved during their stays abroad.[42]

By the mid-1970s, Shaykh Kishk's taped sermons had become a ubiquitous part of the Cairene soundscape, his sharp criticisms of the Sadat regime echoing from stores, taxis, and buses, and private balconies and living rooms throughout the popular quarters.[43] One effect of Kishk's great popularity was to give the cassette its particular status as a technology of the Islamic Revival, as a media form conjoining a contestatory Islamic discourse on state and society, an ethical exercise, and a popular distraction. Kishk's acrid criticisms of the Sadat government and its religious authorities, as well as of Western forms of culture and consumption, defined the cassette sermon as a contestatory Islamic media form, one whose use over the ensuing years would become increasingly suspect in the view of both the government and secular-leftist factions of Egyptian society. As Wagdi Ghunaim, a popular *khatib* from Alexandria whose cassettes sell widely, notes: "I have taken up preaching because the *'ulama'* [religious scholars] at al-Azhar have forsaken their duty. When they once again fulfill their responsibility to preserve our society, then I'll give up preaching" (*'Aqidati* 1996). The cassette offered the revival a site where *du'at* could speak truth in the face of power, and frequently suffer the consequences. Indeed, instances of a *khatib* having suffered at the hands of the state for his taped pronouncements are often now cited as evidence of the *khatib*'s commitment to Islam and of his courage to speak its truth.[44]

Notably, attempts to use the cassette medium to promote arguments sympathetic to the government have continued to be largely unsuccessful. For example, as mentioned earlier, taped sermons of Shaykh Sha'rawi, a "state-approved"[45] *khatib* whose television and print popularity rivals that of all other contemporary religious figures in Egypt, never gained a wide audience. In the years since the height of Kishk's popularity in the late 1970s and early 1980s, the cassette sermon has remained a popular vehicle for the articulation of a critical commentary on the spread of Western social and cultural forms within society. The moral authority of this media form derives less from the classical institutions of Islamic learning, now compromised by the secularizing policies of the state, and more from its embeddedness within the broad domain of *da'wa*, a sphere of religious activity claiming responsibility for the moral direction of Egyptian society in light of the state's failure to perform this role.

According to Egyptian law, all tapes produced and sold commercially require the approval of the Council on Islamic Research (Majma' al-Buhuth al-Islamiyya), the branch of al-Azhar charged with ensuring the conformity of all commercially sold Islamic texts and recordings with a set of orthodox and state-censorship standards. If the council grants approval for a tape, a permit number (*tasrih*) is assigned to it that must be printed on each commercially sold copy. The council frequently requires that certain sections of a sermon or mosque lesson be removed, either on the grounds that they deviate from accepted standards of Islamic argumentation or that they address political issues deemed "too sensitive" by the current government.

While commercial sales of sermon tapes continue to be an important factor in their distribution and use, a far greater number of tapes are recorded, copied, and sold by small-scale entrepreneurs without commercial licenses, contracts with *khutaba'*, or the required permits from al-Azhar.[46] Tapes of this kind are sold in generic cassette boxes, with only the name of the *khatib* and the title of the sermon written by hand on the cover. Although the Egyptian police occasionally confiscate this merchandise from vendors, most of the time they are left alone to sell their wares on the streets outside of mosques or bus stations. However, while a significant number of sermon tapes are produced as objects for sale, the majority of those in use circulate through informal practices of exchange and home duplication, a situation made possible in part by the weakness of copyright laws in Egypt. Tapes are often borrowed and exchanged among friends, groups of university students, acquaintances who have met at the mosque, and so on. In addition, most mosques are now equipped with tape lending libraries. Moreover, preachers encourage people to record, reproduce, and disseminate their sermons, and even commercially produced tapes often include a written statement encouraging the buyer to copy the tape and make it available to others.

For these reasons, sermon and mosque lesson tapes have never been the site of intense capitalization. While a burgeoning export business has been developing over the last couple of decades, in Egypt itself the association of such tapes with suspect political currents has rendered them too precarious a commodity to attract large-scale investment. The fact that the careers of popular *khutaba'* are frequently interrupted by periods of incarceration, house arrest, and the suspension of their right to preach places serious limitations on the marketability of their tapes. By the mid-1980s, the use of advertising to sell cassette sermons had all but ceased, despite the growing popularity of the cassette-sermon phenomenon. In short, the rudimentary market structures that have enabled the production and dissemination of sermons have never been completely untethered from the pedagogical and disciplinary practices of the mosque, nor from the forms of embodied sociability promoted by the *da'wa* movement.

INTERLINKAGES

While the distinction I have made here between state and nongovernmental institutions in regard to the recent history of the sermon is useful, in actual practice the two trajectories constantly intertwine. Many of the most well-known Egyptian *khutaba'* of recent years—for example, Muhammad Mitwalli al-Sha'rawi, Muhammad al-Ghazali, Abd al-Sabbur Shahin, and Abd al-Hamid Kishk—have all been affiliated at some point in their careers both with state institutions *and* with major opposition movements, most frequently with the Muslim Brotherhood. Abd al-Sabbur Shahin, for instance, held an appointment for many years as the chief advisor on religious affairs for the ruling National Democratic Party. At the same time, however, as *khatib* at Cairo's largest mosque, Ibn al-As, he commonly expressed positions on social and legal issues that strongly contradicted those publicly asserted by the state.[47] Even Shaykh Kishk, one of the most unequivocally oppositional public voices of the last thirty years, was never entirely outside the official structures he so powerfully criticized. While Kishk worked for a brief period as an itinerant *khatib* within the system of mosques belonging to the private association al-Jam'iyya al-Shar'iyya, for most of his life he preached for the Ministry of Religious Affairs at the al-Malik mosque in the al-Hada'iq al-Qubba quarter of Cairo. Notably, he retained his position as *imam-khatib* at this mosque from 1964 until 1981, despite having become one of the most virulent critics of the Egyptian government and having been subject to all forms of state repression, including two periods of imprisonment. Then, after having been permanently prohibited from preaching and restricted in his personal movement and communications, he was nonetheless offered a regular weekly column in the Islamic newspaper *al-Liwa' al-Islami*, one of the papers published by the governing party.

The seemingly contradictory positions the state has taken reveal the limits of a political analysis based solely on the distinction between state and private institutions, as well as the error of seeing the state as a monolithic agent. These inconsistencies, of course, can be explained in part by reference to political strategy. The stance of the Egyptian state vis-à-vis Islamist oppositional currents has tended to fluctuate in response to changing perceptions both of state stability and the degree of danger posed by such currents. Overall, the state has applied a kind of political calculus characteristic of democratizing states. This has involved a two-pronged strategy. On the one hand, the Egyptian state has allowed moderate forms of opposition to be expressed within the institutions of public deliberation and representation (mass media and, to a lesser extent, elections) in order to bolster its claims to legitimacy and curtail the appeal of Islamist groups.[48] On the other hand, the Egyptian state has also sought to undermine contestatory movements through wide-scale imprisonment, censorship, and the passage of legislation severely limiting open political expression. In short, what seem to be inconsistencies in the state's approach to Islamist movements often reflect shifting evaluations of the danger that a particular person or group represents, the success of temporary accommodations reached, and changing strategies of co-optation and repression.[49]

Yet such patterns of affiliation and opposition can only partially be explained through an analysis centered on state strategy. Beyond strategic calculation, these inconsistencies also reflect friction and disjuncture between the modernist discourses of the state and the religious traditions it seeks to encompass, reform, and regulate. While the state has tried to harness the Islamic pedagogical, juridical, and homiletic institutions for the twin goals of nationalist propaganda and state security, this has not led to the wholesale abandonment of the practices and discourses that those institutions previously upheld. Many of the state-administered religious organizations include sizable factions sympathetic to the same religious arguments that they have been called upon to officially denounce and combat. The nationalized University of al-Azhar, for instance, has frequently been the site of various challenges to the government. Most recently, new legislation requiring that all *khutaba'* be licensed by the Ministry of Religious Affairs was strongly denounced in a report put out by a group of leading Azhar scholars (*'ulama'*) (see *al-Hayat* 1996a, 1996b).[50] Indeed, many of the al-Azhar faculty members and students I came to know during my stay in Egypt also participated actively in the affairs of independent Islamic institutions associated with revival currents. Conflicts also often occur between different state bureaucracies. In 1995, for example, the minister of education, in a tactic intended to undermine the Islamist trend, asserted that schoolgirls would no longer be allowed to wear headscarves, only to have his decision overruled within a week by Ali Jad al-Haqq Jad al-Haqq, the state-appointed supreme authority at al-Azhar.

State attempts to purge these institutions of the commitments, orientations, and sensibilities that continue to link them with and make them responsive to Islamist currents have been only partially successful. The problem, as viewed by the state, was made clear to me during a discussion I had with a secularly oriented sociologist who had been employed by the Ministry of Religious Affairs to teach one of the supplementary training courses for *khutaba'* mentioned earlier:

We are supposed to give them a background in the sort of fields of science relevant to contemporary life—psychology, sociology, and so on—and to provide them with clear ways to counter fundamentalist claims. Basically, the aim is to secularize them. From what I've seen, however, by the time they arrive here it is too late, as they are far too steeped in traditional Islamic perspectives and thus immune to all our attempts. They've spent years reading and talking about hell, the danger of women's skin, how much beneficence from God they earn by repeating meaningless phrases. And as *khutaba'*, they will go out and spread more ignorance and superstition, even as employees of the Ministry of Religious Affairs.

For those trained in and committed to the practices and modes of reasoning that this sociologist criticizes, many of the Islamist arguments are worthy of serious engagement rather than the outright rejection preferred by the state. The religious institutions now incorporated within state bureaucracies do in fact provide the state with a useful platform: passing fatwas in support of government proposals, authoritatively challenging the arguments put forth by opponents of the state, and retooling the practice of Islamic preaching for the task of state security. At the same time, however, the performance of this function is mitigated by the fact that those who work within these institutions remain deeply entwined with and responsive to the manifold developments within the field of *da'wa* as it has emerged outside the confines of state control. This responsiveness draws force from the ethical attitudes and structures of affect sustained and popularized by the Islamic Revival movement.

THE CONTEMPORARY POLITICS OF HEARING

As I have pointed out in this chapter, the shifts in the orientation and function of hearing that have accompanied the modernizing project in Egypt have not led to the wholesale abandonment or replacement of the earlier tradition of ethical listening. In this last section of the chapter, I want to briefly indicate how tensions between diverse styles of listening are articulated in social and political conflicts in Egypt today. Disagreements about the role of listening do not simply reflect different ideologies of eye and ear, speech and writing, but also concern the range of institutions that embed these practices, the goals they promote, and the forms of sociability they sustain or are indifferent toward.

To cite an example, one of the axes around which contemporary political divisions within Egyptian society position themselves concerns the question of whether the Quran's divine aspect lies in the material word, or only in its symbolic meaning, as discovered through the operation of human understanding. The two models of language authorize very different interpretive regimes, structures of power linked to contrasting social and political projects but also undergirded by diverse repertoires of affect and experience. Arguments on this topic are part of public debate and frequently appear in sermons as well as in the popular press, both state and independent.

For example, in a 1995 article in the Labor Party (Hizb al-ʿamal) newspaper al-Shaʿb, the writer Muhammad Wagdi asserts the validity of a more literalist interpretive approach, drawing on the Quranic account that the divine text entered the Prophet's heart before it was uttered by his tongue. Having cited a verse from the chapter of the Quran (al-Qiyama) that refers to this account, he explains, "And this means that the Quran was inserted into the heart of Muhammad, and thus that he heard it [samʿ] through revelation before he pronounced it. That is, that he memorized it in his heart before he understood it, or, in other words, that the verbal expression preceded the explanation of its meaning" (Wagdi 1995). Wagdi then goes on to speculate on why God imparted such a miraculous nature to the verbal expression itself, suggesting that God did this so that "the beauty of the composition [jamal al-siyagha] [would become] inseparable from the greatness of its message, and this unity [would create in the listener] remembrance [al-dhikr] and humility [khushuʿ]." His argument, in other words, has an ethical dimension, one belonging to the same tradition of sensitive listening I discussed earlier. The ethical dispositions that the author deems essential to a Muslim society (such as humility or a mindfulness for God's commands) depend upon an appreciation for the "sheer words" of the Quran, or rather, on the practices of aural discipline that incorporate such an appreciation (such as sermon audition, Quranic recitation [tajwid], memorization [hifz], and so on). That is, entwined within the debate about the status of the Quranic word is an argument about the virtues that underlie a Muslim society and the role of those virtues within public life (such as within public education).

Said al-Ashmawi, one of the Islamic thinkers whose opinion on this matter is criticized in Wagdi's article and who writes prolifically on matters of Quranic interpretation and history, asserts an opposing view. Writing in a popular leftist magazine, al-Ashmawi argues that it is the meaning of the Quran that is preeminent, a meaning, moreover, that has no necessary relation to a precise verbal form. In his view, an overprivileging of the literal word has been an impediment to free thinking and reason throughout Islamic history and has kept Muslim societies from progressing. While it is not necessary here to rehearse the details of al-Ashmawi's argument, I do want to point to the context in which the argument occurs. Specifically, al-Ashmawi is a legal scholar allied with liberal currents within the judicial and political system in Egypt. For those who support these currents, the virtues cited by Muhammad Wagdi and the institutions that uphold those virtues do not have a dominant role to play within contemporary society. For thinkers like al-Ashmawi—often called "neo-*mu'tazila*" by contemporary Egyptians in reference to the eighth-century rationalist movement in Islamic history—God's wisdom, as embodied in the Quran, must be consonant with, or at least not impede, the modes of reasoning and pragmatic demands that underlie the progressive movement of modern national life. The contemporary reading of the Quran (and it is a *reading*, not a recitation) must take as its goal the uncovering of symbolic meanings through an interpretive approach founded upon the same notions of language, history, and context applied to contemporary literary texts.

This disagreement, I want to suggest, can be usefully illuminated by taking into consideration the contrasting ways of understanding agency and authority in relation to auditory experience.[51] More is involved here than a simple contrast between a literalist and a symbolic interpretive emphasis. For Muhammad Wagdi, writing in *al-Sha'b*, the sound of words lies at the heart of those traditional practices by which the self acquires the virtues that enable moral action. Al-Ashmawi's argument, on the other hand, draws on an expressivist understanding of language, whereby speech is conceived of as a material apparatus for the externalization of a nonmaterial meaning. Too much concern for the sonic qualities of the Quran, mere externalities in this view, threatens to corrupt the purity of the interpretive exercise, to infect one's reasoned engagement with the text with nonrational modes of discrimination. The assumption here is that vocal expression, especially religious expression, can only be an instrument of power applied to a passive listener. These contrastive traditions of language theory and practice presuppose distinct conceptual and disciplinary conditions of their respective readers or listeners; for this reason, without the prior cultivation of certain sensibilities, affective habits of the ear, it will be difficult for partisans of one position to appreciate the force of their opponents' arguments.

❖ ❖ ❖

In this chapter I have traced a set of shifts that have affected practices of ethical listening in Egypt, shifts that have repositioned the pious ear in relation to both the nation and institutions of Islamic authority. The progression I describe is not one of continuous development along a singular axis but rather a series of partial displacements, recuperations, and reorientations. While the ear acquired the features of a national sense organ, it continued to resonate with sensory memory grounded in the tradition of ethical affect and sensibility I began with, a tradition that encompasses the music of *tarab*, Quranic recitation, practices of mystical discipline, and sermon listening. I now turn to this latter to explore the role of the cassette in shaping the ethical sensorium of a contemporary Muslim citizen in Egypt.

[3]

THE ETHICS OF LISTENING

Intellectual life is not an empire within an empire; it is impregnated with affective states which themselves tend to self-expression in movement; it has therefore a constant tendency to play itself out externally.

—MARCEL JOUSSE

AHMAD WAS one of the men with whom I listened to sermon tapes on a regular basis when I was in Cairo. He lived with his mother and sister in the lower-middle-class neighborhood of Ain Shams and worked in an aluminum processing plant on the outskirts of Cairo. Ahmad's father had abandoned the family and gone off to work in Germany some years earlier, and for years now, his father's sole contribution to their family was an occasional phone call and the long-unfulfilled promise that he would someday bring Ahmad to Europe and set him up with a job. After her husband's departure, Ahmad's mother took up a job as a clerk in a government office; her salary, combined with Ahmad's, just barely covered basic expenses. Like many Egyptians in their late twenties and early thirties, Ahmad was desperately trying to put enough money aside to afford marriage, an issue all the more pressing given the increasing impatience of his prospective bride.

Ahmad had become involved in *da'wa* activities as a student during his years at Ain Shams University, from which he had graduated the year before I met him. Approached by other students, he had joined a small group that met regularly in a mosque not far from his house where they received instruction from the resident shaykh. The mosque provided the group with sermon tapes, sheets with devotional sayings, and other instructional materials. The group followed a program aimed at strengthening their knowledge of Islam and their ability to live in accord with its precepts, a program that included the stipulation that they listen to a sermon tape at least twice a week. During one of the many government sweeps aimed at uncovering Islamic militants, a number of the group members were arrested, though most were released after two weeks. This experience led Ahmad to distance himself somewhat from the group and to generally steer clear of Islamist associations on campus. He still had a circle of friends with whom he would exchange tapes, and when they visited his house while I was there, we often listened to a tape together. Thus, while he continued to ascribe great importance to religious practice in his life—praying regularly and attending to his other religious duties, as well as listening to sermon tapes and reading current publications from Islamist presses—he no longer engaged in organized *da'wa* activities or participated in Islamist political associations.

As with other sermon listeners I came to know in Cairo, Ahmad emphasized the utility of sermon tapes as a form of pious relaxation, similar to reading or listening to the Quran, a practice that calmed the mind and body while fortifying the soul. As he described it during one of our meetings:

> Remember when we were sitting at Muhammad's once and we played a tape of [the *khatib*] Muhammad Hassan, you felt relaxed [*istirkha'*]? This is what can happen, this is the opening of the heart [literally, "chest": *inshirah al-sadr*], the tranquility [*itmi'nan*] that makes you want to pray, read the Quran, makes you want to get closer to God, to think [*tafakkir*] more about religion [*din*]. When you listen to a sermon, it helps you put aside all of your worries about work and money by reminding you of God. You remember that you will be judged and that fills you with fear [*khawf*] and makes you feel humility [*khushu'*] and repentance [*nadam*]. The shaykh teaches you about Islam, what it requires of you, so you won't make errors.

As with most of those I met in Cairo who listened to sermon tapes, Ahmad seldom employed them in an exact or rigorous manner. Rarely, for example, would he listen at precise times of the day according to a fixed schedule. He most often put on tapes in the evenings, after he had returned from work, sometimes inviting a friend from the neighborhood to join him, especially if he had a new tape to play. On such occasions I would often be invited as well. We would usually sit in his small living room, drinking tea while listening to the tape on his portable tape player. While listening, Ahmad or someone else would often interject comments on the content of the sermon: "Can that be true?" or "The shaykh's going to get in trouble for saying that!" or "I heard that *hadith* was inauthentic." During the more passional moments of the sermon, however, such verbal interjections were rare.

Often someone would light up a cigarette. When I asked Ahmad about the compatibility of smoking with sermon audition, he commented: "Of course smoking is wrong [*ghalat*]: you are hurting yourself, one of God's creations, and that is forbidden [*haram*]; and to do it while listening to a sermon, you know, that is especially bad: in the presence of Quranic verses, words about God and the prophets?!" Then, cracking a smile, and making a gesture of resignation with his hands, he added: "Yes, of course I know I shouldn't do it, but sometimes I still do. That's the kind of times we're living in!" While many of the people I met rejected cigarettes outright as *haram*, perhaps an equal number expressed views similar to Ahmad's.

Ahmad's brother, Hisham, who lived nearby with his wife and young child and who would drop by on occasion to listen to a tape, would criticize the group for not listening with the appropriate gravity. Hisham worked in the same plant as Ahmad, and the two of them would frequently undertake the one-hour bus trip to the work site together. He had spent many years in a sort of apprenticeship to a shaykh at a local mosque, where he had studied Quranic recitation (*tajwid*), the *hadith*, and various classical exegetical and doctrinal texts. Ahmad would often turn to him whenever he was unsure about the meaning of a particular Quranic verse, the correct form of a ritual act, or the validity of a statement made by a *khatib* on a tape. Hisham was particularly emphatic about questions of ritual practice, and, at our first meeting, spent twenty minutes explaining to me how most Egyptians fail to wash their ankles correctly when doing ablutions. He had begun listening to tapes while under the guidance of his shaykh. He greatly appreciated passionate oratory but also emphasized the benefit of more explicitly pedagogical tapes, those that provide information about such issues as the correct enactment of prayer, the responsibilities of husbands and wives, and the cleansing and burial of the dead, as well as on the proper interpretation of Quranic verses and *hadiths*. Given his taxing work schedule, Hisham could not devote as much time to his study with the shaykh as he used to, but he still liked to listen to sermon tapes in the evening together with his wife and children.

During one of his visits to Ahmad's house, Hisham commented that "most people only listen [*yasma'u*] to tapes, whereas to really benefit from them you need to listen carefully [*yunsit*—literally, to incline one's ear toward] to the preacher's words." The distinction invoked by Hisham is most commonly elaborated in relation to the audition of the Quran. The two terms he contrasts (*yasma'* and *yunsit*), for example, often appear in those *fatawi* (nonbinding legal opinions, sing. *fatwa*) concerned with the proper attitude and state of mind to be assumed when listening to recitations of the Quran. The following, taken from an official publication of al-Azhar *fatawi*, is characteristic:

> One need listen intently [*yunsit*] rather than just hear [*yasma'*], so it is done with intention [*qasd wa niyya*], and directing the senses [*hiss*] to the words in order to understand them, to comprehend their intentions and their meanings. As far as hearing [*al-sam'*], it is what occurs without intention. Close attention [*al-insat*] entails a stillness [*sukun*] in order to listen so as not to be distracted by surrounding words. . . . God ordered man to listen to the Quran with attention . . . [and] listening intently is the means to ponder over [*tadabbar*] the meanings of the Quran. . . . It is a duty on all Muslims to educate themselves, and be guided by the etiquette [*adab*] of al-Quran.
>
> (MAKHLUF 1950)

"Listening with attention," *al-insat*, is figured here as a complex sensory skill, one opposed to mere hearing (*sam'*), understood as a passive and spontaneous receptivity. According to Hisham, such was the kind of attentiveness appropriate to those moments when one's heart is inclined toward God, as should be the case in sermon listening: "Many people in Egypt listen to sermon tapes for entertainment [*ka tasliyya*], as if it were popular music, or they play a tape while doing something else, driving a car, or selling groceries: they don't really follow the sermon with their hearts."

Ahmad disagreed with Hisham. While he concurred that some concentration was required, he argued that the state of ethical receptivity that enabled one to benefit from tape audition did not demand the sort of active concentration indicated by Hisham: "Of course, if you listen as one would read a newspaper or watch the television, distractedly or indifferently, which many do, then the benefit is much less. What is most important, however, is to listen with humility [*khushu'*], with a pious fear [*bi'l-taqwa*]. If you listen with a sensitive heart, filled with humility and faith [*iman*], then even if you are momentarily distracted, or the phone rings, or your thoughts stray for a moment, you will still benefit [*tastafid minu*]. And if the shaykh is good, he will incite in you these feelings, and keep you close to God." Thus, for Ahmad, sermon tapes afford the listener a type of relaxation from which one can nonetheless expect an enriching of one's knowledge and a purifying operation on the soul. For people like Ahmad, tapes enable a strengthening of the will and what many people refer to as an ability to resist the devil's whispers (*wasawis*). With repeated and sensitive listening, they can also help lead a listener to change his or her ways. In short, for Ahmad and others, listening to sermon tapes is understood as a means by which a range of Islamic virtues could be sedimented in one's character, enabling one to live more piously and avoid moral transgressions.

For many sermon listeners, the regular practice of audition also serves as a constant reminder to monitor their behavior for vices and virtues. Tapes help one to maintain a level of self-scrutiny (*muraqaba*) in regard to one's day-to-day activities and, when possible, to change or modify one's behavior. As Beha, a taxi driver with whom I would often exchange sermon tapes, told me:

> One of the main things gained from listening is that one is reminded what Islam really entails. It then becomes more likely that one will correct one's behavior and be guided from one's state of being astray. See, I am not very Islamic [pointing to his cigarette], I smoke, but when I hear these things on tape, I am encouraged, steered toward correct practice [*a'mal saliha*]. I gain enthusiasm [*hamas*] for doing what is right.

Beha lived in Imbaba, which is one of the poorest quarters of Cairo and is often viewed as a hotbed of Islamic militancy (see chapter 4, note 35). He frequently put in eighteen-hour days behind the wheel in an attempt to feed his wife and two kids, and on such long days sermon tapes were his constant companion. As his comments suggest, Beha recognized that he often acted in ways that contradicted what he held to be morally appropriate behavior. While he viewed such contradictions as moral lapses of greater and lesser degrees, they were lapses he sought to overcome within a teleological process of learning, one that included, among other things, the audition of sermon tapes. Many of the young men I worked with in Egypt related their decision to become diligent in the performance of their Islamic duties to having been moved by a particularly powerful sermon, heard either on tape or live at the mosque.

There are other pleasures and benefits that sermon tapes provide as well. For example, for those who work in public transportation, sermon audition may simultaneously help them to achieve a state of closeness to God and allow them to remain calm and relaxed in the face of Cairo's maddening traffic conditions. As Beha commented on another occasion:

> I listen to sermons while I am driving because it soothes and relaxes me. So I don't get upset and begin to shout at the other drivers. Reading the Quran is even better, but I can't read and drive. Sometimes music works as well, but sermons are better. They give you religious knowledge, and make me remember God when I get too caught up in making a living. When I hear the tape while I am driving, and the shaykh talks about the Quran, or the Prophet, or death, or the grave, then I start to remember that everything I do will be judged, that my money, work, children all will be gone, and I will be judged for my good works alone. Then I say "I fear God in His Glory [ataq allah ʿazim]." "May God forgive me [astaghfar allah]." This gives me strength, and calms me and leaves my heart open [munsharih].

The tape produces in those already rightly disposed the sensorially rich experience of *inshirah*—the Quranic concept referring to the opening of the heart that accompanies drawing near to God—and in doing so, allows one to better meet the stress and monotony of urban labor. In contexts where reading the Quran or praying is impractical, a sermon tape on the Death of the Prophet or the Heavenly Pool of Kawthar that awaits the virtuous in the hereafter delivers diversion with a mild ethical elixir to the right place at the right time.

Muhammad Subhi, the *khatib* from whom I took lessons in the art of preaching for over a year, would often emphasize this calming and bolstering effect of recorded sermons, at least sermons by those *khutaba'* he considered masterful at the art.

> Listening to the Quran or sermon tapes, it leads you to a state of relaxation, or *sakina*. What does *sakina* mean? It means the calm one feels knowing that only God can determine when one will die. A calm by which one can stand firm before all oppression. It means one can let the winds of the mass media blow—all their silly words about Islamic terrorists, the [Islamic militant organization] *al-gamʿat al-islamiyya*, all the lies they throw out, all of the seductive images they surround us with—one can live in this swirl

of falsehoods but not follow or be moved by them, remain calm and sure before them.

Here, the modulation of affect performed by the preacher on the tape enacts an ethical therapy on the listener, both relaxing the body and enhancing the listener's capacity for discernment in the face of moral danger—in Muhammad's example, the danger of being deceived by state propaganda and corrupted by impious entertainment. Muhammad, like many of those I worked with, would frequently put on a tape upon coming home from work after a day of frustrations and difficulties. The mechanical manipulation and modulation of affective-kinesthetic experience enacted by the tape made him feel, in his words, lighter, fresh, and relieved, and turned his thoughts to God and religion. In this way, cassette sermons offer a portable, self-administered technology of moral health and Islamic virtue, one easily adapted to the rhythms, movements, and social contexts characteristic of contemporary forms of work and leisure.

In addition, sermon tapes may even serve to automatically reorient the heart in relation to God when one has inadvertently committed a moral error. One of the men I met once while visiting Cairo University was a twenty-three-year-old student named Saif. Saif had grown up with sermons: his father had been a *khatib*, though he now worked as a censor (*mufattish*) for the Ministry of Religious Affairs, which sent him round to different mosques each week to ensure that preachers were not straying into "sensitive" (*hassassi*) topics. Despite his father's official position, both Saif and his father emphasized to me on a number of occasions their strong preference for the more oppositional *khutaba'* associated with the *da'wa* movement. On one occasion Saif explained to me why he made a point of regularly listening to sermon tapes:

> Let's say that you looked at a woman desirously during the day, without even being aware you were doing it. In other words, you committed an act of disobedience to God. You should immediately ask for God's forgiveness, but let's say you are rushing somewhere and by the time you get there you don't even remember what you did. Well when you hear the shaykh in the bus on the way home talking about Judgment Day, or the tortures of the grave you get worried and start to fear. Your predicament becomes clear: you are going to die. You had forgotten to fear, and without it, you were probably preparing a place for yourself in hell. Then you will say, God, I seek

your forgiveness for my disobedience. Of course, you don't need a tape to do this, and you should do it automatically. But the tape helps if you forget. Especially if the tape is a really scary one.

Here, sermon media sustain one of the primary affective conditions of virtuous conduct, an active fear of God, consumed as both ethics and entertainment. As a device for the reanimation, modulation, and embodiment of pious sensibilities, cassette technology may be seen as a prosthetic of the modern virtuous subject: a mnemonic instrument that both enhances and supplements the capacity for memory, ethical feeling, and moral discernment while providing many of the pleasures of popular entertainment.

THE PHYSIOLOGY OF THE QURAN

As I discuss in chapter 2, the utility of tape audition for the task of ethical self-improvement is founded on a language ideology foregrounding the performative dimension of godly speech and its capacity to reform and attune a rightly disposed heart.[1] The effect of sermon speech on a "rusted heart," as the *khatib* and prolific writer on the craft of sermons, Ali Mahfuz, describes it, is not just one of cleansing. Sermons are understood to evoke in the sensitive listener a particular set of ethical responses, foremost among them, fear (*khawf*), humility (*khushu'*), regret (*nadam*), repentance (*tawba*), and tranquility (*itmi'nan* or *sakina*). These terms appeared constantly in the descriptions of the people I worked with, as in the following comment by Beha:

> Tapes are always of benefit, whether on the torment of the grave ['adhab al-qabr], Judgment Day [yawm al-qiyama], death [al-mawt], on the most dangerous of sins [kaba'ir], or the headscarf [hijab]. You learn things you didn't know, and this is useful. And they restore you to [moral] health [biyashfuna]. Listening to a tape of a sermon you've already heard is a way of reinforcing what you've learned, strengthening the fear of God's punishments, so you won't commit a moral error [ma'asi]. This leaves your heart calm [mutma'in]. There are some people who just do what they should. Many others, however, they realize that the devil [shaytan] has got into their heads [yuwaswisu—literally, whispers to them], and is making them think that what is evil [haram] is actually good [halal]. By listening, they strengthen themselves against this, as it gets them to pray and read the Quran. Then they begin to regret [nadam] what they have done, and ask God for forgive-

ness [*istighfar*]. The tape, in other words, helps them to fight [*bijahiduna*] against the devil.

As elaborated within classical Islamic moral doctrine, the affective dispositions Beha describes that endow a believer's heart with the capacities of moral discrimination necessary for proper conduct (see Fakhry 1983; Izutsu 1966, 1988; Sherif 1975). They are both virtues and states of emotional receptivity and response. Traditional texts on the task of moral refinement (*tahdhib al-nafs*) elaborate these dispositions extensively, as does contemporary *da'wa* literature. In order to understand how this terminology of ethical affect was employed by the men I worked with, however, it will be useful to draw on some of the contemporary writings that they themselves used and frequently referred to. The following discussion comes from an article published in *al-Tawhid*, a monthly journal put out by the *da'wa* association al-Ansar al-Sunna al-Muhammadiyya, and often purchased or referred to by those I worked with. The article focuses on the effect of particular Quranic verses, when used by a *khatib*, on the moral condition of a faithful Muslim listener. Drawing from the exegetical works of classical scholars in regard to the interpretation of a verse from the Quranic chapter entitled "al-Zumar" (The throngs), the author notes:

> What is meant here is that when the true people of faith, the people of the eternal and deeply rooted doctrine [*al-'aqida*] hear the verses of warning [*al-wa'id*] their flesh trembles in fear, their hearts are filled with despair [*inqabadat qulubuhum*], a violent angst shakes their backs [*irta'adat fara'isahum*], and their hearts become intoxicated with fear and dread. But if they then hear the verses of mercy [*al-rahma*] and forgiveness [*istighfar*], their flesh becomes filled with delight [*inbasatat juluduhum*], their chests are opened and relaxed [*insharahat suduruhum*], and their hearts are left tranquil [*itma'annat qulubuhum*].
>
> (BADAWI 1996B:11–12)

What is described here is a kind of moral physiology, the affective-kinesthetic experience of a body permeated by faith (*iman*) when listening to a *khatib*'s discourse. The description is derived directly from numerous verses of the Quran depicting the impact of godly speech on a rightly disposed listener, as in the following verse from the chapter entitled "al-Anfal" (Spoils of war): "Believers are only they whose hearts tremble whenever

God is mentioned, and whose faith is strengthened whenever his messages are conveyed unto them" (Quran 8:2). This particular responsiveness constitutes what might be termed a Quranically tuned body and soul. This attunement, according to Badawi, is a characteristic of a person who is close to God. For such a person, auditory reception involves the flesh, back, chest, and heart—in short, the entire moral person as a unity of body and soul. To listen properly, one might say, is to engage in a performance, the articulated gestures of a dance.

The moral physiology that is invoked and refined in the context of sermon listening is elaborated in a plethora of visually striking images, found both in the Quran and in a vast body of exegetical and ethical writings. Note, for example, the author's description above of how one relaxes in the process of hearing the verses of mercy and thus moves closer to God. The term used both here and by those I worked with in Cairo to denote this state of calm and relaxation is *inshirah* (literally, opening of the chest). As an ethical concept indicating the joyous relaxation that often follows acts of supplication or seeking forgiveness, it embeds strong affective and kinesthetic contours: to convey its meaning to others almost always involves an act of opening up the arms, raising and relaxing the chest, turning the face upward. The experience of *inshirah* has its origins in an event mentioned both in the Quran (in the chapter entitled al-Sharh)[2] and in many *hadiths*. It is recounted that on the night of the Prophet Muhammad's ascension to heaven (*al-isra'*), God opened his chest and took from his heart all the resentment, rancor, and lust and replaced them with virtues of faith and knowledge. The account, in other words, connects the purity of the soul with the powerful image of God opening up the chest—what Muhammad, the *khatib* I studied with, described to me as a "surgical operation" (*'amaliyya jirahiyya*). This connection provides the authoritative textual basis upon which a particular pattern of gestural and kinesthetic reponse is both conceptually *and experientially* linked to a moral state (*inshirah*).[3] For insomuch as the reading—or rather, recitation—of the event occurs within the disciplinary context of a Quranic education, it contributes to the training and inculcation of sensory habits. The account is not a dispassionate description but a story whose contours are learned with the body, in all of its kinesthetic and synaesthetic dimensions.

THE GESTURAL SUBJECT

In order to deepen this inquiry into such affective-gestural aptitudes and their place within contemporary practices of sermon listening in Egypt,

I want to draw on one of the most interesting and neglected figures of early-twentieth-century anthropology, Marcel Jousse. Jousse had the good fortune to have studied under two of the most fertile thinkers of his generation on questions of thought and human embodiment, the pathological psychologist Pierre Janet and the sociologist Marcel Mauss. Based on his ethnological study of traditions of recitation in preliterate societies, Jousse came to formulate a theoretical account for the stylistic features common to oral genres.[4] He was particularly fascinated by the prevalence of rhythmic gestures among storytellers and reciters, and he eventually came to see mimetic gesture as fundamental to both speech and memory:

> All reception, internal or external, triggers in the organism "a complexus of which kinesthetic elements [ocular, auricular, manual, etc . . . gestures] form the stable resistant portion . . . they ensure continuity. When our past experiences [our gesticulations] are submerged in us, they nevertheless subsist and are even active (facts prove this). What remains of them if not that portion which is their "support tissue", that which most easily does without consciousness? It is this [this infinitude of past gestures lying under the threshold of consciousness and setting each other off] that makes possible [revivification] of past states and the totality of their multiple connections."
>
> (JOUSSE [1925] 1990:27)[5]

Jousse's ideas bear the imprint of the physiology of vibration that oriented much of eighteenth- and nineteenth-century thinking on the senses and that was largely inspired by Isaac Newton's work on vision.[6] Language and consciousness are constructed upon a substrate of rhythmic motions, determined both by the mnemonic faculties of the senses and the dynamics of bodily rhythms (respiration, pulse, heartbeat, and so on). Humans are "essentially balancing, undulating beings" (Jousse [1925] 1990: xx), awash with pulsations and reflexes through which the body registers its involvement in its sensory surroundings. The "human compound," as Jousse glosses the indivisible unity of body and mind, is the product of a complex dance of rhythmic gestures, or "gesticulations," the motor actions by which the body "intussuscepts" the world it inhabits, incorporating what is outside within it. These gesticulations traverse the entire human organism in its diverse physiological, psychological, and autonomic modes of functioning, from the motions of the sense organs (ocular reflexes, auricular vibrations), to the movement of the muscles and limbs, to the unfoldings of thought. Memories are precisely these "gestural reviviscenses," this repetition of past receptions for which the body in its sensory entirety has served as medium. Memory, in other words, is not built upon ideas, and much less upon visual images, but rather on the reactivation of gestures, understood as the sensory sediments of prior perceptions. It is founded, we might say, on the body's potential for reproducing its sensorimotor past without the mediation of thought, as in such activities as walking, or riding a bicycle.[7]

While particular percepts might recruit some parts of the sensorium more than other parts—as when one has been trained to attend to a very limited range of sensory experience, such as in modern academic reading—to at least some extent, the organ of reception remains the body in its entirety. Jousse uses the example of a spectator to a fencing match:

> "Without our knowing it, all that we see projects itself instantaneously into our musculature" (Verriest: 46). "As a spectator at a fencing session follows the movements of attack and defense, each one of these movements repeats itself with lightning rapidity in his own musculature. Motor waves run through his whole body; in his person he fights, attacks, fends off, wins or succumbs. The associated sensation of ease and well-being at the right movement, of embarrassment and pain at the wrong movement are felt by him in the same way as by the fencers themselves" (44).
>
> (JOUSSE [1925] 1990:24)[8]

The mimetic reception of the event involves the sensorium in its entirety, entwining proprioception with various forms of synaesthetic experience—the patterned interconnections of touch, vision, hearing, smell, and taste that tend to remain outside of awareness in adult perception. These gesticulations, as Jousse labels them, constitute a substrate of latent tendencies, dispositions toward certain kinds of action operating independently of conscious thought. As sensory memory, these tendencies may be reactivated with greater or lesser degrees of intensity, from fully elaborated gestures and movements, perceptible to others, to gesticulations that are merely "sketched," as in acts of imagination (Jousse [1925] 1990:29).[9] Generally, however, they remain outside of consciousness, present as a sensory background, the body's affective involvement with the world that forms the constitutive outside of our consciously directed actions.

While aspects of Jousse's physiology are now outdated, his expanded notion of the gestural provides a particularly useful tool for thinking about the practice of ethical sermon listening I am concerned with here. Within the Joussean analytic, oratorical performances are viewed in their capacity to organize the sensorium, to install and attune affective-gestural potentialities at the level of sensorimotor processes, within the mnemonic folds of visceral, kinesthetic, and tactile experience. Jousse's exploration of the way speech and audition work to sculpt the body extends a line of inquiry opened up by his mentor, Marcel Mauss. For Mauss, as Talal Asad notes,

> the human body was not to be viewed simply as the passive recipient of "cultural imprints," still less as the active source of "natural expressions" that are clothed in local history and culture, as though it were a matter of an inner character expressed in a readable sign, so that the latter could be used as a means of deciphering the former. It was to be viewed as the developable means for achieving a range of human objectives, from styles of physical movement (e.g. walking), through modes of emotional being (e.g. composure), to kinds of spiritual experience (e.g. mystical states).
>
> (T. ASAD 1993:76)

Following leads opened up by Jousse's provocative notion of gesture, I want to think of sermon listening as a practice predicated on the developability of the body as an auditory instrument. To "hear with the heart," as those I worked with described this activity, is not strictly something cognitive but involves the body in its entirety, as a complex synthesis of patterned moral reflexes. Indeed, as I describe below, the imaginative response evoked in the course of sermon audition runs along a progression from full-voiced interjections and dramatic gestural movements, to whispering and subtle postural shifts, to a slight moving of the lips and tongue, to an apparently invisible response, with all gradations in between. Listening invests the body with affective potentialities, depositing them in the preconscious folds of kinesthetic and synaesthetic experience and, in doing so, endows it with the receptive capacities of the sensitive heart, the primary organ of moral knowledge and action. Importantly, Islamic ethical traditions give explicit recognition to this kind of somatic learning, as we see in Badawi's invocation of the faithful listeners whose "flesh trembles," who are seized by "a violent angst [that] shakes their backs," whose "chests are opened and relaxed." Contemporary sermon listening, in other words, inherits and extends a practical tradition for the formation of a pious sensorium.

THE RECITATIONAL BODY

To flesh out the perspective I am developing here, it is useful to examine some of the body techniques deployed in the context of Quranic recitation, especially as they both inform the practice of sermon audition and depart from it in certain crucial aspects. All of my informants had memorized portions of the Quran and learned at least the rudimentary skills of recitation by the time of adolescence, either through lessons at Quran schools for children known as *katakib* (sing. *kuttab*),[10] in classes within the secular public school system, or under direct tutelage from their fathers and mothers. A few only began to learn it as young adults when, like many Egyptians of their generation, they came to see Islamic practices as increasingly important to their lives. The recitational techniques taught today are founded upon longstanding Islamic traditions, and even the most popularized literature on the practice relies heavily on classical models found in medieval sources.[11] While such works provide instruction in a particular tradition of vocal performance, the performance itself is understood to involve a kind of audition, insomuch as a skilled reciter should attempt to "hear the speech of God from God and not from [the voice of the reciter] himself" (A. H. al-Ghazali 1984:80).

Among the demands of this audition cited by the eleventh-century theologian Abu Hamid al-Ghazali are both practices of mental concentration and a variety of affective, gestural, and verbal responses, some of which require the listener to assume the ethical dispositions corresponding to the recited or audited verses: humility, awe, regret, fear, and so on. Al-Ghazali elaborates this in terms of "fulfilling the right [*al-haqq*]" of the verses:

> Thus when the Quran reader reads a verse necessitating prostration before God, he will prostrate himself. Likewise, if he hears [the recitation of] a verse of prostration by another person he will prostrate himself when the reciter prostrates. He will prostrate only when he is physically and ritually clean. . . . Its perfect form is for him to utter *allahu akbar* [God is Great!] and then prostrate himself and, while prostrate, supplicate with that supplication which is appropriate to the verse of prostration recited.
>
> (1984:44–45)[12]

For al-Ghazali, listeners and reciters must feel the emotion appropriate to each verse, foremost among them, fear.

Whenever the Quran reader's knowledge [of the meaning of the verses recited] is perfect his fear will be the most predominant of the states of his soul ... when reading a verse which warns and restricts divine forgiveness to those who fulfill certain stipulations, he will make himself so small as if for fear he is about to die. When a verse on the promise of forgiveness is recited he will rejoice as if he flies for joy. When God, His attribute and names are mentioned, he will bow his head in submission to His majesty and in awareness of His greatness. When he reads a verse on the infidels' belief in an impossible thing for God (great and mighty is He!)—e.g. their belief that God (great and mighty is He!) has a child and a consort—he will lower his voice and be broken hearted in bashfulness because of the evil of what they have believed.

(75–76)

The word of God demands a range of ethical performances from the reciter/listener. She must not only seek to understand God's message, in the cognitive sense; she must also make herself into an adequate "host" for the presence of divine words, by bodying forth the attitudes and expressions corresponding to the verses heard or recited.[13] Through practice, she must make her body and heart into an instrument capable of resonating (re-sounding) the words she submits to (see chapter 2 for an elaboration of the ethical and doctrinal bases of this model). Training in such skills begins in earliest infancy, as the interwoven practices of audition, memorization, and recitation are central to the ethical upbringing of children in Egypt. Parents, upon introducing me to their children, would commonly ask a child to recite part of a *sura* (a chapter of the Quran) he or she had mastered. Beyond such instruction, however, the Quran—as well as other traditional Islamic genres such as *hadiths*, *qisas* (Islamic stories), and *siyar* (biographies of Muhammad and other early Muslim figures)—are woven into much of daily life, with verses often punctuating the succession of devotional, ritual, public, and family activities occurring in the course of a day (Graham 1987; Schimmel 1994). Moreover, just as individual Quranic verses invoke ethical responses, so also do ethical situations often give rise to the citation of verses, whether in acts of giving advice, instructing children, making decisions, or arguing a point, particularly among those Egyptian Muslims more observant of the demands of piety. In this sense, the Quranically tuned body, with its repertoires of affect and expression, makes possible the form of pious sociability that the Islamic Revival has sought to enhance and extend, a phenomenon the next chapter explores at length.

While sermon audition facilitates the development and formation of the virtues, the practice is distinct from Quranic recitation and other disciplinary programs geared to this task. Insomuch as sermon tapes are used as a kind of background or environmental sound, attended to in a relaxed manner, often with shifting degrees of focus, their reception needs to be theorized at the level of the somatic more than the programmatic. Instead of the fully elaborated sequences of gesture, speech, and bodily movement that accompany the act of Quranic recitation, tapes produce a modulation of affect registered kinesthetically and viscerally, one experienced as an ethically enhancing form of relaxation. In this sense, what is acquired through the practice are less honed dispositions, moral skills as delineated and organized within disciplinary regimes, than the somatic and affective potentialities from which such dispositions draw sustenance.

This point can be usefully elaborated by drawing on a distinction made by Brian Massumi (2002) between affect and emotion. Massumi reserves the term "affect" to describe the myriad emotional movements within the body occurring below or outside of consciousness, the vast sea of emotionally charged perceptual responses that traverse the body without being assimilated as subjective content (2002:27–28). Affects are part of the presubjective interface of the body with the sensory world it inhabits, a linkage registered at the level of the visceral, the proprioceptive, and other sites where memory lodges itself in the body. (While I write these words at an outdoor café, a bird lands on the table in front of me. I casually watch the staccato motions it makes with its head. Each of these jerky movements rebounds off of my neck and upper body as a sort of shock wave. Now imagine a similar pulsation, though one carrying ethical potential, say the "shock wave" that accompanies a reaction of moral disgust.) Emotion, on the other hand, refers to culturally qualified affect, affect elaborated and codified within sociolinguistic frames, inscribed within scripted action-reaction circuits, and made the property of a subject inhabiting a world of constituted objects and goals (Massumi 2002:26). "*Khushu'*" or "*taqwa*," the Islamic virtues with strong affective dimensions that I mentioned above, are examples of such discursively defined emotional content.

Cassette-sermon listening, I want to suggest, intervenes precisely at the level of what Massumi calls the affective. The relaxed attentiveness of this auditory practice invests the body with affective intensities (Jousse's "gesticulations"), latent tendencies of ethical response sedimented within the mnemonic regions of the flesh. The vocabularies of ethical affect, bodily sensation, and moral actions invoked both by preachers and sermon listeners, in this regard, function as instruments for objectifying and organizing sensory material, in accord with long-standing discourses on ethical cultivation. Following Foucault, we might describe the practice as "a technology for the constitution of the self that cuts across symbolic systems while using them" (1984:369). The practice addresses the self in its capacity of sensorimotor instrument, exploiting possibilities of thought and action born of the body's pervasive and largely inaudible dialogue with the world.

William Connolly's discussion of micropolitics points toward the sort of techniques of the sensorium I describe here. Elaborating on Nietzsche's use of the notion of instinct, he notes:

> Instincts are proto-thoughts situated in culturally formed moods, affects and situations. They are not even entirely reducible to implicit thoughts, since they undergo significant modification and refinement when drawn into a linguistic network of complex contrasts. And these modes of appraisal are often intensively mobilized, often carrying considerable energy and fervency with them. This "invisible" set of intensive appraisals forms (as I will call it) an infrasensible subtext from which conscious thought, feeling and discursive judgments draw some of their substance. Moreover, instincts that are culturally formed can sometimes be modified by strategies applied to groups to themselves and by arts of the self.
>
> (2002:17–18)

Cassette-sermon listening may be seen as just such a strategy.[14] In their ability to mold both soundscapes and human receptivity, sermon tapes help fashion and sustain the sensory conditions for a modern Islamic ethics. One of my key arguments in this book is that such undisciplined disciplines play a far more pervasive role in shaping traditions, both religious and secular, than their more "serious" (rigorous and systematic) counterparts.

In order that the claim I am making not be misunderstood, let me clarify one point. Some readers might object that the analysis of cassette listening I am suggesting here rests on a generic model of human perception, one of questionable universality. This is not my argument. As I have shown, the practice of sermon listening is informed by those Islamic traditions of ethical cultivation that highlight the role of affective, kinesthetic, and gestural modalities of bodily experience within processes of ethical learning—those traditions, in other words, that take the sensorium as an object of pedagogy and ethical attunement. My recourse to such theorists as Marcel Jousse and Brian Massumi, in this regard, is to sharpen our appreciation of certain aspects of these traditions rarely attended to by scholars of ethics—not to demonstrate the universal validity of the perceptual models these thinkers articulate. I should also point out, however, that the theoretical accounts of sensory experience I have drawn upon have clear filiations as far back as Greek harmonic and vibrational theories, theories that also shaped the development of Islamic traditions of philosophical and mystical inquiry (see Carruthers 1990; Chittick 1989).

LISTENING AS PERFORMANCE

A more detailed look at the sensory elements of this active and ethical listening practice is needed. Many of the protocols of sermon audition are transferred over from the live context in the mosque to the cassette, though in attenuated and abbreviated form. At times, one follows the ethical movements of the sermon with its appropriate gestural, vocal, and subvocal responses with same sort of automaticity and spontaneity by which commuters intone popular radio hits with only a vague awareness they are doing so. The more times one has heard a particular sermon tape, the more one enacts its demands without the support of conscious thought. To begin with, the sermon necessitates a voiced or subvocal accompaniment, as listeners are repeatedly required to enact a range of illocutionary acts. The preamble is a collective utterance[15] composed of acts of remembrance (*dhikr*), praise (*thana'*), and supplication (*du'a'*). While the *khatib* provides the guiding vocalization for these acts, it is incumbent on the audience to accompany him in this with their hearts, an act that often involves the mumbled or whispered utterance of the appropriate devotional formulas. The preeminent *khatib* Shaykh Kishk on occasion called on his audience to repeat word for word the invocations he recited or, more frequently, had them repeat one phrase over and over (such as "I seek forgiveness from God"), exploiting the pathetic momentum such rhythmic repetitions evoke in an audience.

Listeners also must be ready to pronounce the *basmala* ("In the name of God, the compassionate, the merciful") each time the *khatib* begins to recite a verse from the Quran and the call for prayers upon the Prophet ("God bless him and grant him salvation") each time his name is mentioned. Additionally, throughout a sermon listeners are frequently enjoined to vocalize a wide variety of supplicatory locutions, or *du'a'*, that relate to the argument the *khatib* is making or the situation he is describing. For example, in warning his audience about the dangers of gossip (*ghiba*) or backbiting (*namima*), a *khatib* will call on them to implore God for forgiveness from moral error. When lecturing them on a topic such as proper burial technique, he will have them ask God to increase their knowledge, to lessen the agonies of dying, or to illuminate the darkness of their graves. While discussing the plight of Muslims in Chechnya, he will pause to have the audience ask protection for Muslims who face affliction elsewhere in the world, for the defeat of their enemies, for the strength to persevere through the hardships they suffer. The popular *khatib* Umar Abd al-Kafi punctuates his sermons with such rapid-fire enjoinders, continuously recruiting his listeners to vocally and morally participate in the oratory he performs. In the context of cassette audition, listeners may respond with clearly audible utterances, with whispers, with a silent movement of the lips, or without visible or audible gesture. When the response of tape listeners passes the threshold of audibility, it may simply consist of an abbreviated acclamatory expression, such as *"amin"* (amen), or a longer phrase repeating the verb invoked in the supplication ("strengthen us, defeat them . . .").

The final section of a sermon is composed solely of such acts of supplication, strung one after another by the *khatib* in a rhythmic crescendo that gathers emotional momentum as it proceeds. During the live performance at the mosque, this is the point when the pathos of the audience reaches its peak, and it is not uncommon at this point for the entire assembly to weep without restraint. While a particularly moving *du'a'* will also often provoke tears among cassette listeners, the intensity of the expression is relatively less in the absence of the emotional dynamics put in play by a large crowd. Nonetheless, many of the men I worked with appreciated this section of the sermon for the ethical-affective progression it could initiate, leaving them with a sense of closeness to God and the accompanying experience of relief and tranquility (*itmi'nan* and *sakina*). As I have argued, this should not be thought of through a generic, psychophysiological model of catharsis but as an experience of moral relief whose specific contours have been honed through a range of ethical practices, including sermon audition itself. The listener, for example, must have cultivated the capacity for humility and regret: these are both felicity conditions (in Austin's [1994] sense) for the act of supplication as well as soma-ethical[16] conditions for the body's experience of *itmi'nan*,[17] the relief and kinesthetic relaxation that follows—via regret and repentance (*nadam* and *istighfar*)—from such an act. If these conditions are not met, then the listener will not be able to adopt the attitudes, the dispositions of the heart, upon which successful and beneficial acts of audition devolve. One's listening, in short, will be impaired.

Much of the substance of sermons is drawn from those pieces of text that form the common stock of cultural wisdom: Quranic verses, *hadiths*, biographies of the Prophet, accounts of the lives of early Muslims, and various traditional story genres that have been elaborated on the basis of these primary sources. Sermon listeners come to the sermon already familiar with many of these narratives, though sermons are also one of the contexts where new ones are learned. As with storytelling in other cultural contexts, the listening pleasure found in such narratives does not reside in the presentation of something entirely new but in the effective and stirring performance of a known account, one reinterpreted and revised through its retelling in a new narrative context.[18] Often while a group of us were listening to a tape, for example, on the signs that precede and indicate the arrival of the Day of Judgment, a person would note with interest and satisfaction that he had never before heard a particular detail mentioned by the *khatib*, such as the blue eye of the Antichrist (*al-masih al-dajjal*) or the sun turning red. Saif, the Cairo University student, would on occasion tell me with surprise and skepticism about a particular rendition of the eschaton recounted by the *khatib* at his mosque during the Friday sermon. A few times, when the issue had really piqued his curiosity, he went and either checked in a book on the subject or asked the shaykh in his mosque.

Knowledge of these Islamic narrative forms, as the sermon listeners I knew visibly demonstrated in explaining the sermons to me, consists not simply in the ability to recite a given text, but also in performing its emotional, gestural, and kinesthetic contours, the bodily conditions of the text as memory. While listening to taped sermons with these men, they would often interrupt with comments and gestures intended to help me understand the particular *hadith* or story being recounted by the *khatib*, sometimes stopping the tape to elaborate in more detail or introduce relevant passages from the Quran or other traditional textual sources. In doing so, they would bring a common expressive-gestural repertoire to their explanations: in the context of recounting a *hadith*, the narrowness of the grave (a common sermon topic) is expressed by a drawing up of the shoulders; the exit of the soul from the neck of a good man is distinguished from that of an infidel by the smoothness of the hand movement tracing the passage and the relaxed muscles of the face and hand, which are tightened and contorted in the case of the infidel; encounters with respected Muslim figures in heaven are accompanied by the joyful relaxation of the chest, the upward glance of delight. The events surrounding Judgment Day, a very common sermon topic on which many *khutaba'* have produced extensive cassette series (drawn either from sermons or mosque lessons),[19] all have a strong gestural component: the grasping of the book of one's deeds from above the right or left shoulder; the testifying of the individual parts of one's body as to the deeds they have committed; the binding of the hands by the guards of hell. While these stories all have a striking visual intensity, they are in fact rarely given visual representation; their most visible aspect therefore lies in the gestures and emotional expressions that accompany their verbal performance. The narratives are rooted in physically grounded imagery, insomuch as their ethical dimensions have affective and bodily correlates. It is the sensual experience of the body accustomed to such performances that attunes the heart to their appropriate reception. A listener does not enact the performance, but his experienced body shapes his response and reception of it. Recall Jousse's spectator to a fencing match, whose nerves and muscles register each gesture of attack and defense, of humiliation and victory.

The stock of Islamic narrative forms that provide the raw material for many sermons also has a strong bilateralism, each gestural text having its right- and left-side variants, the former always associated with moral probity in accord with classical Islamic body schema. Thus, the angel that counts one's good deeds sits on the right shoulder, the one counting evil deeds on the left; a virtuous person will take the book of his deeds from his right on Judgment Day as he or she stands before God, the sinner from the left. The positive valence given to the right side within Islamic societies extends to a vast range of activities, a pattern scholars have frequently noted in other societies as well (see Hertz 1909; Needham 1973). This includes devotional acts such as ablutions and prayer, where each movement is specified in terms of the bilateral axis: the Quran is held only with the right hand; one looks first to the right after completing prayer; for ablutions, the limb on the right is washed first then the left. All sorts of mundane daily actions also incorporate right/left organization: one enters the house with the right foot but the bathroom with the left, one must wash the teeth of a corpse only using the right hand, and so on. On many occasions, someone would correct me for having entered a room with my left foot instead of my right, or picking up the Quran with my left hand. This bilateral training of the body and the repertoires of gesture, movement, and speech learned in accord with such a coding were further conditions shaping the sensory orientation of listeners to the narrative fragments composing a sermon.

Notably, the young men I knew in Cairo did not always agree with each other in regard to the truth status of some of the accounts commonly found in sermons. Often, for example, one person would refer to a narrative element (such as the throne of God) as a symbol (*ramz* or *kinaya*), while another would claim it as "real" (*haqiqi*), though in a way beyond human comprehension (*bila kayf*). The student Saif would often describe as "metaphors" those parts of a sermon he understood to be somewhat far-fetched: for example, the writing of the word "infidel" on the forehead of the Antichrist, or the blackening of the heart that follows from sin. In contrast, Ahmad and his brother Hisham, as well as most of the *khutaba*' themselves, insisted that these were statements of literal truth. In some instances, one informant might not know the meaning of some of the key terms used by the *khatib*. Yet despite these differences of opinion and comprehension, all of the young men I worked with would mimetically represent the narratives from which these elements were drawn in more or less the same way, including the corresponding facial and postural expressions of fear, delight, or tranquility. I do not mean to imply that these differences of interpretation are insignificant. Indeed, arguments about the ontological status of Quranic references have been extremely consequential throughout Islamic history. What I am pointing to here is that beneath the level of expressed belief and opinion, those I knew who participated in sermon listening shared a common substrate of embodied dispositions of the sort I have described as instrumental to the task of sermon audition. It is these sensory dispositions, I argue, more than a commitment to a normative rationality, that constitute the common ground upon which the discourses of a tradition come to be articulated, the "reflexes" that make arguments about the status of Quranic references meaningful and worthy of engagement.

THE LIGHTNESS OF ELECTRONIC VIRTUE

When I first asked the *khatib* Muhammad Subhi what he thought about the fashion of cassette-sermon listening and its contribution to al-Sahwa al-Islamiyya (the Islamic Revival movement), of which he considered himself to be an active proponent, he responded, much to my surprise: "They're not important. How can tapes be important when the people who listen to them will turn around and deny they do so!" This response made little sense to me at the time, though I assumed the reference to denial had to do with the fact that in the context of the current government crackdown, many people had become more circumspect about the practice, fearing it might make them appear suspicious in the eyes of the police. The comment became even less comprehensible as I got to know Muhammad and discovered that he not only avidly listened to sermon tapes himself but had also recorded many of his own for personal use and to give to friends. It was only much later, after having encountered a range of preoccupations concerning the practice, that I came to understand his criticism as reflecting an aporia within the practice engendered by the cassette medium itself, though one also related to the broader reorganization of Islamic authority I describe in the previous chapter.

Among listeners, this aporia was usually expressed in terms of a skepticism about the efficacy of the practice. As with modernity's other popular technologies of the self, such as *Eight-Minute Abs* or learning Chinese subliminally while you sleep, the beneficial effects of recorded sermons often didn't live up to initial expectations. One of the men who expressed such a view was Ahmad's friend Ibrahim, who I mentioned in chapter 1 together with his sister Huda. Ahmad and Ibrahim had both graduated from the geography department at Ain Shams University and had participated in the same Islamic study group during the period of their studies. Unlike Ahmad, however, Ibrahim had a solid job waiting for him after graduation at a publishing company where his father served as acting director. His father had studied business back in the 1960s and had been fortunate enough to secure a position consonant with his level of education, a rare accomplishment in contemporary Egypt.

During one of my visits to Ibrahim's house, he told me of his initial enthusiasm for and subsequent disappointment with sermon tapes:

> When you first hear a tape by Abd al-Hamid Kishk or Muhammad Hassan, you feel very enthusiastic, enthusiastic for Islam, for doing right, visiting my relatives, encouraging others to stop disobeying God. I used to listen all the time, always giving tapes to friends, telling them we should go to the mosque together. Now I still like to listen sometimes but it is not as important to me as it was before. I mean, there is clearly benefit in sermon listening, and moreover you get merits with God in doing so, but unless you pray regularly and read the Quran often, the benefit will be limited. That's the way it is most of the time: someone will hear a really moving sermon on the afterlife or the grave. It will scare them and strengthen their resolve to do good. Then you see them a few days later and they have gone back to the way they were.

Many listeners expressed similar concerns that the effects of the practice might not extend beyond the moment of listening itself. Indeed, an ambivalence regarding the practice is evident in the way the notion of the tape recorder is used metaphorically in popular speech. As a figure used to designate a specific human quality, for example, it carries both positive and negative valences, suggesting a prodigious capacity of memory, on the one hand, but a kind of learning that remains somewhat superficial on the other.[20] Tapes are good for you, but the benefits may be insubstantial and short-lived.

This concern was raised with far more urgency and intensity by *khutaba'*. One of the signs that many people take as evidence of a *khatib*'s virtuosity is an ability to move an audience to tears. Weeping has an important place within Islamic devotional practices as a kind of emotional response appropriate for both men and women when, with humility, fear, and love, they turn to God.[21] Many *khutaba'* today, however, are concerned that people are crying during sermons for the wrong reasons. Note, for example, the following remark by the popular Egyptian *khatib* Fawzi Said, made in response to a question by an audience member during one of his mosque lessons about why he didn't do more to evoke the passions of his listeners in his sermons:

> Lots of people today just look forward to crying during sermons; they feel they are being cleansed, like Christians at baptism. But the sermon that just leads you to cry doesn't imprint upon the heart. It doesn't get people to change their actions. It is only through a careful engagement with the texts, reading the Quran and *hadith* literature, that knowledge gets rooted in the heart. Not that the sentiments are unimportant; but many people no longer know why they are crying.

Said's manner of distinguishing sentiment from action signals a rupture within the Aristotelian foundations of the practice of ethical listening. As I note above, the model of cultivation invoked by those who undertake the practice is premised on a notion of affect as integral to action. Sadness (*huzn*), humility (*khushu'*), and pious fear (*khawf* or *taqwa*) are not internal, subjective states appropriate to the performance of certain actions. They are actions in and of themselves.[22] As an attribute of character, *khawf* entails and is expressed through the performance of a vast range of ethical actions, from prayer, to giving alms, to visiting one's parents. To perform these actions without *khawf*, to walk away from a group of acquaintances drinking alcohol impelled by something other than pious fear, is to do it incorrectly, poorly. To have pious fear and drink alcohol is not to have pious fear, or to have an inadequately developed capacity for it.

In short, Said's comment registers a breakdown in the continuity that binds affect to action, and thus in the tradition of the virtues from which that model is derived. The anxiety it gives voice to, and that informs Muhammad Subhi's offhanded dismissal of the practice, is bound up with the cassette medium itself. As I note in chapter 2, the cassette removed the sermon from the structures of authority and discipline that previously grounded its ethical functioning. As a result, the "machinery of affect" mobilized by the sermon is now truly a machine, one only contingently related to a subject who operates it on his or her own prerogative (see Keane [1997, 2002] on affect and materiality). This displacement not only separates the affects from the institutional moorings that ensured their ethical cultivation, but also from the subject itself: "people no longer know why they are crying," for the production of the tears is now determined by the functional possibilities of cassette technology. Tapes exteriorize an entire circulatory system that had remained invisible, submerged within the practical and institutional conditions of community life. Floating free of subjects, cassette piety is now left to the whims of subjective appropriation, or equally possible, as Muhammad Subhi noted, simply denied.

This displacement effected by the cassette also contributes to a broader epistemological crisis within the oral tradition of which the sermon is a part: for Said, writing (and reading) must be called in to guarantee the validity of the oral forms of knowledge, a particularly surprising gesture for a *khatib* to make and one reflecting the status of written texts within the contemporary economy of meaning. Saif and Ahmad would often tell me that the best way to confirm the validity of a *khatib*'s assertion was to "check in books" [*yu'akidu fi kutub*]," though exactly how one might do so and with which books remained notably vague. Calls for textual fact checking, in other words, revealed more about epistemological tensions within the ethical project of *da'wa* than about actual procedures undertaken.

These fissures within the practice of sermon audition frequently emerged in conversations I had with Muhammad Subhi and other *khutaba'*. In a discussion on the problems of preaching today, for example, Muhammad noted:

> When people today listen, they hear about Judgment Day and the torment of hell and they feel relieved and exalted [*intisha'*]. *Intisha'* is what you experience when you drink alcohol and feel that all of the pressures and difficulties of your life have been lifted. Or when you hear a really beautiful song, that touches all of your emotions ['*awatif wa masha'ir*] and sensibilities [*ihsas*]. You feel a kind of comfort and relief [*tanfis*], a calm [*raha*], a kind

of catharsis [*kathrasis*]: this is *intisha'*. If I am a Muslim, when I listen to the Quran or a sermon on tape I feel this relief [*nashwa*]. But things must not stop at this feeling, as so often happens. It must be transformed into part of one's practical reality.

Much like Fawzi Said, Muhammad worries about the disjunct between affect and action, though his use of a nonethical vocabulary to describe the experience of listening further accentuates the split: "calm" (*raha*) instead of the Quranic "opening of the heart" (*inshirah*); "comfort" (*tanfis*) and "relief" (*nashwa*), instead of the stillness of the soul suggested by the term *itmi'nan* and the numinous quiet of *sakina*. In his recourse to "*kathrasis*," a transposition into Egyptian Arabic of the English "catharsis," the secularization of the emotions and their detachment from ethical life reaches its apogee. As with Said, the specter of "entertainment" hangs over this comment. People may be listening for little more than the momentary experience of catharsis and pleasure. This concern may partly derive from the fact that, by convention, cassettes are a medium of (musical) entertainment. Indeed, while sermon tapes may be described in ethical terms by their users, their mode of employment differs little from other popular cassette-based media. Insomuch as one of the interpretive conventions distinguishing the category of entertainment is precisely its *unseriousness*, its irrelation to what Muhammad Subhi refers to as "practical reality," attempts to assign ethical significance to practices of cassette audition will be aporetic, the medium itself throwing into question the very project for which it serves as instrument.

This concern can be heard again at the beginning of a recorded mosque lesson on the topic of Judgment Day by the popular *khatib* Muhammad Hassan:

> Maybe you will go home today and tell your wife, husband, or children about the good stories you heard. It will just become, "Once upon a time, when the Prophet lived . . . ," as if it were no longer an issue of today. But this is not some escape from reality, not entertainment, or cold culture which only addresses the intellect [*al-adhhan*] and the rational mind [*al-'aql*]. Belief in Judgment Day is one of the foundations of Islam, along with belief in God, His prophets, His books, and His angels. Unless you understand Judgment Day and know of its circumstances, how can you believe in it? Thus, we need to grasp [*nastaw'ib*] this knowledge, and live by it [*na'mal bihi*].[23]

Knowledge of the events of Judgment Day must not become assimilated to the category of entertainment, Hassan is saying. The very operation by which this is overcome, however, is itself already premised on a rupture that the category produced, evident in the copula dividing the grasping of knowledge from living by it. Knowledge, in other words, does not designate a teleological process of ethical becoming but, in accord with a liberal notion of the autonomous subject, a possession, first acquired, then deployed. ("*Tatbiq*," "implementation" or "execution," a term with strong echoes of the "Five Year Plans" frequently announced and rarely carried out by the Egyptian state, is the term I heard most often to describe what Muslims today were failing to do.) In another comment, made this time in the context of an interview with the newspaper *al-Liwa' al-Islami*, Muhammad Hassan advises:

> Every Muslim must enact a practical *shahada* [*shahada 'amaliyya*] on the ground of our lived reality after they have pronounced a verbal *shahada* [*shahada qawliyya*] with their tongues. The smallest libraries today are full of books and [sermon and mosque lesson] cassettes, but this theoretical project does not equal the value of the ink which it was written with until we transform it into a practical reality and a way of life.
>
> (AL-LIWA' AL-ISLAMI 1996)

Hassan's use of the terms "theory" and "practice" invokes a sort of Platonic division between a world of ideas and a world of action and thus diverges sharply from the model of ethical cultivation invoked by preachers and listeners. According to doctrinal sources, the uttering of the *shahada*— "There is no God but the One God, and Muhammad is his apostle [*la ilaha illa allah wa muhammad rasul allah*]"—is the minimal sufficient condition for becoming a Muslim. There is considerable argument, however, over what precisely is entailed in making the utterance. Ibn Taymiyya, a fourteenth-century theologian whose doctrinal writings have had considerable influence on contemporary Islamic thought, especially within those currents represented by the *khutaba'* of my study, argued that to utter the *shahada* without fulfilling the prescribed duties of Islam, such as prayer, fasting, and giving alms, is not to have truly uttered the *shahada*. The enactment of these duties, in other words, was understood by Ibn Taymiyya as a felicity condition for the illocutionary act of the testimony of faith (see Ibn

Taymiyya n.d.). Admittedly, Hassan does not break entirely with this tradition. While he distinguishes between words (*al-qawl*) and practices
(*al-ʿamal*), he locates the *shahada*—fundamentally, a speech act—on both
sides of the divide, thereby complicating any notion of a clear division.
Nonetheless, his way of framing the problem is haunted by the modern
split between the order of knowledge and the order of the body. The strains
I identify here run right through the entire ethical project.

The discursive conventions of the media form introduce an aporia into
the practice, a constant danger to the integrity of its ethical subject. This
condition, of course, is also embedded in "practical reality" itself, as a fragmented moral space often inhospitable to the rationalities and protocols
of comportment characteristic of the tradition of the virtues toward which
cassette listeners aspire. It is not surprising, in this regard, that much of
the Islamic Revival aural and written media involve attempts to provide
consumers with strategies for adjusting to social and work conditions incompatible with a virtuous life—for example, where norms of dress, sociability, financial transaction, and medical treatment contradict what are
understood to be Islamic precepts. And while the revival movement has
dedicated much of its energies to attempts to create spaces of social and
economic existence where such contradictions are minimized, few people
I worked with could afford to entirely restrict their lives to the mosque and
its affiliated network of institutions. Such tensions within the ethical project to which sermon listening contributes often surface in the form of irony,
as in Ahmad's burst of laughter when I asked why he smoked even while
recognizing it as a moral error.

For *khutabaʾ*, this aporia inaugurates a debate over rhetorical style, one
framed around a rhetoric of surface and depth: by what rhetorical techniques can an instrument of surfaces—the tape recorder—achieve results
of depth—ethical action? As a well-trained *khatib*, Muhammad Subhi
had memorized a veritable encyclopedia of stories, poetry, and *hadith*
geared to the task of eliciting emotions of fear (*khawf*), sadness (*huzn*), or
terror (*ruʿb*), a genre of literature often designated by the term *tarhib* or
waʿz.[24] The rhetorical techniques of *tarhib* (from the verb *rahhab*, to terrify, frighten) and *waʿz* (from *waʿaz*, to warn or admonish) are employed
in order to instill fear into the heart of a listener so as to steer him or her
toward correct practice. They are the subject of an extensive literature, both
classical and contemporary, a body of work of key importance to the art of
preaching. Muhammad demonstrated his mastery of this preaching style
to me on a couple of occasions where, in order to provide me an example

of classical *tarhib* techniques, he would improvise a sermon, stringing one piece from this memorized stock of texts after another with extreme rapidity and precise cadence. His point in making such a display of virtuosity, however, was to highlight what he saw to be an improper practice on the part of many *khutaba'*, those who, in his view, "mechanically produce emotional responses [*bishaghalu al-ʿawatif bi tariq makanikiyya*] by such means without grounding those emotions in a useful and lasting knowledge rooted in the lived reality of the audience." A virtuoso *khatib*, in contrast, constantly weaves the classical narratives into the fabric of lived experience in an ongoing attempt to mend the fractures within ethical life with voice, image, and ear.

BETWEEN ETHICS AND ENTERTAINMENT

The tensions I have located within the ethical project of Islamic audition in Egypt today do not lead inexorably to the project's failure. Rather, they shape the fractured terrain upon which that project is pursued. As a continual source of friction mediating the realization of the project's ethical goals, such tensions find expression among those who promote and sustain the project in moments of ethical contradiction, in inconsistencies of action, or in experiences of vulnerability. Importantly, it is precisely from the vantage point of an ongoing attempt to impose discursive and practical coherence on this modern ethical regime that such moments of rupture acquire their meaning within lived experience.

One of the ways Islamic Revival activists like Ahmad, Saif, and Ibrahim coped with such conditions of ethical ambiguity was to draw upon popular discourses on the distinctions between Islamic and non-Islamic cultural forms. As I describe above, the very diffuseness of the affects associated with taped-sermon audition, along with the structural similarity of the practice to other forms of listening, introduces a worry into the practice: How is the experience produced by the tape different from the nonethical senses of pleasure, fear, or well-being produced by other popular media? Many of the people I spoke to invoked the example of music in order to explain to me the kind of relaxed feeling one feels when listening to a sermon. Beha described for me the workings of *tarhib* in a good sermon, and then compared it to the experience of music:

> When you hear about the tortures in the grave, you get scared, you fear God, then you start to feel regret, between you and yourself, for what you've done

wrong, so you ask God for forgiveness, you repent, and then you remember his mercy and you feel calm [*raha*], your chest opens [*munsharih al-sadr*], open to Islam, the Quran, God, and knowing that you will get close to him. When you listen to music, you also feel calm and relaxed, but that doesn't mean you're really close to God. With a sermon or Quran tape you can attain that closeness, so the feeling is better and more intense than when you are just relaxed.

Many of the sermon listeners I spoke with in Egypt suggested that although they listened to taped sermons as a means to ethical improvement, there were also times when, feeling tired or tense, they might choose a music tape over a sermon. Both could bring one to a state of relaxation. Yet, as Beha's comment begins to suggest, there is a key distinction to be drawn between the two experiences. As opposed to music, the sermon sets in motion a moral (and, as I have suggested above, affective and somatic) progression from fear, to regret, to asking for forgiveness, to repentance, and eventually to a sense of closeness with God, an experience that was described to me through terms such as *inshirah al-sadr* (opening of the heart or chest), *itmi'nan* (tranquility), and *sakina* (stillness). This progression constantly reappeared in the comments of the people I worked with in Cairo. Again, in Ahmad's words: "If a Muslim sees hell close to him [through a good *khatib*], he won't find peace until he asks forgiveness for his errors, repents, and returns humbly and tearfully to God." Such is the movement that a listener's body/heart makes, one learned in the soma-ethical dispositions I discuss above, under the guidance of a skillful *khatib*. Importantly, this is not the *raha* (calm) produced by soft music but rather a moral state conceptually articulated within the traditions of Islamic self-discipline.

Similarly, listeners distinguish pious fear (*khawf* or *taqwa*) from other forms of fear. When I asked Ahmad's brother Hisham to compare the experience of listening to sermon tapes on hell and death with horror films, he explained:

There is no comparison. True, when people watch scary films, terror may grip them and become imprinted on their brains [*fi mukhkhihim*]. Then, when they hear a door creak, or see a mouse, they get scared. This kind of terror is also caused by *'afarit* [demons], but it has nothing to do with hell, Judgment Day, or the tortures of the grave that the shaykh is talking about. Fear of these doesn't make you jump or scream; it is a fear implanted deep in your heart, and you can tell this because it keeps you from committing impious acts. Besides, most of those films are foreign anyway.

In his comment, Hisham contrasts two opposing structures of motivation, two psychologies of action, one moral, connected with the virtues, the other almost instinctual, a kind of animal reactivity. The fear and terror produced by popular films is morally neutral in this view, neither corrupting nor ethically fortifying. It is similar to the fear evoked by demons, a class of sometimes frightening otherworldly creatures within Islamic supernatural taxonomies, whose existence does not carry the existential significance nor demand an ethical responsiveness as do the facts of the brevity of life and the events of the eschaton. In short, for Hisham, the emotions induced by reflection on the grave presuppose and are integral to a structure of moral action, one presupposing a particular kind of motivation. Note also the different loci of the contrasting types of fear, one literally in the brain (*mukhkh*), the other in the heart, the organ of moral knowledge and practice. An even more common distinction drawn by people I worked with was between a kind of hearing that only engages the mind (*al-ʿaql*) and one that stems from the heart (*al-qalb*). As should be clear, their use of this distinction is not simply grounded in a metaphorical conceit. Instead, they are pointing to two contrasting modes of sensory organization, one purely intellectual, the other ethical and grounded in the honed patterns of sensorimotor responsiveness I discuss earlier.

As historians of media have often remarked, our tendency to speak of hearing as something achieved with the ears does not simply reflect a physiological datum but a variety of historically grounded assumptions embedded in our concept of hearing and in the cultural practices that organize and give form to our sensory experience. Specifically, we hear speech with our ears because, among other things, our alphabetic technology has encouraged us to conceive of speech as sounds produced by the mouth, tongue, and lips; it is only sound (of an extremely limited range) that such a technology can give visual form to.[25] The remnants of another kind of hearing can still be seen in such expressions as "to learn by heart" or "open your heart to what she is saying." As Illich notes, for the Greeks, "utterances could be articulated by the lips, tongue, or the mouth, but also by the heart when it spoke to a friend, by the *thymos* (which we might call 'gall') which rose in Achilles and drove him into battle, or by the onrush of a wave of blood" (1993:39).[26] To listen to an Islamic cassette sermon with the heart means to bring to bear on it those honed sensory capacities that allow one to "hear" (soulfully, emotionally, physically) what would escape a listener who applies only her "ear" or *al-ʿaql* (mind). Sermon audition is one of the means by which such capacities are developed and deepened.

Hisham's reference to the foreign origin of such films points to a certain mapping of moral space onto a political and cultural one. The virtues toward which the practice of sermon media is oriented, in other words, presuppose a nationalist political geography. More than this, however, the abrupt shift of argument—from the ethical content of emotions to the site of their manufacture—betrays an underlying anxiety of the sort I note earlier in the chapter: the film's foreign origin is called in to shore up a distinction that is threatened with dissolution or irrelevance, namely, the distinction between ethical and nonethical practices, and specifically media practices, in contemporary Egypt. In the face of this threat, the reference discursively bolsters the bond between the cassette-mediated experience of fear and the forms of ethical comportment in which it ideally finds expression.

SERMON RECEPTION AND ETHICAL SEDIMENTATION

As should now be clear, sermon oratory recruits the body of the listener in multiple ways. Beyond its referential content, the sermon can be seen as a technique for animating and organizing a stratigraphy of bodily experience and for endowing the human compound with gestural potential, in Jousse's vocabulary. The auditory apparatus consists of an experienced body in its entirety, one learned in the gestural vocabularies by which the sermon's ethical narratives have been woven into the autonomic and motor responses of this compound. Sermons impart not simply moral lessons but affective energies of ethical potential, a background of sensory and motor skills considered by those I worked with to be necessary for inhabiting the world in a manner appropriate for Muslims. The many performances involved in a sermon—such as the *khatib*'s visually striking depiction of extracting the soul of a sinner with a labored and trembling gesture of the hand rising above the neck—enliven and deepen the affective-gestural experiences that make possible—in the view of the sermon listeners I knew—the practices, modes of sociability, and attitudinal repertoires underlying a devout Islamic community. The task may be compared to that of an actor who, when playing the part of King Lear, must hone the strained gait, the movement of the hands, the manner of labored breathing, and the contortions of the face that express the tortured soul of one so betrayed (although in the cassette context, as I have argued, it is more an affective substrate that is honed, not fully elaborated performances). Note that I am not referring to the symbolic coding of the body, the attribution of meaning to its surfaces, movements, and speech. Rather, it is more like what rhetoricians call "attitude," a kind of "non-self-referential mode of awareness"[27] not reducible to mental states or symbolic processes.

The reference to rhetoric here can be extended further. In learning the art of rhetoric—one of the pillars of both classical education and the Christian curricula well into the early modern period—students not only acquired a capacity for eloquence but also skills of character, comportment, and affective expression. For example, *pronuntiatio*, or delivery, one of the five categories of rhetorical analysis, focused on the role of voice and gesture as they express the character of the speaker, character being a condition for the persuasiveness of one's argument.[28] As the Roman orator Quintilian explains: "And, indeed, since words in themselves count for much and the voice adds a force of its own to the matter of which it speaks, while gesture and motion are full of significance, we may be sure of finding something like perfection when all these qualities are combined" (1963:9). It is worth noting that such an analysis blurs the boundaries between language and character, and between speech and action.[29]

While for Aristotle (and later Augustine), rhetoric was a neutral art (*techne*), equally deployable for both good and evil aims, another school of thought (one more indebted to Quintilian and continuing up at least until the Renaissance) postulated a necessary relation between rhetorical excellence and moral virtue, that is, between speaking and being. As the historian Nancy Christiansen suggests in her discussion of the teaching of rhetoric during the British Renaissance, the discipline involved a strong ethical component: in learning to speak and act with decorum, to be persuasive in one's demeanor, one necessarily mastered the ethical attributes of upstanding character and, in that sense, became wise. Our modern inclination, of course, is to dismiss such skills as mere acting. However, while a distinction between inner self and outer acts is relevant in this context, that distinction indexes mastery, rather than degrees of truthfulness. As Christiansen notes:

> While the "role" and the person can be distinguished, the person is recognized by his or her roles. While the speaker may change roles, the choice and the manner of playing each role reveals the speaker's sense of decorum.

As a consequence, "sincerity" and "insincerity" name the good and the poor "act," not "being" versus "acting." Because universal principles of decorum guide the ordering of mental, spoken, and non-spoken discourse, every "act" is by nature in some measure sincere or insincere.

(CHRISTIANSEN 1997:319)

When discussing the Islamic sermon and its role in shaping ethical dispositions, it is important to distinguish between a rhetorical practice of evoking or modulating the passions as a means to sway an audience toward a point of view, and one aimed at constructing the passions in accord with a certain model. In regard to the former, Aristotle dedicated considerable attention to the possibilities of rhetorically manipulating the passions, examining the means by which anger, fear, or pity might be intensified or attenuated by an orator to his advantage (1991). We also find in Augustine an emphasis on the utility of arousing the emotions as a means of moving people to do what they know they should yet have failed to.[30] Such a technique is predicated on the instrumental use of emotions for purposes to which those emotions have no necessary relation. By contrast, in the practice of Islamic sermons, as I have noted, the objects of discourse and the emotions that are elicited in the context of their discussion are interdependent, such that those emotions only achieve their proper formation through that relationship.[31] The *khatib*'s task, in other words, includes not just the modulation of emotional intensities but also the orienting of those emotions to their proper objects.

If one responds to a given passage of a sermon with tears and sadness (*huzn*), one is not simply expressing the spontaneous movements of an autonomous inner self. The response of the heart, while never entirely knowable by others, nonetheless produces a performance—often an affective-gestural expression. Indeed, as I mention above, for some classical Islamic theologians such as al-Ghazali, each verse of the Quran summons forth from the pious listener both a corresponding disposition of the soul, such as fear or hope, and movements of the body and tongue, for example, an act of requesting forgiveness involving prostration, or one of supplication expressed through a gesture of the hands. As a skilled response of the learned body/soul to the *khatib*'s oratory, the performance of *huzn* both hones and expresses the listener's ethical character as enacted and practiced in accord with authoritative standards of moral rectitude.

On what basis can we compare contemporary practices of taped-sermon audition with scholarly exercises focusing on rhetorical exempla? Clearly, in the moment of listening to a sermon, one does not act out all of the gestures and movements corresponding to the particular account being narrated by the *khatib*, nor vocalize each and every response solicited. Rather, and this is an important part of my argument, an experiential knowledge of the gestural and emotive elements of the story constitutes a condition for its ethical reception. That is to say, one is capable of hearing the sermon in its full ethical sense only to the extent one has already cultivated the particular modes of sensory responsiveness presupposed in the discourse's gestural vocabulary, a vocabulary rich in affective, kinesthetic, and visceral dimensions. Collingwood makes this point in regard to the phenomenon of synaesthesia in aesthetic appreciation: we hear the sounds, colors, movements, and emotions that a composer has written into his music only insofar as we have an ear—and a body—trained in the sensibilities the composer brought to bear on his work (1966:146–51). One does not hear "the raw sound" and then elaborate upon it an imaginary experience of motion and color. One simply "hears" the emotion and color. The sensibilities that allow one to do so are not something purely cognitive but are rooted in the experience of the body in its entirety, as a complex of culturally and historically honed sensory modalities.

> The art of painting is intimately bound up with the expressiveness of the gestures made by the hand in drawing, and of the imaginary gesture through which a spectator of a painting appreciates its 'tactile values.' Instrumental music has a similar relation to silent movements of the larynx, gestures of the player's hand, and real or imaginary movements, as of dancing, in the audience.
>
> (COLLINGWOOD 1966:242)

The synaesthetic experiences of movement, color, touch, and emotion that occur when we listen to music are not produced through the free creative activity of the mind but are grounded in the actual sensual experience of the body as a complex of culturally honed perceptual capacities.[32] Our sensory responses are similar to those of other listeners or viewers to the extent that our capacities for hearing or vision have been shaped within a shared disciplinary context. They possess a specific affective-volitional structure as a result of the sensorial practices by which we have been formed as a member of a specific community.

This way of construing audition in terms of tactile, kinesthetic, and visceral responsiveness is strongly reminiscent of Jousse's gestural subject, one whose anemone-like body ripples with the rhythmic motions of the universe. Jousse's psychophysiology (which has clear Aristotelian roots) rests on a vision of the cosmos as a dynamic whole in constant rhythmic interaction, a vision with a definite affinity to aspects of Islamic mystical thought.[33] For Sufi mystics, such as Ibn al-Arabi, it was by means of the sound, rhythm, affect, and harmony afforded by both poetry and recited Quranic verses that imaginal knowledge of the right and true (as opposed to rational knowledge) could be achieved, or, in Ibn al-Arabi's term, "tasted [*dhawq*]" (see Chittick 1989; Schimmel 1994). While the contemporary *da'wa* movement rejects many aspects of Islamic mysticism, it has incorporated this tradition of linking the realization of ethical being with the resonant body. Jousse's own framing of this kind of linkage is worth citing here:

> We know and think first of [our gestures, and that] in order to act; and of the things we know, not one is a biological luxury. We have seen that every [reception, external or internal] contains, besides its representative elements, an affective element and [above all, which constitutes its substratum] and active [gestural] element. . . . This applies also to . . . [reviviscenses of every kind] and to ideas properly speaking, whose primary function is to direct the action [of the various gestural systems].
>
> (JOUSSE [1925] 1990:96)

PASSIONAL REASON

The kind of affective dispositions acquired and enhanced by the men I knew through taped-sermon audition (among other practices) are precisely the kind that worried Plato in *The Republic*. In his view, those performances that engaged an audience in ways that bypassed a reflective, philosophical understanding—such as poetry, theater, or song—had a power to impact and mold individuals that rendered such arts especially dangerous. As a present-day interpreter of Plato notes:

> The problem with uncontrolled mimesis, as Plato sees it, is not just the character of the likenesses it brings into our presence. It is how these likenesses gradually insinuate themselves into the soul through the eyes and ears, without our being aware of it. . . . It is as if eyes and ears offer painter and poet entry to a relatively independent cognitive apparatus, associated

with the senses, through which mimetic images can bypass our knowledge and infiltrate the soul.

(BURNYEAT 1998:8)

Recognizing the power of such arts to shape moral character, Plato advocated the prohibition of those performances that depicted human qualities not corresponding to the Athenian virtues he saw as foundational to the ideal city. Later Christian thinkers, in contrast, have tended to place more emphasis on the positive contribution of embodied forms of knowledge. Arguing along lines much closer to those suggested by the men I worked with, Christian theologians from Aquinas to Luther to John Henry Newman have asserted that a certain disposition of the passions was necessary in order to assess the validity of claims for the truth of Scripture; that ethical affects such as gratitude, humility, and love of God have an epistemic value, allowing one to evaluate evidence for the authority of the Bible in the proper light (see Wainwright 1995).[34] According to Newman, it is precisely in living piously that our emotions, imagination, and attitudes (our senses and sensibilities) are shaped so as to appreciate Christian arguments. Conversely, sinning renders one's faculties over time incapable of evaluating the evidence of religion.

The sermon listeners I worked with in Cairo held a similar view of the positive contribution of passional factors to acts of moral reasoning and saw the practice of sermon audition as a means by which such affective orientations could be honed in accord with models of Islamic moral personhood. In my analysis of this auditory practice, I have—following Joussean tracks—chosen to view the body as a kind of fluid medium, one animated and traversed by an ensemble of interlinking movements: the gestures of the hands, the face and eyes, the nerves, muscles, and breath that in their synthesis and complementarity form the sensitive heart of an ethical listener. This ensemble of sensorimotor reflexes, Jousse argues, "constitutes the warp upon which [and by means of which] consciousness weaves its designs" ([1925] 1990:8).

There is an echo of Benjamin's storyteller that merits being heard here. As I note in the introduction to this book, for Benjamin, the craft of storytelling depends upon a particular coordination of "the soul, eye, and hand" that has been lost with the disappearance of artisanal modes of production and their replacement by forms of labor that do not entail or engender such affective-gestural skills (1969:108). While the sermon-tape listeners I have described inhabit this postartisanal world, this is not the end of the story. Nor, for that matter, have the soul, eye, and hand simply parted ways, despite their current reliance on tape recorders, TVs, automobiles, and commodity markets. For boredom—the relaxed attentiveness produced by artisanal labor that, in Benjamin's view, enabled listeners to assimilate the story material—has not been overcome, although its somatic rhythm and texture have changed considerably for the taxi drivers, store clerks, and aluminum plant workers of today. Within such moments of modern boredom, the cassette sermon, with its distinct rhetorics, technology, and circulatory modes, offers up a collective wisdom to the senses. Benjamin's analysis of how the perceptual regime ushered in by modernity renders traditional worlds silent, invisible—in short, imperceptible—needs to be complemented by a recognition of the ways in which practitioners of a tradition, through innovation and adaptation, attempt to cultivate and sustain the sensory conditions and the modes of attention and inattention that make that tradition viable within modern contexts. While Benjamin was clearly correct to point to such processes of sensory erosion, we must avoid the tendency—encouraged by the concept of modernity—to interpret these as instances within a totalizing historical process, as disparate manifestations of a singular teleological development. As scholars have increasingly recognized, an account of modernity can no longer be told simply in terms of the destruction of the old and its replacement by the new; modern lives have been shaped both by the maintenance of continuities with past practice and by revivals, reworkings, and rediscoveries, including rediscoveries of buried sensory experiences.[35]

[4]

CASSETTES AND COUNTERPUBLICS

S CHOLARS EXPLORING the incorporation of modern mass media into religious practices have frequently approached the topic in terms of a polarity between what are assumed to be two contradictory processes, the deliberative and the disciplinary. Analyses focusing on the deliberative aspect have emphasized the possibilities of argument, contestation, and dialogue that have been afforded by the advent of universal modern literacy, the diffusion of printed texts, and the operation of electronic mass media.[1] Following conventional histories of the Protestant revolution, this scholarship has given particular emphasis to the role of print and other media technologies in propelling a democratization of religious authority. The new objectlike quality of religion and the universal accessibility of religious texts, it is argued, transform ritual speech into individual assertion, oral mnemonics into analytical memory. Equipped with these newfound sophistications and the autonomous reasoning that they facilitate, a growing number of individuals engage with and revise the religious traditions they have inherited.

Scholars emphasizing the disciplinary functions of religious media, on the other hand, have stressed the ideological over the dialogic aspects of the phenomenon.[2] Media technologies, in this view, enable an extension of an authoritative religious discourse. The resultant public is less a site of discussion than of subjection to authority, part of a project aimed at promoting and securing a uniform model of moral behavior. In short, the public arena constituted by the media practices of religious actors tends to be identified *either* as a deliberative space of argument and contestation between individuals *or* as a normative space for education in community-oriented virtue. The assumption is that the more truly deliberative a public, the weaker its disciplinary function, and vice versa.

This way of framing the inquiry reflects, in part, a tendency within liberal thought to view the individual as necessarily in conflict with the community and the forms of collective discipline that undergird it. As Michael Warner has recently noted, the idea of *public* privileged within the modern social imaginary tends to exclude any recognition of the institutional and disciplinary conditions that enable it (2002:67–74). For the public to be seen as both autonomous and sovereign with respect to the state, Warner suggests, it must be understood as self-organizing, constituted solely by the circulation of its own discourse beyond the reach of any external norms or formal mediations. Even those institutions through which a public enacts its agency, such as voting or polls, are normatively interpreted to express, not produce, the public opinion that they make available. To sustain this fiction of a purely self-organizing discourse, this conception of a public builds in a structural blindness to the material conditions of the discourses it produces and circulates, as well as to the pragmatics of its speech forms: the genres, stylistic elements, citational resources, gestural codes, and so on that make a discourse intelligible to specific people inhabiting certain conditions of knowledge and learning. Such material conditions of discourse are obscured through a language ideology that circumscribes meaning to propositional content and construes the speech situation as one of rational-critical dialogue, a universal speech form unhindered by conventions of affect and expressivity or by the pragmatics of particular speech communities (Warner 2002:114–15). Deliberation, in this way, is conceptually immunized from what are understood as the necessarily distorting effects of power.

The form of public I explore in this chapter contrasts with this model in some of its basic features. For this reason, I will refer to it as a "counterpublic."[3] While clearly structured around some of the assumptions of modern publicity, this idea of a "counterpublic" rests upon a conceptual edifice in which deliberation and discipline, or language and power, are regarded as thoroughly interdependent. In contrast to a space for the formation of political opinion through intersubjective reason, the discursive arena wherein cassette sermons circulate is geared to the deployment of the disciplining power of ethical speech, a goal, however, that takes public deliberation as one of its modalities. Within this context, public speech results not in policy but in pious dispositions, the embodied sensibilities and modes of expression understood to facilitate the development and practice of Islamic virtues, and therefore of Islamic ethical comportment.[4] For contemporary Egyptian Muslims who participate in this sphere of dialogic engagement, the definition and articulation of Islamic ethical norms and their embodiment as practical aptitudes are critically dependent upon the communicative practices and discursive conventions of this public arena.

Although shaped in various ways by the structures and techniques of modern publicity, the form of Islamic public I discuss here exhibits a conceptual architecture that cuts across the modern distinctions between state and society and between public and private that are central to the public sphere as a normative institution of modern democratic polities. In their objects, styles of reasoning, and modes of historicity, the entwined deliberative and disciplinary practices that constitute this arena reflect the way Islamic notions of moral duty and practices of ethical cultivation have been mapped onto a national civic arena by Muslim reformists over the course of the last century. As mosques in Egypt over the last fifty years became the site for new kinds of social and political organization and expression, everyday practices of pious sociability gradually came to inhabit a new political terrain, one shaped both by the discourses of national citizenship and by emerging transnational forms of religious association. In the course of this shift, forms of practical reasoning tied to the tradition of the virtues became oriented not simply toward a notion of moral community (an *umma*) but toward what we would recognize as a public as well: the practice of the virtues and the deliberation of issues of public concern were fused together in a unique manner. The cassette sermon has provided the discursive vehicle wherein this interdependency has been most extensively and intensively worked out.

As opposed to the private reader, whose stillness and solitude became privileged icons of a distinct kind of critical reasoning within the imaginary of the bourgeois public, it is the figure of the ethical listener—with all of its dense sensory involvements—that founds and inhabits the counterpublic I describe here. Informed by a language ideology emphasizing the poetic and performative dimensions of speech and its ethical resonances across multiple sensory registers, the form of public reason and sociability I describe remains dependent upon and positively oriented toward its own affective, gestural, and kinesthetic conditions.[5] Through the deployment of new styles of moral exhortation and critique and their circulation within an aural media geared to the honing of sensibilities and the cultivation of pious habits, a fragmented history of soma-ethical experience found new coherence and expression as the sensory background for an emergent form of public sociability. This public is a fragile and unstable accomplishment, the contingent product of the way embodied forms of historical memory have congealed within new social and political spaces as the visceral substrate for a modern Islamic ethics. I say fragile because the practices that constitute this arena are continually subject to rival and more powerful discursive framings that are tied to the market, the regulatory institutions of the state, and conditions of governance more generally.

The moral and political project that I explore in this book does not lend itself easily to the dominant binaries of contemporary political debate: liberalism/communalism and democratic/authoritarian. To the extent that I use these terms, I do so lightly, to avoid obscuring what I consider to be the unique and politically challenging aspects of Egypt's Islamic counterpublic beneath the analytical umbra cast by these terms. The notion of fundamentalism is even less useful. As I will argue in my concluding chapter, the interpretive grid fundamentalism provides is entirely inadequate to the arguments and histories of contemporary Islamic activism. Worse, it deafens us to some of the ways that the contemporary struggles of pious Muslims speak to our own moral and political conundrums. Learning to hear, in this regard, is as important a political precept *for us* as it is an ethical one for sermon publics in Egypt today.

CASSETTE *DAʿWA*

The production and consumption of sermon tapes has, since their beginnings in the early 1970s, been associated with the broad movement known as *al-daʿwa* (literally, a summons or call), and, as noted in chapter 2, almost all of the preachers who make use of this medium refer to themselves and are referred to by others as *duʿat* (sing. *daʿiya*), that is, those who undertake *daʿwa*. The term *daʿwa* has historically encompassed a wide range of meanings. When found in the Quran, it generally refers to God's invitation, addressed to humankind and transmitted through the prophets, to live in accord with God's will.[6] Over the early centuries of Islam's development, *daʿwa* came to be used increasingly to designate the content of that invitation, and in the works of some classical jurists it appears to be interchangeable both with the term *shariʿa* (the juridical codification of God's message) and *din* (often translated as "religion").[7] *Daʿwa* also, however, carried another sense from early in Islam's historical career, one that has been central to contemporary Islamic thought: that of a duty, incumbent upon some or all members of the Islamic community, to actively encourage fellow Muslims in the pursuance of greater piety in all aspects of their lives.[8] It is the performance of this duty, one now charged with new social and political functions, that founds the Islamic counterpublic in Egypt.

The contemporary practice of *da'wa* can be illustrated through a conversation I overheard during a taxi ride through downtown Cairo and that is rather typical of the kind of public interactions for which cassette sermons have played a constitutive role. Taxis in Cairo frequently pick up more than one passenger. In this case I was sharing the ride with two other people, a teenage boy and a young woman who wore the *hijab* (headscarf). The taxi driver, who had a long beard and was dressed in a *jallabiyya* (a male form of pious dress), was listening to a sermon tape by the popular preacher Umar Abd al-Kafi. At a certain point during the ride, as the tape came to an end, the boy sitting in front next to the driver asked him if he had any song music he might put on instead. After a few moments of awkward silence, the driver responded that music was *haram* (forbidden) in Islam. The boy looked surprised and irritated but kept quiet and turned away. The driver, noting the boy's irritation, said: "Don't just look away, tell me what you're thinking. We can talk, there's no problem."

"How can singing be *haram*?" said the boy, "Who told you that?" The driver replied, "Do you or don't you believe in the Quran and the *sunna* [the Prophetic traditions]?" The boy responded that of course he did. The driver continued, "Shouldn't we do everything in our lives to follow the *sunna*? Doesn't it tell us not only the rules of God, but as Muslims, isn't it also a model for us?" Again, the boy, now getting impatient, concurred. On a roll, the driver moved to clinch the argument by means of a *hadith*, an account of one of the Prophet's deeds or sayings: "When the Prophet used to hear songs, he would put his fingers in his ears, and considered music to be one of the devil's snares [*madkhal al-shaytan*]." The boy quickly retorted that the driver's *hadith* was "*da'if*," a classificatory term referring to a category of *hadith* whose authority is of the weakest kind. Not ready to concede the point, the driver continued: "Do you believe there is nothing that is *haram* in religion [*din*]?" "Of course," the boy countered, "but I must know where the proof [*dalil*] is for the *haram*. Someone can tell you today that driving a car is *haram*, and you'll stop driving. Then later you'll find out it was wrong, and start to drive again, unless you found out from the beginning whether what was called *haram* was really *haram* or just an erroneous invention."

The driver, realizing now that he had better take another tack, asked, "Don't you think that drinking alcohol is *haram*? Do you know why? Because it interferes with prayer. It's the same with songs; when you hear songs your mind goes somewhere else and you can't pray." The boy retorted vigorously: "Alcohol is one thing, but the Quran says nothing about music. I pray, fast, and do all my obligations of worship [*ibadat*], and what is wrong if I hear songs as well? I am not doing anything *haram*!"

At this point, the woman sitting in the back next to me entered the debate: "But all the words of songs are about love and all of these things, so that when you go out you think about that rather than think about God. Your ears get used to hearing the songs, until you don't like to listen to the Quran. Well, then songs are prohibited so that at an adolescent age you don't think about things that would lead you to illicit desire [*shahawat*] and sin [*al-dhanb*]. Especially in this era and time, when the world is full of seductions that are always seeking to occupy your thoughts [*tishaghallak 'ala tul*]. The sermon, on the other hand, makes you think of God, and brings you feelings of humility [*khushu'*] and regret [*nadam*]." She then quoted a verse from the Quran, but the boy immediately pointed out to her that the verse made no mention of music. "Yes," she concurred, "but it leads you to the reasoning of why music is *haram*." The driver nodded in agreement. The boy, not to be defeated, countered, "Love is not *haram* in Islam."

This conversation reveals a number of characteristics of a kind of public deliberation that has become increasingly prevalent in Egypt in recent decades. Note, to begin with, the rather unstructured and informal character of this exchange. Situated outside the boundaries of prescribed ritual practice or scholarly instruction, this form of discussion cuts across generational and gender lines in ways not possible within the traditional institutions of Islamic authority. The relationship between the speakers is not that of teacher to pupil, nor of social superior to social subordinate, but rather of coparticipants in a common moral project, their speech structured around an orientation toward correct Islamic practice. Importantly, this structure of motivation is less a prerequisite for the exchange than the collective achievement toward which it is teleologically disposed. One acquires the will and capacity to act morally precisely though participating in such conversations: to speak publicly on ethical issues is one of the ways one both hones and enacts ethical knowledge. Moreover, reference to authoritative Islamic sources does not close debate. Instead, the lines of argument pivot precisely upon the proper interpretation and understanding of those sources.

Admittedly, notions of gender equality have played little role in the *da'wa* movement. Participants in the movement, and the *khutaba'* who are its most prominent exponents, generally emphasize a certain patriarchal order as essential for the organization of social and individual conduct in a Muslim society. In the field of preaching, for example, arguments about the dangers to male piety inherent in the female voice continue to sanction a long-standing prohibition on women delivering sermons to mixed audiences in mosques in Egypt.⁹ That being said, the actual practice of *da'wa* has been one area where women's subordinate status has been relatively attenuated and where many of the arguments commonly used to disqualify women from domains of political and religious authority are not seen to apply. As Saba Mahmood notes in her ethnography of the lives of pious women in Egypt, one of the apparent paradoxes of the *da'wa* movement lies in the fact that while its participants generally insist on upholding Islamic edicts that subordinate women to men within social life, the movement itself has been more open to women's participation than have other currents of the broader Islamic Revival (Mahmood 2005).

The impact of the cassette sermon on gendered practices of public discourse are also important in this respect. Tapes and tape markets have enabled the extension of sermon oratory into dialogic contexts where women are active participants, arguing with men over doctrinal matters, the competency of particular preachers, and social and political concerns addressed in the recordings. On a number of occasions I was told of women having deployed tapes to pressure male kin to uphold their familial responsibilities. Moreover, the fact that women make up a large percentage of sermon listeners has led preachers to increasingly address topics considered germane to women, from the rights women may demand from husbands to the sexual pleasures that await them in heaven.

The exchange among the taxi passengers also points to a new familiarity with bases and styles of Islamic argumentation, evidenced, for example, in the boy's knowledge of the specific *hadith* as well as its classification within the authoritative traditions. The advent of modern mass education, literacy, and the wide availability of written texts has equipped recent generations of Muslims in the Middle East with new competencies in styles of scholarly argumentation and their associated textual materials, both classical and modern (Eickelman 1992; Eickelman and Anderson 1999). There is a sense among many young Muslims in Egypt today that adherence to Islam requires a personal knowledge of Islamic ethical and juridical traditions and that one cannot rely on the viewpoints of others in regard to doctrinal issues—a point underscored by the boy. Ahmad and his friend Ibrahim, as well as others I worked with, frequently emphasized the importance of checking out the veracity of doctrinal claims by seeking out corroborating statements in the Quran or *sunna*, referring the issue to someone known to be more learned in religious matters, or finding a tape by a reputable shaykh where the topic is addressed. Both Ahmad and Ibrahim claimed that cassette sermons and recorded mosque lessons had enabled them to expand and bolster their knowledge of Islamic ethical and doctrinal literatures during times of the day when the sort of concentration demanded by written texts would be impossible. In short, for many Egyptians today a practical competence in skills of religious reasoning and argumentation has increasingly become part of what is entailed in being a Muslim, a trend indebted in no small way to the proliferation of new institutions of Islamic learning associated with the revival movement, such as mosque study groups, private Islamic institutes, *da'wa* centers, and a vibrant market in Islamic books and tapes.[10]

Note that this practice does not map onto the constitutionally demarcated separation of public and private but rather traverses this distinction in a way that is often uncomfortable to those with secular-liberal sensibilities. *Da'wa* is undertaken in the street, on public transportation, at the workplace, or in the home. From a liberal perspective, *da'wa* is seen as encouraging an unwarranted intrusion into the privacy of others, especially as it entails entering into what are considered to be personal matters of religious faith. *Du'at* render public issues that the liberal state relegates to the private sphere of individual choice—the modesty of one's dress, the precision of gesture in prayer, the danger of gossip, and the proximity of unrelated men and women in both the workplace and the home, as well as other more overtly political issues (as I discuss below). For liberals, these issues tend to be viewed as either insignificant (such as precision in prayer, gossip) and thus unworthy of public attention or, alternatively, as matters of individual preference (such as dress, gender conventions, and so on) and as such protected by private law. *Da'wa*, for this reason, constitutes an obstacle to the state's attempt to secure a social domain where national citizens are free to make modern choices, as it *repoliticizes* those choices, subjecting them to a public scrutiny oriented around the task of establishing the conditions for the practice of Islamic virtues.

While *da'wa* frequently takes the form of discussion and deliberation, its paradigmatic speech genre is the sermon. As I discuss in the preceding chapters, the interpretive norms informing Islamic homiletic traditions foreground the capacity of ethical speech—particularly one imbued with the language of the Quran and the teachings of the *sunna*—to move the sensitive heart toward correct practice. A well-crafted sermon is understood to evoke in the listener the affective dispositions that underlie ethical conduct and reasoning and that, through repeated listening, may become sedimented in the listener's character. Enabled in part by the mediatization of sermons on cassette, some of the norms governing sermon practice have been extended by the *da'wa* movement to the dialogical context of public discourse.

Within this arena, speech is deployed in order to construct moral selves, to reshape character, attitude, and will in accord with contemporary standards of pious behavior. The efficacy of an argument here devolves not solely on its power to gain cognitive assent on the basis of its superior reasoning, as would be the case in some versions of a liberal public sphere, but also on the ability of ethical language and exemplary behavior to move human beings toward correct modes of being and acting. A language ideology foregrounding poetic and affective aspects, sensory modes of understanding outside the realm of semantics narrowly construed, provides conceptual scaffolding here. What joins the practice of delivering or listening to a sermon with that of arguing with a neighbor is a conception of the rhetorical force of ethical speech to shape character, as I outline in the preceding chapters. In other words, if in the earlier tradition the ethical mediation of divine speech required the voice of either the Quran reciter or the *khatib* in the mosque, now a deliberative public also performs this function. Deliberative and disciplinary moments, in other words, are thoroughly interwoven and interdependent within this arena.

MODERNIZING MORAL DUTY

The contours of a distinctly modern *da'wa*, exemplified in the taxi conversation, emerged gradually over the course of the last century. *Da'wa* seems to have received little systematic elaboration from the late medieval period through the early twentieth century. While the "rediscovery" of the notion cannot be tied to any particular figure or institution, its current salience owes primarily to its development within Islamic opposition movements, most notably within the Muslim Brotherhood.[11] From the late 1920s, Hassan al-Banna, the founder of the Brotherhood, appropriated the classical notion of *da'wa* to define the goals of the organization, namely, the restoration and strengthening of the Islamic community (*umma*) in the face of its increasing secularization under khedival rule (Mendel 1995:295).[12] As previously mentioned, the Brotherhood was particularly critical of the marginalization of Islamic doctrines and practices within the projects of social and political reform being promoted by nationalist thinkers, and of the failure of the established institutions of Islamic authority to oppose this process. By employing such modern political methods as media campaigns, large-scale rallies, and training camps for Muslim activists, the Brotherhood quickly went from a local grassroots association that encouraged pious conduct to an international organization embodying considerable religious and political power and authority.[13]

As elaborated by al-Banna, *da'wa* defined the mode of action by which moral and political reform was to be brought about. Brotherhood members were advised to go to mosques, schools, cafés, clubs and other public locations and speak with whomever would listen about Islam, the Brotherhood, and the task of building a pious Muslim society. The Brotherhood also encouraged the Islamic practice of *isti'dhan*, wherein a member of the mosque assembly asks permission to address the gathering on matters relevant to the Muslim community. This practice, which became increasingly widespread during subsequent decades, had the effect of enhancing the dialogical structure of social discourse within the mosque and orienting it within a national political frame, thereby expanding its role as a key site of public discussion.[14] The Brotherhood also pioneered the use of mass media as an instrument of Islamic activism and reformism. Books, short tracts, pamphlets, and flyers by reformist writers, as well as magazines covering national and international events considered relevant to Muslims, were widely circulated and competed with the more secularly oriented publications of the nationalist movement. For *da'wa* speech and print (and, later, audio) media, the sermon provided a paradigmatic rhetorical form, a practice that stood in contrast to the European models of political oratory increasingly adopted by Egyptian secular nationalists. Al-Banna's sermons in particular became massively popular in Egypt and other Arab countries and were widely distributed in book and pamphlet form.

In many ways, al-Banna and his followers fell within a long tradition of preacher-reformers within Islamic societies.[15] Speaking to ordinary Muslims rather than scholars, these reformers had to engage the practical and political constraints on moral action in a way that those working within the institutions of Islamic learning and authority did not. As a result, they have often been viewed by their scholarly contemporaries as either dangerous innovators or ignorant popularizers, garnering public approbation at the expense of doctrinal rigor (a charge frequently leveled against al-Banna at the time from within al-Azhar and its affiliated institutions).[16] Such challenges aside, some of the most productive experiments in responding to the ethical challenges of modern political discourse, of which al-Banna's is an early and influential example, have taken place precisely within this space of everyday practical action and concern opened up by the notion of *da'wa*. Indeed, one of my arguments in this chapter is that *da'wa* has provided the conceptual site wherein the concerns, public duties, character, and virtues of an activist Muslim citizen have been most extensively elaborated and practiced.

While the Brotherhood was eventually banned by the Egyptian state in the 1950s and many of its members imprisoned or driven underground, the practice of *da'wa* itself did not disappear.[17] On the contrary, over the last half century *da'wa* has increasingly shaped a space for the articulation of a contestatory Islamic discourse on modern society, a discourse embodied in a diversified array of institutional forms, including educational centers, preaching associations, thousands of private mosques, and an expanding network of publishing houses and other media organizations.[18] A wide variety of other activities in some way oriented toward promoting and fortifying the ethical practices that constitute Islamic modes of piety and community have also come to be understood through the concept of *da'wa*—from providing social and medical services to the poor, to tutoring children at mosques, to selling Islamic books or tapes. *Da'wa*, in other words, has come to describe a particular way of linking public activism with moral reform. Placed under the rubric of this notion, a wide range of commercial, educational, and welfare activities essential to the reproduction and maintenance of modern society have been assigned moral significance, as contributions to the goal of building a community oriented around the practice of the virtues.

Cassette sermons have played an important role in Egypt since the 1970s in the transformation of *da'wa* from an organizing principle within specific institutions (such as the Brotherhood or the Islamic welfare associations) to a popular form of public practice and participation. Largely because of the mass popularity achieved through cassette circulation, popular preachers (most notably Shaykh Kishk) became rallying points and exemplary figures within an emerging counterpublic of *da'wa* practitioners.[19] Many of the young men I worked with explicitly identified cassette sermons as an alternative to the televisual and press media promoted by the state. As Ahmad, pointing to his cassette recorder, told me shortly after we met: "This is the only mass media [*al-i'lam*] I need. The [state-controlled] television and the newspapers never discuss the important events and issues. We would never find out about what is really going on even here in Egypt without these tapes." There now exists, both in audio and booklet form, a substantial number of works offering instruction in the practice of "individual *da'wa*," understood to be an ethical form of speech and action aimed at improving the moral conduct of one's fellow community members. As a result of the dissemination of such techniques of ethical self-improvement and the establishment of their associated institutional networks, the virtues and skills of the *da'iya* have come for many to provide a model for the attributes of the Muslim-citizen. These attributes find expression within many different moments of daily life, including the occasional taxi ride.

PUBLIC ISLAM

To gather up the threads of my argument so far, the media and associational infrastructure put into place by the *da'wa* movement has created the conditions for a kind of publicness grounded in the deployment of certain classical Islamic concepts within a context increasingly shaped by the normative modes of discourse of a modern public sphere. That is to say, reformers like Hassan al-Banna and Abd al-Hamid Kishk revived a notion of *da'wa* as a moral duty, the performance of which, conceptually and historically, had long been defined as a condition for the vitality of the Muslim collective. In its contemporary elaboration, *da'wa* defines a kind of practice involving the public use of a mode of reasoning whereby the correctness of an action is argued and justified in the face of error, doubt, indifference, or counterargument. To assume the position of a *da'iya* (one who undertakes *da'wa*) is to adopt the rhetorical stance of a member of the Islamic *umma* acting on behalf of that particular historical project (and thus not simply as an individual concerned for his or her own moral conduct).[20] Although such a *da'wa* counterpublic has only become possible with the contemporary emergence of a range of public institutions and media practices, it is less an empirical entity than a framework for a particular type of action. *Da'wa* is constituted whenever and wherever individuals enter into that form of discourse geared toward upholding or improving the moral condition of the collective, as, for example, illustrated in the taxi conversation above.

Deployed in a political context structured by the discourses of citizenship and nation, *da'wa* has come to fuse what are in effect two models of agency: one ethical, grounded in the Quranic moral psychology I discuss in chapter 3, the other embedded in the liberal notions of public that accompanied the state's attempt to fashion a modern political order. A discourse on the ethical impact of pious speech on the sensitive listener provides the interpretive frame for a public sphere geared to the deliberation of the common good. This attribution of ethical agency to a broader deliberative arena also found resonance with an interpretive trend within modern Islam whereby the consensus (*ijma‘*) required to establish the veracity of an interpretive judgment was increasingly seen to necessitate not simply a restricted group of entrusted scholars but the *umma* as a universal collective body (D. Brown 1996). While the nineteenth- and twentieth-century scholars who advocated this view rarely elaborated it in explicitly national terms, their more catholic interpretation of the jurisprudential notion of *ijma‘* clearly draws sustenance from democratic conceptions of a deliberative public. In other words, while the Islamic *umma* is fundamentally a moral space, the types of action it encompasses and that serve to delineate and sustain it have come to be structured by the normative mode of articulation of the public sphere. Inflected by the discourse on moral action organized under the rubric of *da‘wa*, the new form of public is grounded in the tendency of ethical public discourse toward self-correction, toward an approximation of what is understood to be divinely sanctioned comportment. As politics, both national and global, impinge on the structures of moral life, the ethical discourses of *da‘wa* necessarily extend to political topics. As a type of activity aimed at both revealing and realizing Islamic ideals of moral life through persuasion, exhortation, and deliberation, it is fundamentally a political practice. Indeed, *da‘wa* emerges not at a point of commonality but precisely at one of difference, where a discrepancy in practice makes argument necessary.

DA‘WA AND THE NATION

While participants in the *da‘wa* movement clearly consider themselves to be Egyptian citizens, they also cultivate sentiments, loyalties, and styles of public conduct that stand in tension with the moral and political exigencies and modes of self-identification of national citizenship. In this sense, they inhabit a counterpublic: a domain of discourse and practice that stands in a disjunctive relationship to the public sphere of the nation and its media instruments. While in practice *da‘wa* often entails an oppositional stance in regard to the state, this type of public does not in its present form play a mediatory role between state and society. In other words, the practice of *da‘wa* does not take place within or serve to uphold that domain of associational life referred to as civil society. When the state acts in ways that foreclose the possibility of living in accord with Islamic standards promoted by the movement—such as forbidding schoolgirls from wearing headscarves, broadcasting television serials that show behaviors that are considered indecent, or cutting back on the amount of time dedicated to learning the Quran in schools—*khutaba'* use the mosque sermon to publicly criticize these actions, a critique that is then quickly distributed on tape. On some occasions, the broad mobilizations that have ensued have led the state to reverse a decision (as happened with the ruling banning the use of headscarves in public schools).

Having said this, it is important to recognize the extent to which the nation is a political condition of the *da'iya*'s speech: the position of utterance he inhabits and the contestatory discourse he articulates have been shaped by the concepts and institutions of national political life. I have used the notion of counterpublic precisely to register the relationship of complementarity and interdependence linking this arena to the nation. While the nation inhabits the *da'iya*'s discourse as a necessary object of reflexive self-identification, it is as an object embedded in (and subordinate to) the broader moral project of an Islamic *umma*. As performatively enacted within *da'wa* discourse, the nation's claims on loyalty and identity are relativized in light of the demands of this moral project, a project understood to be irreducible to the concepts of territory, ethnicity, and collective historical experience upon which the nation is founded. The *da'iya*'s narrative locates itself within the temporal frame of an Islamic *umma* and in relation to the succession of events that characterize its mode of historicity.[21] The temporality of these tapes, for example, does not index the nation, the daily unfolding of events, or "news," through which the newspaper reader or television viewer participates as national citizen. Rather, the ethical listener sees both recent sermons and those from two decades past as contemporary, and they are combined and interspersed through listening practices. The ethical and political content of these sermons bear on the present—a present structured by the notion of *sahwa*, or revival , the period of moral renewal that repeatedly succeeds eras of decline and corruption.[22]

As opposed to the national public sphere centered around the press and televisual media, the *da'wa* counterpublic reveals a more marked supranational focus, evident, for example, in the considerable attention given in sermons to the plight of Muslims worldwide as well as the interest shown by cassette-sermon audiences in such issues. Sermon tapes often mediate debates on the geopolitical boundaries of ethical responsibility, as in the following conversation that took place in the Karim Coffee Shop in Bulaq-Dukrur, a lower-class quarter of Cairo that I visited with Ibrahim one day.

When we arrived, the owner of the shop was wiping down the counters while listening, on his tape player, to a preacher's passionate evocation of the current suffering of Bosnian Muslims at the hands of Serbian aggressors. His three clients, all men from the neighborhood, accommodated to the languorous rhythm of their water pipes as the account of Serbian atrocities and European indifference echoed around them. At a certain point, the preacher, his voice straining with grief, halted his description to ask: "Where are the Muslims?! Where are the Muslims, while Muslim girls are being raped, mosques are being burned?! Where?!" "Enough, O shaykh," the man sitting closest to the counter called out, "They're not Muslims; they're Europeans!" Turning now to the owner of the shop, he continued, "Why all of these tears for the Bosnians? They dress like Europeans, they act like Europeans. There is nothing Islamic about them." "How can you say that," the shop owner retorted as the preacher continued behind him, "Didn't you hear? They have mosques; they pray; they stand in the same line [nafs al-saff] as we do. They worship . . ." His client cut him short: "No, no, no. They may have been Muslims once, but they became Westerners long ago [yatagharrabu min zaman]. Whatever little Islam they had was extinguished by the Communists." Ibrahim, who knew the man from previous visits to the café and was visibly irritated by his comment, weighed in: "Shame on you, Samir [haram ʿalayk, ya Samir]. Muslims are Muslims, wherever they are. The shaykh is right: the shame is on us that we sit by and do nothing while our brothers [ikhwanina] are being slaughtered. The mosques collect a little money, the prime minister says, 'we support the rights of the Bosnians,' and nothing is done." Samir again rejected the argument: "We Arabs have enough problems. Palestinians are being murdered and you want us to save the Bosnians?! Maybe the Bosnians are our cousins, but our brothers, the Arabs—the Iraqis, the Algerians, the Palestinians—they're the ones we should be concerned with."

As the preacher began a collective prayer calling for an end of Bosnian suffering, the shop owner returned again to the theme of Muslim solidarity: "So we should only help Arabs. That's exactly the reason why Muslims are so weak today. That's exactly what our enemies want us to do: 'Those Muslims are different from us; those over there don't speak our language; those there, their clothes are strange.' No. If you say 'There is no God but the one God' then you are a Muslim. That's in the Quran. The Serbs destroy houses of God, full of people praying, and you say, 'It's not my business [maʿlish daʿwa]'! Listen to the shaykh, Samir." Attempting to bolster the shop owner's argument, Ibrahim now cited a well-known prophetic tradition (*hadith*) on the equality of Arab and non-Arab Muslims: "No Arab is superior to an non-Arab ['*ajami*] except by righteous conduct." The exchange was interrupted as a boy from the store next door called out for the shop owner to bring over another round of tea. Samir, turning to finish the last of his water pipe, suggested that he didn't have time to complete the conversation now but would take it up with Ibrahim on their next encounter. Ibrahim, in obvious frustration, turned back to me.

Informal exchanges of this sort, a common element of daily experience for many Egyptians, point to the way tapes have contributed to reshaping contemporary discourses of Muslim solidarity and community. *Khutaba'* often address themselves to an Egyptian audience but from a standpoint that takes a universal Muslim collective as its framework of concern, as the category of belonging and commitment necessary to acts of moral and political judgment. When I asked Ibrahim why he had chosen to speak up in the way he did, he replied: "If I am a Muslim, then I must ask myself every day, what have I done for Islam? If I had stayed silent, I would have done nothing for Islam. What would I say to God on Judgment Day, that I was busy, that I didn't have time? No, *da'wa* is not a choice, Charles. And that is something that many Egyptians don't understand." One effect of the Islamic Revival, in other words, has been to articulate the links between global political issues and practices of moral reform. The stakes here include both one's own salvation and the moral health and fortitude of the community as a whole.

This concern for Muslims worldwide has also given impetus to new practices of moral reflection. As Ibrahim told me after hearing a tape by an Egyptian *khatib* on Muslims in the United States, "When one hears these things, that people in the U.S., or in Bosnia, are becoming more diligent in the performance of their religious obligations, one is stirred. You ask yourself, if they are turning to Islam there, how is it that I as a Muslim, living in an Islamic country, am not even committed in my practice? What do they have over me? We are all equals after all. So hearing this moves me toward committing to Islam, and reforming my practice." Cassettes and other media have transformed the political and religious context wherein Islamic virtues are cultivated and practiced, endowing this context with a distinctly transnational dimension.[23] This tendency has been further enhanced, first, by the fact that many of the *khutaba'* whose tapes are popular in Egypt are from other Muslim countries, particularly Saudi Arabia, but also Jordan and Lebanon; and second, by the fact that the leading contemporary *khutaba'* and other significant figures of the *da'wa* movement participate in networks of mosques and Islamic associations whose reach extends from Arab countries to Europe, the United States, and Canada. These various factors have contributed to the morally inflected cosmopolitanism evident in the comments of Ibrahim and others above.

SAMᶜ AND THE CITIZEN

Cassette technology has played a key role in shaping the social imaginary of contemporary *daʿwa* in Egypt, in fashioning its forms of reflexivity and collective action into what I have called a counterpublic. By dislodging print from its privileged position within the national imaginary of publicness, the cassette sermon, I want to suggest, introduces a rupture into *daʿwa's* mode of articulation with the normative structures of public discourse. Tapes allow listening to go public, not simply as the figure of an ideal receptivity but as a model on which an emergent notion of the public could be conceptualized and imagined. By replacing print and the image of the private reader with resonant sound and sensitive hearts, the cassette gives new purchase to a history of reflection upon the virtues and specific agency of sound. The faculties of the ethical listener—an appreciation for and attunement to the affective and expressive dimensions of divine speech—now come to define the proper attributes of a public subject. This shift entails not simply the circulation of a discourse on pious affect but the dissemination of auditory practices whereby such ethical dispositions are cultivated and expressed (such as those I discussed in the last chapter), as well as a general revival and renewed interest in such long-standing techniques of ethical discipline as Quranic memorization and recitation.

In their privileging of the listener, cassette sermons have made possible the reanimation of the ethical tradition I discuss in chapter 2. The forms of sensory memory, affect, and expression at the heart of this tradition have often been associated with Islam's more mystical side, but they also infuse the pedagogical practices of those traditions considered more orthodox. This is not a sensory world at great remove from the experience of the social classes who have formed the backbone of the *daʿwa* movement. Sufism has remained one of the dominant forms of Islam for many Egyptians and continues to be especially influential in many popular quarters, despite the strong rationalist tendencies within Islam's modernist intellectual currents.[24] Paradoxically, while the *daʿwa* movement has often adopted the anti-Sufi rhetoric of *salafi*-modernist trends, the techniques of social discipline it has facilitated have privileged ethical and affective dispositions historically linked to Islam's more mystical variants. Thus, Sufi poetry and the breathing techniques of *dhikr*—the vocal practice of giving remembrance to God, often through the extended repetition of the divine names—are frequently employed within the sermons of contemporary *khutaba'-du'at*. Giving priority to eschatological and thanatological themes and incorporating Quranic repertoires for the acoustic modulation of emotion, popular preachers draw upon this substrate of sensory-emotive experience, one that had been largely circumscribed to specific ritual occasions and circumstances, and effaced from the dominant discourses mediating public memory.[25] These fragments of buried experience have found new coherence and expression within a contestatory movement focused on the ethical, as the nondiscursive background for an emerging form of public reason, virtuous comportment, and moral agency.

The *khutaba'* whose cassettes mediate this discourse frequently contrast its passional and embodied character with the forms of discourse found in state-run media, what the widely popular *khatib* Muhammad Hassan criticizes as "cold culture [*al-thaqafa al-barida*] addressing only the intellect [*al-adhhan*]," or "the dead, dry, trivial language of 'culture' or 'history.'" For these preachers, a language consonant with the eschatological drama of human existence must not engage the rational-critical faculties alone but must also address the heart—the seat of ethical sensibility, affect, and will. That said, it is wrong to view the *da'wa* public as an affective collectivity, a unity galvanized around a rhetoric of shared emotional experience.[26] The intensely passional character of sermon rhetoric does not address a collective subject of affect. For the affects invoked and refined through sermon audition do not refer to the category of subjective experience but of ethical action: they are actions of a heart properly disposed toward God, actions that accompany and serve to refine practices of moral conduct and reasoning. Rather than standing opposed to reason, they provide it affective-volitional substance—the epistemic and passional conditions for its proper exercise; not interior states accompanying ethical action but the honed repertoires of expression by which actions acquire moral excellence. For this reason, we might say *da'wa* public discourse presupposes and performatively enacts not shared affects but a shared moral orientation, one that finds embodiment in a coordination of gestures, bodies, and hearts fashioned as a mode of pious sociability and public engagement.

The *da'iya* in this sense is not a "sentimentalist," the term Stokes used in his discussion of twentieth-century musical trends in Egypt to describe the highly subjectivized emotional style of the singer Abd al-Halim Hafiz

(Stokes in press). Instead, the *da'iya* finds his musical correlate in the *mutrib*, the performer of *tarab*, whose accomplishment is at once individual and collective and whose "enchantment" is as much a social relationship as it is a form of experience (see chapter 2). In referring here to divergent musical styles, my point is not simply to elucidate through analogy. My argument, rather, is that the fault lines that characterize Egyptian political life today owe their force to the contrasting structures of affect and subjectivity that traverse contemporary Egyptian political, ethical, and aesthetic practices. Arguments over the appropriate place of Islam within Egyptian social and political life derive their force and meaning not only from the unequal distributions of wealth and power they map onto but also from the way such arguments articulate with sensory habits and with patterns of sensibility, affect, and memory cultivated within daily life.

Within sermon rhetoric, the dynamics of impassioned response are organized around two overarching themes. The first, which I will discuss in greater detail in chapter 6, is death: the drama of human mortality and the terror of divine judgment evoke in the sensitive listener a series of affective responses, from fear and sadness to joyful release in the face of God's mercy. The subject of this progression is the isolated individual, stripped of social and familial bonds and left trembling before an omniscient and all-powerful judge. Vivid renarrations of this scene pervade contemporary sermon rhetoric. The second pole of affective investment within sermon discourse centers on the current plight of the *umma*, as a historical community now riven with moral corruption and profoundly suffering all forms of injustice, disrespect, and insult. Within the structure of the sermon, this theme reaches its apogee during the supplementary prayers at the conclusion, where the *khatib-da'iya* calls for prayers for the many Muslim communities currently facing adversity in Palestine, Chechnya, the Philippines, Bosnia, and elsewhere. It is here that the rhetoric of pain—now a collective one—reaches its greatest intensity, and where the entire congregation often weeps without restraint.

SOUND AND SENSIBILITY

One of the developments contributing to the formation of the public arena I describe here has been the creation of a pious soundscape.[27] The role of sound (and particularly the call to prayer) in regulating and auditizing the social rhythms of Muslim societies has often been noted by anthropologists concerned with Islam (see, for example, Lee 2003). As most of Cairo's thousands of mosques broadcast the call to prayer (*adhan*) over externally mounted loudspeakers, five times a day the city is engulfed in a sort of heavenly interference pattern created by the dense vocal overlayings. These soaring yet mournful, almost languid harmonic webs soften the visual and sonic tyrannies of the city, offering a temporary reprieve from its manic and machinic functioning.

The common practice of playing Quran and sermon tapes in shops, cafés, taxis, and buses has also reshaped the moral architecture of such places.[28] Sermon and Quran tapes tend to bring with them some of the norms of sociability associated with the mosque: when they are played in a public location, such as a store or a bus, they produce an environment wherein certain styles of speech and comportment become marked as inappropriate and are likely to draw public censure from others present. "Don't act so rudely in the presence of the Quran"; "Shame on you, while the shaykh is talking about the Prophet." Such comments, I want to suggest, should not be taken simply as evidence of a more religiously oriented clientele. Nor can they be understood solely as the enactment of a norm (as opposed, say, to similar reprobations given at a mosque, where such a norm does exist). Rather, such responses need be seen in light of the acoustic construction of public space and the affective intensities that such an architecture mobilizes.[29] Quran and sermon tapes don't simply frame space discursively but also shape it sensorially by animating, below the threshold of consciousness, the substrate of visceral, kinesthetic, and affective experience that is integral to the tapes' ethical reception (see chapter 3). As the intensifying background for practices of embodied sociability and moral discernment, such qualities may give rise to ethical performances, as in the acts of public reprimand mentioned. The presence of this sonic background is also frequently registered in the listener's lips as they subtly trace the salutation to the Prophet following the *khatib*'s mention of his name, in the barely audible phrases of supplication uttered when a certain dire event of the eschaton has been described, in barely uttered bits of prayer or in adjustments of posture. These are the motions of the heart, limbs, and will—what Jousse called "the entire human compound"—as they continuously accommodate themselves to the familiar demands of a sonorous moral acoustics.

Such an acoustic unconscious is at work in a wide range of habitual actions. Once, while listening to music at Ibrahim's house with a couple of friends, I noticed Ahmad get up and proceed to walk over to the cassette player to turn down the music. As the sound of the *adhan* (the call to prayer) became audible to me, the conversation immediately tapered off, then returned, with hardly a sense that there had been an interruption—all this unfolding with an automaticity and a spontaneity analogous to the reflex adjustments of the muscles of a driver approaching a curve. It was as if no one had noticed, yet everyone had moved, introducing a pause that was not a break but an integral part of the grammar of the conversation. Over time I began to recognize this responsiveness among the men I worked with in many moments where before it had passed me by unnoticed.

Viewed in this light, cassette sermons emerge as more than just a technology of ethical self-fashioning. Such tapes contribute to the creation of a sensory environment from which the subject draws its bearings, an environment that nourishes and intensifies the substrate of affective orientations that undergird right reasoning, as I describe in chapter 3.[30] These forms of embodied action and thought are patterned in accord with a particular form of life, and its repertoires of postural, gestural, and affective expression. Animated or "played" by the rhythms, lyrical intensities, sound figures, echoes, and resonances of the recorded performances, the sensorium acquires a moral orientation. The performances call forth, mimetically, sensory elements at the heart of what I have called the tradition of ethical listening. These elements constitute the affective basis of moral attitudes and dispositions, the embodied attributes of a Muslim public subject.

PUBLIC NOISE

For those Cairenes who are critical of the *da'wa* movement and its soundscape, the acoustic world I have described here, one that embeds and sustains the practices of the *da'wa* counterpublic, is a space of noise pollution. Articles in secularly oriented newspapers routinely complain about the "assault on the ears" produced by mosque loudspeakers and cassette recorders, perceived as the violent imposition of religious discourse onto the nonreligious space of public life. "The call to prayer, when I first heard it as a child, was beautiful to hear. It wafted over the city in soft and sometimes musical tones," notes the Egyptian writer and activist Nawal El-Saadawi in a recent interview. "Now it has become a cacophony of strident voices, a threatening call shot through with violence" (S. Smith 2005). Another Cairo resident interviewed links the amplified call to prayer with religious discrimination:

Each mosque should be allowed their own call to prayer but only in their own voice without the aid of loudspeakers. My neighbourhood sounds like a rock concert each morning and has become nearly uninhabitable; I now sleep with earplugs. Compounding the problem is that other faiths are not granted the same privilege. Christians are forbidden to ring bells, broadcast Christmas carols or religious songs. As in many Islamic states, religious freedom is suppressed and the verbal onslaught each morning is merely one of many powerful tools used to dominate other faiths. When I was young I used to enjoy the lone, clear voice calling us to prayer but no longer.

(S. SMITH 2005)

For these listeners, as for those who respond positively to such religious media, the experience of the soundscape created by amplified Islamic oratorical performances is deeply visceral, more a result of aural sensibilities than a reasoned commitment to the liberal notion of religion as private worship. This public space offers little resonance for the kind of subjectivities predicated on the silent internality of belief and the soft tonalities that accompany and express it in moments of private worship. In contrast, for many of those who participate in the *da'wa* public, such acoustically configured spaces sustain and amplify the affective-gestural repertoires of pious civility.

The Egyptian state, for its part, is anxious not about noise but rather about the loyalties and sensibilities of the religious subject being forged within the *da'wa* movement, and it has sought, in response, to construct a domain of private life to which they might be confined. There is a steady flow of advice and speculation in the government-controlled press about how this is to be achieved. The following editorial regarding the correct use of mosques is characteristic:

We should restore mosques once again to their proper function as places of worship, and provide young people with plenty of other accessible leisure activities, so that they can live like normal young people, studying or working in the morning, going to their place of worship to pray, and then in their leisure time going to the cinema, theatre or library, or taking part in their favorite sport.

(*AL-AHRAM WEEKLY* 1993).

For "normal young people," Islam—as individual spiritual practice—should stand as a brief interlude between the two primary modes of existence around which the times and spaces of daily life are arranged: work and leisure. Indeed, it is precisely this disjuncture between the kind of public subject fashioned within the *da'wa* movement and one who will perform the role of national citizen inhabiting a private domain of unconditional immunity that has made "culture" into a site of considerable struggle.[31]

For *khutaba'* and their audiences, the danger of Western cultural forms and popular-media entertainment lies in the fact that they engender emotions and character attributes incompatible with those that in their view enable one to live as a pious Muslim. As my preaching instructor Muhammad Subhi told me, echoing a widely held opinion, "The enemies of Islam use art [*fan*], literature [*adab*], culture [*thaqafa*], and fashion [*muda*] to attack Islam," a comment explicitly acknowledging the Western and secular genealogy of these categories of discourse and practice. Much of the criticism found in cassette sermons is directed at media entertainment, film stars, popular singers, and television serials. Thus, some of Shaykh Kishk's most well known sermons are his critiques of popular singers, while the *khatib* Umar Abd al-Kafi is best known for having convinced a number of famous film actresses to give up their acting careers. Muhammad Hassan, in a sermon entitled "al- Shahawat" (The illicit desires), takes issue with a religious scholar who has recently stated that it is permissible to listen to popular music (*al-ghina'*). To emphasize his point, Hassan mentions a music tape that was quite popular in Egypt at the time, noting,

> We all know that cursed tape "Luna." It has sold more than eighty million copies, and there is nowhere you can go to escape from it. Young people listen and sing the words. It puts these words full of illicit desires [*shahawat*] into the mouths of the young people until they go out and commit sins [*ma'asi*]. It pulls them to the disco, boys and girls, where they engage in evil, filthy dancing. Muslims! Our young Muslim sons and daughters!

For these *khutaba'*, popular music, and much of television and film, corrupts the heart or soul, instilling desires in people that lead them to take up un-Islamic activities.

What is at stake here is not simply a case of political criticisms being deflected onto the safer realm of culture. According to many *khutaba'* in Egypt, most of the programs presented on state-controlled television engage and direct the senses toward moral dispositions, states of the soul, that are incompatible with the virtues upon which an Islamic society rests.[32] In response, proponents of *da'wa* have sought to develop and encourage the use of alternative, Islamic forms of popular diversion. There has been a proliferation of Islamically suitable songs for weddings, Islamic summer camps for children, "Islamic theatre" based around stories of early Muslim historical figures, and various forms of Islamic literature. *Khutaba'* frequently recommend to their audiences the use of *anashid* (epic stories performed to music, often based on the lives of heroes from early Islamic times) or sermon tapes as media practices suitable for Islamic gatherings. These recommendations and practices, I suggest, are part of the revival's attempt to create an ethically sustaining lifeworld.

PIUS SOCIUS

The development of the *da'wa* counterpublic depended crucially on the way the circulation of cassette-mediated discourse articulated with practices of embodied sociability and corporeal expressivity that were concurrently being nurtured by the new assemblage of mosque-centered institutions. As mentioned in chapter 2, the arrival of the cassette sermon in the 1960s and 1970s coincided with the recuperation of the mosque as a center of public life within many of Cairo's popular quarters. With a weakening of the state's ability to provide education, health, and welfare services in the context of the economic liberalization programs of the 1970s (Sadat's program of *infitah*), many mosques began to take on the character of community centers, offering an array of moral and material resources for the neighborhood communities they served. Larger mosques, and the Islamic welfare associations that frequently adjoin them, now offer free supplementary courses for schoolchildren in all subjects,[33] funds for individuals who cannot afford medical treatment, and even assistance locating jobs. The growth of open-air markets set up adjacent to mosques on Fridays has further served to centralize community activities around the mosque. One effect of the growth of these networks of self-defined Islamic institutions has been to give these neighborhoods a degree of autonomy vis-à-vis the state. Indeed, in the late 1970s and early 1980s, some mosques, including those of renowned *khutaba'* Abd al-Hamid Kishk and Ahmad al-Mahlawi, came to be explicitly identified by those who frequented them as "counter-states" (Kishk 1986; al-Mahlawi 1991).[34] While only a small number of mosques in Egypt adopt such a radical posture, many have become centers and agents of neighborhood revitalization.

When the young men I worked with wished to indicate the positive effects of *da'wa*, most of them referred to specific popular neighborhoods where, in their view, the residents' neighborly conduct accorded with Islamic ethical standards: assistance was provided to the sick and poor by the community; those behaving improperly (for example, drinking, swearing, fighting, dressing inappropriately) were readily confronted by community members; and most people prayed, read the Quran, and attended mosque regularly. In short, these were contexts where a general ethic of mutual assistance and collective responsibility prevailed. When describing this character of Cairo's lower-middle-class neighborhoods, Beha, the taxi driver introduced in chapter 3, emphasized the benefits for the women in his family:

> My sister comes home from school on the bus, and then has to walk a long way from the bus stop to get to our house. There are many places in Cairo where I would be worried about her, but not in this neighborhood. If a man insults her, or tries to touch her, people will come right out and confront him. Do you think this would happen in [the elite neighborhoods of] Zamelek, or Muhandeseen? Maybe, but I wouldn't count on it. Here, in contrast, people are more religious [*mutadayin*], so they are not afraid to speak out, even if they may get hurt by doing so.

As Beha's remarks suggest, one of the most pronounced effects of this agglomeration of activities and associations around the mosque in popular quarters has been the reinforcement of a normative civility, one grounded in the sort of ethical sensibilities foregrounded by popular *khutaba'* but also embodied in a variety of publicly enacted expressive forms. The collective wailing that occurs during sermons, for example, is one such form. While crying has always been part of the pious responsiveness of sensitive sermon listeners, in Egypt it has only been in the last few decades that such intense collective expressions of public sadness and pious fear have become commonplace. The headscarf is, of course, another expression of this public civility, and in popular neighborhoods, a male version of pious dress—the white *jallabiyya*, or tunic-shirt—has become almost as widespread.[35] In addition, a certain style of personal grooming elaborated on the basis of regnant ideas of moral and bodily purity, demonstrated in such things as closely clipped fingernails, trimmed facial hair, neat beards, and newly washed and pressed clothing, has become prevalent in these neighborhoods. Men here routinely use musk and other scented oils and perfumes, many of which are sold outside the mosque. Indeed, certain smells carry a strong moral valence, and they are frequently commented on publicly. Moral uprightness, for instance, is understood to bring a sweet smell, one that may remain even after death. Ibrahim once recounted that the mechanic who lived next to him had been digging up his floor in order to expand his workshop when a sweet smell began to come up from the ground. Taking this as a sign that a pious man must have been buried below, he decided to convert the workshop into a mosque. It is also believed by some that the meaning of dreams can often be uncovered by the smells that accompany them. For example, when Ahmad once expressed anxiety about the significance of a dream in which he found himself tightly thronged by a circle of men in *jallabiyyas*, Ibrahim suggested he try to recall the smell that pervaded the dream, so as to decipher its correct meaning. Smell, in other words, is a salient perceptual feature of the moral landscape for those who practice *da'wa*. The mode of sociability that the *da'wa* counterpublic has created has been crucially enabled by the kinds of embodied practices (of sounds, smells, gesture, and so on) I describe here. This pious sensorium distinguishes this arena, giving it a palpable presence in urban Cairo.

THE VIRTUES OF DELIBERATION

Within *da'wa* literature and among the young men of my study, the performance of *da'wa* is understood to be predicated upon a prior cultivation of virtues.[36] As I describe in this section, virtues play more than an instrumental role in relation to the activity of *da'wa*: as with other obligatory practices—such as prayer, fasting, or alms giving—*da'wa* has conditions of enactment that include a particular set of virtues. In this sense, it is both an activity that upholds the possibility for the virtuous performance of other Muslim practices and a virtuous act in itself.

As I mentioned earlier, much of the Islamic print and audio media today concerns the qualities the *da'iya* must possess in order to perform the moral and civic duty of *da'wa*.[37] Such discourses fall within a long and continuing tradition of Islamic ethical and pedagogical writings on the virtues that uphold individual piety. Where they depart from this tradition is in addressing the virtues, not simply from an ethical point of view but also from a rhetorical one, as conditions for the persuasiveness of speech and action within the public domain of *da'wa* practice. Virtuous conduct, in other words, is seen by the movement both as an end in itself and as a means internal to the dialogic process by which the reform of society is secured. Although a concern for individual salvation continues to inform the disciplinary exercises of the movement, it is coupled with an emphasis on the construction of an ethical sociability conceived as a vehicle of moral and political reform.

The virtues of the Muslim citizen qua *da'iya*, as cultivated and practiced within daily life, tend to be understood behaviorally, as disciplined ways of being and acting, ways for which the body's performances and expressions constitute an integral part (on virtue ethics, see MacIntyre 1984; Williams 1985; Lambek 2000a). They are cultivated gradually through the disciplinary practices I describe in chapter 3, such as prayer, Quranic recitation and memorization, *hadith* study, and listening to sermons, as well as by undertaking the practice of *da'wa* itself. Some of the virtues specific to *da'wa* are addressed within *da'wa* literature under the term *adab al-da'wa* (loosely, etiquette of *da'wa*) and include those qualities that ensure the orderliness and civility of public interaction.[38] Much of *da'wa* print and cassette media focus on the task of developing these qualities. For example, a recently published book entitled *al-Da'wa al-Mu'athira* (Effective *da'wa*) lists among the principles undergirding the character of the public subject the following:

> First Principle: Who takes no interest in the affairs of the Muslims is not one of them. Expressing interest in others draws them toward you. To be given concern, one must show a concern for others. This is one of the effective qualities of the Muslim individual, that he be useful to those around him. Thus, one need be skilled at placing oneself in the service of others; and extending a useful hand to others, with sincerity and free from personal interest or egoism. . . .
>
> Fourth Principle: Speak of good or stay silent. This means listening well and saying little. For the hurried speaker is also a hurried listener. Be a good listener and don't interrupt while your interlocutor is speaking. Rather, listen to him as you would want to be listened to. Many people fail to leave a good influence on the souls of those they meet, because they don't listen to them closely with attention and interest.
>
> (MADI 1995:23, 27)

The *da'iya*, as figured here, must be an active and concerned citizen, one who, having honed the skills of public concern and careful listening, is able, through example and persuasion, to move fellow Muslims toward correct forms of comportment and social responsibility. The book provides exercises, including a list of questions at the end of each chapter, to help the reader learn and polish the requisite skills.

Similarly, a tape by the popular *khatib* Wagdi Ghunim, entitled "The Muslim as *Da'iya*," provides the listener with a list of thirteen requirements that every individual in his or her capacity as *da'iya* must adhere to. Among these he includes friendliness, gentleness of speech (*al-rifq wa al-lin*), temperateness, and neatness and cleanliness.[39] Throughout the tape, Ghunim provides numerous illustrations of how *da'wa* should be undertaken, as in the following:

> Say we are sitting and speaking with a fellow who then gets upset. I'll say to him, Oh my brother, may God be generous with you; Oh my brother, may God open your heart and mine [*yashruh sadrak wa sadri*]. Or say someone is sitting nearby smoking a cigarette, and then comes and offers you one. Take advantage of the opportunity. Don't try to take the pack of cigarettes away from him. No. *Da'wa* always entails politeness [*adab*]. Say to him: Oh Brother, may God restore you to health. I ask God that you stop to smoke. May God protect your chest [*sadrak*] from [the consequences of] your act.

The prior cultivation of such virtues as friendliness, temperateness, and gentleness of speech ensures that *da'wa*, as a public act, is conducted in a calm, respectful manner, protected from the kind of passions that would vitiate the act and the social benefit that it seeks to realize. The *adab* of *da'wa*, in other words, entails not a simple suppression of the passions but their moderation or attunement in accord with an authoritative model of the virtues. A speech devoid of passion—the "cold culture [*al-thaqafa al-barida*] addressing only the intellect [*al-adhhan*]"—lacks the rhetorical force to move others toward correct behavior.

The virtues of sincerity (*ikhlas*), humility (*khushu'*), and fear of God (*taqwa* or *khawf*) are also frequently associated with the performance of *da'wa* and are given great emphasis in sermons and manuals on the practice. As elaborated within classical Islamic moral doctrine, these dispositions endow a believer's heart with the capacities of discrimination necessary for proper moral conduct and reasoning. In the rhetorical context of public deliberation discussed here, this understanding has implications for both speaker and listener. For the speaker's discourse to result not merely in abstract understanding but in the kind of practical knowledge that affects how one lives, it must be imbued with those virtues that enable it to reach the heart of the listener. This was spelled out for me by Muhammad Subhi: "The speaker must soften the listeners for what he has to tell them. This will depend on how well they are moved by the Quranic verses, the tone of the *khatib*'s voice, by the warnings of divine punishment and the promise of the hereafter. But only if one speaks with humility, fear of God, and sincerity will their hearts open in this way, and the listeners will be moved and want to do good."

Alternatively, from the perspective of the listener, without having first imbued the heart with the requisite emotional dispositions, he or she will be incapable of actually grasping and digesting what is at stake in the discourse. The virtues, that is to say, are a condition for both the effectiveness of the *da'iya*'s utterance and the listener's audition. As affective-volitional dispositions sedimented in one's character, they form the evaluative background enabling one to act and speak reasonably and effectively within the public realm.

AFFECTIVE REASON

As I suggested earlier, the virtues I have mentioned here are not valued simply because they undergird the protocols of polite speech upon which public argumentation depends. These virtues imbue such argumentation with its proper form, orient it toward its correct goals. Another way to put this would be to say that the practices of deliberation and argument articulated by this concept have goods internal to them and do not simply serve an instrumental function. The internal goods of a practice are those that can only be specified in terms of the practice and are only achievable in the course of undertaking the practice itself. They contrast with those goods that may be realized by means of a practice but that are only contingently or externally related to it. For example, while playing the violin may win one respect or renown, these goals may equally be won through other means. Playing a difficult sonata with fluidity, clarity, and expressiveness, on the other hand, is an accomplishment unique to violin playing, and one that, to some extent, can only be fully judged by those with experience in the practice. The virtues, in this context, refer to those qualities that, once cultivated and refined, enable one to achieve such excellence at a practice.[40]

Let me clarify these points by reference to an event in Cairo that generated considerable discussion within Egypt's *da'wa* public, as well as in the national and international media: the case of the Cairo University professor Nasr Hamid Abu Zayd, who was initially denied tenure on the grounds that his writings showed him to be an apostate. The Abu Zayd affair became a cause célèbre for both liberal and Islamist currents within Egypt: for liberals, the case epitomized what they saw as an ongoing attack on liberal freedoms, while for Islamists, Abu Zayd was viewed as yet another agent of secularization seeking to undermine Islam from within Egypt's own educational institutions. Many of the details of the case are now well known (see Dupret and Ferrié 2001; Hirschkind 1995). I want to focus here on how the issue was addressed by those I worked with in the field of *da'wa*. While many of the sermon listeners knew little about the case beyond the charge, reiterated by many *khutaba'* at the time, that Abu Zayd had denied the divinity of the Quran, a few were interested enough not only to follow the debate in the national press closely but even to read some of the published writings of Abu Zayd that were coming out in magazines supportive of his case. Muhammad Subhi expressed his opinion on the matter in this way:

> Many of those who dismiss Abu Zayd out of hand must never have looked at his work. For clearly he demonstrates considerable knowledge of the Quran and is doing important work in terms of bringing new theories to bear on its study. We need this. Unfortunately, his irreverent and dismissive attitude toward classical Islamic scholars [*al-salaf*] is incompatible with serious work in this field by a Muslim. He writes of the Quran without humility [*khushu'*], respect, or fear of God [*taqwa*]: while this may be fine for other books, it is not acceptable for a Muslim to do so with the Quran. I don't think he should be treated the way he has been, but he should be made to understand that such an attitude is injurious both to Islam and his work.

The suggestion made here is that the Islamic virtues of humility, fear, and respect endow the scholar—or the *da'iya*—with the commitments and orientations that ensure right reasoning and action. Without these qualities, the performance of either *da'wa* or scholarly inquiry may achieve a kind of technical proficiency but never the standards of excellence internal to these activities as Islamic practices. Another man put the argument to me this way:

> Abu Zayd just mimics being a Muslim in order to attack it. The basic foundation that defines a Muslim is belief in his books, prophets, angels, Judgment Day, and fate. Even the *mu'tazila* who drew on Greek philosophy in their critiques never challenged this foundation. A Muslim should affirm [*yu'min bi*] these elements—above all the Quran—and not seek to deny them or treat them with cold indifference. Abu Zayd's work differs little from arguments the *mu'tazila* made centuries ago, except in one key area. For him the Quran is a book like any other and holds no place in his heart.

Note that the claim being made here is not that Abu Zayd's argument contradicts scholarly opinion as established within authoritative Islamic traditions (as found, for example, in the exegetical works of al-Tabari or Ibn Kathir). Rather, as in the previous comment, the assertion here is that Abu Zayd's writing betrays an attitude or an emotional disposition incompatible with and subversive of the intellectual and social good realizable through an engagement with the Quran. We would be tempted to read both of these criticisms in terms of a concern with tone over substance. In framing the matter this way, however, we fail to acknowledge the extent to which the affective register alluded to here is recognized to be of considerable consequence for the scholarly excellence of the work, its potential contribution to the Islamic society wherein it has been produced. Insomuch as the reading and recitation of the Quran play a role for Muslims in the shaping of virtues, the text cannot be approached as an abstract statement to be assessed dispassionately. A properly disposed heart—a figure for something like "the right attitude"—is necessary in order to learn from the Quran, to achieve sound judgment in one's engagements with it *as a Muslim*. The verb used by the man cited above, *"yu'min bi,"* from the root *"amana"* (to have belief in),[41] implies far more than a simple cognitive orientation: it implies an act of submission and resignation to God. It was an apparent lack of this disposition in Abu Zayd's writings that those I worked with saw as the greatest flaw in his work. In stating this I am not making a claim about Abu Zayd's inner psychology but pointing to the grammar of certain Muslim virtues.[42] While the words, behaviors, and predispositions that constitute and exemplify a well-disposed heart may be understood to refer to and express such an interiority, in themselves they are "external" and, as such, are subject to observation, comment, and criticism by others. I am not suggesting, of course, that those who criticized Abu Zayd were all motivated by this concern: as in all such media events, petty motives and political opportunism undoubtedly played a significant role in pushing the case as far as it went.[43] My point here is simply to note how, among many of those active in the field of *da'wa*, of primary importance are the affective dispositions, or virtues, that one must possess in order to achieve excellence in a scholarly engagement with tradition.

I also note that the context of assessment presupposed by the above statements is not the university, with its academic standards largely derived from the Western disciplines it has adopted. Rather, Abu Zayd's writings came to be evaluated by these men and many others according to criteria internal to the sphere of *da'wa* practice, and thus as an act directed toward the moral health of the Islamic *umma* rather than the nation and its secular institutions.

The classical argument for why religion should be prevented from entering the domain of politics is that it is grounded in passional attachments and faith, and thus incompatible with rational argument. Religious sentiments, such as those expressed in the criticisms of Abu Zayd above, are entirely appropriate within the private sphere of personal belief, but they threaten the integrity of public discourse by introducing nonrational matters of individual faith. While in secular society the civic role of such dispositions—what we might call prediscursive modes of appraisal—are not explicitly thematized, among participants of the *da'wa* movement they are understood to be of the utmost importance. As ethical dispositions grounded in traditions of Islamic discipline, they create the moral space within which public argumentation takes place, orienting the interlocutors toward the goals and goods that define that space. As I emphasize in relation to the conversation in the taxi cited earlier in this chapter, these culturally honed affects and attitudes, rather than producing a unity of opinion, help sustain the shared background of values and assumptions that make disagreements amenable to reasonable deliberation.

Debates of the kind that emerged around the writings of Abu Zayd occur in a highly charged political context in Egypt today. Specifically, the rationalist hermeneutics advocated by Abu Zayd, one that privileges a metaphoric interpretation of many Quranic verses over the more literalist and orthodox interpretation supported by most of those involved in *da'wa*, is linked with certain liberal trends within Egyptian politics and law.[44] Proponents of these trends argue, for example, that the sections of the Quran that are understood to authorize harsh punishments for a variety of moral offenses or that undergird inheritance rules that privilege male kin over female or that prohibit the charging of interest within lending practices may have been applicable at the time of their revelation but no longer carry a mandatory status. In this view, the virtues emphasized by the *da'wa* movement and the institutions and structures of authority that uphold those virtues, while important for individual practices of piety, do not have a dominant role to play within the politics, economics, and law of contemporary society.

This brings us to an important point: while debate and argumentation are ascribed a salient role within the Islamic counterpublic I have examined here, this does not imply a move toward liberalism. Indeed, many of the social norms that the practice of *da'wa* has helped to strengthen in Egypt are not acceptable for most liberals, Egyptian or otherwise. *Da'wa* is not geared toward securing the freedom of individuals to pursue their own interests but their conformity with a divine model of moral conduct. The field of power brought into existence by this movement has made such actions as publicly expressing affection for someone of the opposite sex, or choosing not to wear the headscarf, more difficult, especially in the lower- and lower-middle-class quarters where the movement is most active. Many in Egypt today resent the social and political pressures that they feel the Islamic Revival movement has imposed on them. And while the *da'wa* public contrasts with the public sphere articulated by the national media in remaining open to non-Egyptian nationals, Egypt's six million Christians are a priori excluded from participation, despite the fact that this discursive arena has increasingly reshaped the social conditions of their lives.

Although this Islamic counterpublic is far from universal in its scope (neither are liberal publics, for that matter), its boundaries of inclusion and exclusion are not fixed but are continuously redefined by the practices of exchange and argument that constitute the arena. As in the conversation in the taxi, this arena is shaped by disagreements, the outcomes of which are not predetermined by reference to any overriding set of principles or doctrines. This public is not static, a labor of timeless repetition, but involves a historical dynamism derived precisely from the sort of practices of reasoning and argument foregrounded by the *da'wa* movement, practices that depart from the assumption of an authoritative corpus by which the status of current practices may be assessed but that do not presuppose a prior agreement on how that corpus is to be interpreted.[45] Indeed, many of the *da'wa* activists I came to know held divergent views on such issues as the proper role of women in social life, the desirability of a national legal system founded on the Islamic *shari'a*, and even on the ethics of disagreement itself. *Da'wa*, in other words, does more than simply enforce a normative moral order. It makes that order dependent upon the activities of ordinary Muslim citizens acting within changing historical circumstances in such a way that mediates against claims to closure and certainty.

GOVERNMENTALITY AND MODERN ISLAMIC ETHICS

For some scholars of the Middle East, the discursive arena I have explored in this chapter is best understood in terms of the norms and practices of a modern consumerist public (Salvatore 1998, 2001b; Schulze 1987; Starrett 1995b). This viewpoint has been elaborated with great rigor and insight by the Italian scholar Armando Salvatore. Focusing on televisual and print media, Salvatore has sought to document how publicity has increasingly become a condition of all religious practice in Egypt. For Islamic arguments and practices to remain viable, he argues, they have been forced to remake themselves in accord with the canons of self-abstraction and generality that govern the modern public sphere. In this way, "religious knowledge and modes of disciplining are restyled in public forms through increasingly standardized (and marketable) communicative patterns" (1998:91). The activities of leading *khutaba'*, according to Salvatore, no longer anchor Islamic traditions of ethical practice but shares of media popularity and regimes of religious consumption:

> Actors within the religious field organize their interests, fulfill their functions, acquire their cultural capital and social prestige and reinvest them in the culture market according to dynamics that increasingly involve stakes of public definition along with skilled crafting and marketing of religious services and products. This is not a "free market" but a highly oligopolistic one, however, as the new religious media star (like Mustafa Mahmud or Shaykh Sha'rawi, who migrate through different print and electronic media and are well-established TV celebrities) resembles a media notable who chases after market shares at the same time as having to make show of a personal virtue, of a charismatic energy that is still comparable with the one shaykhs have to use in order to check the loyalty of adepts and clients.
>
> (SALVATORE 1998:104)

Salvatore's argument is both insightful and persuasive in regard to the two media figures mentioned above—Mustafa Mahmud and Muhammad Mitwalli Sha'rawi. The extent to which it can be generalized to all "actors within the religious field," however, is less convincing. Among popular religious figures in Egypt today, these two men have been exceptional in terms of the degree of their marketization and television exposure. Moreover, Shaykh Sha'rawi's popularity must be understood in light of his status as a state-promoted religious figure, one deployed precisely to counter the oppositional impetus of the popular Islamic Revival *khutaba'*. Although the preachers of the *da'wa* movement are also media phenomena, the interpretive conventions and modalities of sensory engagement put into play by the discourses they mobilize presuppose and enable a distinct form of embodied sociability and moral reason whose locus is within the *da'wa* counterpublic I have described.

Drawing on another theoretical vocabulary, we might say that Egypt's Islamic counterpublic is inscribed within the governmental rationalities and institutions of national public life but also oblique to them, incorporating orientations and modes of practical reason that exceed or cut across modern normativity. This contradictory relation derives from the fact that in postcolonial contexts like Egypt, the forms of discipline and control undergirding modern governmentality are themselves fractured by historical multiplicity, embedding forms of memory, experience, and practice irreducible to the imperatives and rationalities of the modernizing state.[46] Governmentality, the technical and institutional matrix enabling what Foucault refers to as "the conduct of conduct" (1991), depends on the creation of dense networks of social and individual discipline, many of which remain inchoate and discontinuous within the Egyptian context. Take the mosque as an example. Since the late nineteenth century, as I describe in chapter 2, successive projects of reform have attempted to transform mosques into pedagogical instruments for the training of a modern citizenry, and particularly for narrowing the scope of religious authority within the lives of Egyptian Muslims to matters of private worship. Yet, despite having been rendered an object of bureaucratic organization and expertise, the mosque has continued to encompass modes of authority, practices of association, and sensibilities that stand in tension with nationalist reforms (see the section entitled "Interlinkages" in chapter 2).

Practices of cassette audition similarly extend governmental rationalities and displace them. Sermon audition embeds many of the conventions governing other audio media, in relation to the places and times of listening, the modalities of self-regulated discipline they enable, the linkages they establish between practices of consumption and the organization of religious authority, and so on. In this sense and to this extent, they adjust and accommodate their users to the structures of political and social governance. That being said, insomuch as the sensibilities that listeners cultivate are oriented toward the structures and practices put into play by the *da'wa* movement, they diverge from the political and consumerist rationalities characteristic of other media. In short, the Islamic counterpublic must be seen as a contingent assemblage, erected upon a social and political terrain fractured by historical plurality, embedding temporalities and layers of historical experience never fully functionalized or erased by the powers of modern normativity.

DEMOCRACY, DEBATE, DISCIPLINE

The kind of public arena that has been created by the *da'wa* movement in Egypt is both normative and deliberative, a domain for both subjection to authority and the exercise of individual reasoning. As I have argued, it is less an empirical structure than a framework for a kind of action, one intertwining moments of learning, dialogue, and dispute as practices necessary for the moral guidance of the collective. In this sense, we can see that one does not undertake sermon audition and the associated practices of *da'wa* with a preformed or unchanging set of interests and goals. Rather, one comes to acquire an understanding of the good and the virtues that enable its realization in the course of participation in this domain. This learning is not simply a process of acculturation or of ideological indoctrination: both of these notions fail to capture the extent to which one's participation within this arena necessarily involves practices of argument, criticism, and debate. Although some shared orientations and languages are a prerequisite for this type of public engagement, and one participates with the assumption that there is a proper and divinely sanctioned form of life to which one aspires, this does not imply a uniformity of thought and action. Rather, the aim is to uphold those practices understood to be essential to an Islamic society, practices whose proper form, however, must be continuously determined by public acts of guidance, argument, and discussion by all members of the collective.

As I noted earlier, the concept of *da'wa* has taken on a variety of meanings and institutional forms over the history of Islamic societies. This is also the case today. In contemporary Saudi Arabia, for example, *da'wa* has been instituted as a kind of moral security apparatus deployed by the state; for the Tablighi Jama'at in India and Pakistan, it authorizes a project of international proselytization; and in Indonesia, the term designates a leading political party. My argument here is that in Egypt, over the course of the last century, *da'wa* has been elaborated in such a way as to define a mode of public life that incorporates practices of argumentation and debate about the orthodoxy of current practices. The aim of this discursive activity is not "public policy" but the formation of Islamic public virtues. In articulating itself against the modernizing programs of the Egyptian state, the *da'wa* movement has drawn on the universalist discourses of the Islamic tradition to create a form of community and identity that accommodates and transverses the moral and geographic boundaries of the nation.

Most analyses of emergent forms of public life privilege nationalism as the historical frame within which an account must be located. Admittedly, the discourses and practices of nationalism have also been important in my own account of the rise of *da'wa* public engagement. While the notion that Muslims have a duty to speak in the face of moral error for the sake of the *umma* had clear precedents within earlier Islamic societies, the contemporary institutionalization of this notion owes considerably to the idea and experience of national citizenship and the notions of civic responsibility implied in that status. Yet although nationalism changed the conditions within which Islamic traditions could be elaborated and practiced, we should be cautious about assuming that all forms of Islamic activism were henceforth assimilated to the nationalist project or some variant thereof. As I have sought to demonstrate, it would be wrong to understand the practices of public sociability articulated around the concept of *da'wa* in Egypt as nationalism cast in an Islamic idiom. Although the views and attitudes cultivated within this domain sometimes find application in the public sphere of the nation (as when participants in the movement vote for Islamist party candidates), the concerns, loyalties, sentiments, and practices that *da'wa* has given rise to presuppose a form of community for which the nation is an essential yet partial and qualified source of identity.

There are, of course, currents within the Islamic Revival movement that can rightfully be called nationalist. To cite one example, Islamist political parties, such as Hizb al-'amal (the Labor Party) in Egypt, view the state as the form of agency through which Egyptian society is to be transformed, and they direct their efforts to securing its control through the electoral process. As a type of association presupposing and organizing its activities in accord with the political categories of the nation-state, such parties in my view may be convincingly described as nationalist. It is therefore not surprising that many of those engaged in this sort of political activity find the *da'wa* movement to be valueless, if not counterproductive, for the tasks that Egyptian society currently faces. As one Hizb al-'amal official I spoke with put it, "The *da'wa* movement produces little more than religious chatter [*tharthara dinniyya*] about unimportant details of ritual practice. This not only distracts the mass of Egyptians from the real issues of the day such as democracy, political rights, and an Islamic legal code, but leaves them ever more mired in superstition and long irrelevant debates about trivial matters." *Da'wa*, in this view, channels social energies in directions that are of no direct benefit to the nation and its goals of development.

Should the public practices of *da'wa* be seen as yet another product of the intensified global circulation of media, capital, and labor—in short, of globalization? Not in any strong sense, I would argue. Indeed, the very fact that *da'wa* has been instituted in such diverse ways within different Muslim societies today suggests a much more contingent process than that indicated by the framework of globalization, at least in its more technological determinist versions. Globalization highlights for us the transnational context of the movement's institutional forms and modes of mass communication but cannot tell us why these features have been articulated as they have. Discussions of the emergent Islamic publics often leave unexplored the specific categories and traditions invoked by the participants, since it is assumed that the true determinations giving rise to these practices lie in the international circuits of media and commodity circulation. It is not surprising, in this light, that such religious movements are understood to be expressions of either one or both of the two models of political organization seen to underlie and be viable with this circulation: the nation, on the one hand, and the new transnational forms of diasporic religious association, on the other.

My argument is that we should not view *da'wa* as simply an Islamic rendition of the normative structure of the public sphere, one enabled and produced through an incorporation of Islamic symbols and culturally grounded frames of reference. To focus solely on the process through which the concepts and modular institutions of modern liberal democracy have been inflected by non-Western traditions is to fail to explore the often parallel projects of renewal and reform launched from within the conceptual and practical horizons of those traditions. This is not to reinstate the binary of tradition and modernity but, on the contrary, to point to processes that cannot be adequately analyzed through this opposition. It is for this reason that I find discussions of contemporary Islamic movements unhelpful in terms of the notion of an "invented tradition," as a modern institution in the guise of an ancient one. An approach adequate to the historical form I have described here will necessarily understand tradition as a set of discourses and practices that, while enabled by modern power, nonetheless articulates a politics and a set of sensibilities incommensurate with many of the secular-liberal assumptions that attend that power.[47] Of course, the Islamic tradition is not the only framework within which the actions of the participants of the *da'wa* movement are meaningful, nor by any means the most powerful.

{ 5 }

RHETORICS OF THE *DA'IYA*

A s a required component of Friday's communal prayer, the sermon
has continued to occupy a well-defined location conceptually and
ritually within Islamic practice. As with the other acts of worship
prescribed within Islam, the sermon has its authoritative basis in the example set by the Prophet Muhammad's words and acts, what is collectively referred to by Muslims as the *sunna*. Documented in the classical biographies
of Muhammad's life (*al-sira*, pl. *al-siyar*), as well as in numerous *hadiths*
(the preserved records of the Prophet's words and deeds), the Prophet's
sermons have provided a set of authoritative guidelines upon which the
tradition of Islamic homiletics has been built.

The doctrinal requirements for the performance of sermons (*khutab*;
sing. *khutba*) have remained relatively stable since the practice was instituted early in Islam's history. As I mention in chapter 2, classical sources
generally limit their description of the *khutba* to the following few specifi-
cations. The *khutba* precedes the Friday prayer (*salat*) and is delivered by
the *khatib* from a raised podium/platform called the *minbar*. The *khutba* is
divided into two sections, with the *khatib* sitting down briefly between the
two. The opening includes the customary locutions of praise to God (the
hamdala), prayer to the Prophet (*salat 'ala al-nabi*), and the *shahada*, the
testimony to the unity of God and the status of Muhammad as his messenger. According to some jurists, the Prophet should also be given praise
(*al-thana' 'ala rasul allah*). The *khatib* should recite verses from the Quran
during the first section and end with an invocation to God (*du'a'*).

Sermons in Egypt today generally conform to this basic structure. This is not to say that contemporary sermons have not undergone significant change in recent decades but simply that such changes have not been at the level of the sermon's basic, doctrinally defined elements.[1] Indeed, if the national imaginary is one of the spaces for the contemporary sermon's rearticulation (see chapter 2), then, as I explicate below, the mass media (with its profound transformation of the subject's potential to hear and visualize) has indelibly marked the rhetorics of today's sermons, particularly those associated with the Islamic Revival.

Most of the sermons that circulate on cassette, especially those produced by small-scale entrepreneurs, simply reproduce the live version, including all of the ambient sound occurring at the time of the performance (traffic noises, sirens, audience response, and so on). In the case of tapes put out by licensed companies specializing in Islamic media—by my estimate, roughly one-third to one-half of those in circulation—the recording is frequently embellished within the studio. Sermon tapes produced by the company al-Nur, one of the largest distributors of cassette sermons in Egypt, open and close with a brief segment of electronically simulated bird chirping. Most companies also splice in a studio-recorded preface, greeting the listener and announcing the company's name, the title of the sermon, and the name of the *khatib*. Even more elaborate framing devices have been developed by some companies, such as a slow repetition of the sermon's title, interspersed with both sound effects and phrases extracted from the sermon itself and coated with a heavy dose of reverb.

This refashioning of the sermon in commodity form and the increasing recourse to conventions used in the production of other media products have had an impact on the oratorical performance itself in a variety a ways. One striking example of such innovation is the introduction of titles, or prefatory statements about the subject to be discussed, into the body of the *khutba*.[2] As an edifying and ethically nurturing oratory given before prayers as part of Friday worship, sermons never previously had titles per se.[3] Instead, *khutaba'* would usually begin (following the preamble) by reciting a verse from the Quran and then proceeding to explicate one of its themes. With the increasing popularity of cassette-recorded sermons, *khutaba'* have begun to introduce a preface into the sermon, immediately after the preamble, in the form of either a title or a short description of the topic, as well as a set of subthemes through which the topic is to be elaborated. Muhammad Hassan, for example, always provides his listeners with an outline of the sort one would expect in an academic lecture, as in the following excerpt from a sermon on the war in Bosnia:

> Allow me to speak to you today under the title: "Bosnia: Between the Ser-
> bian slaughter and the slaughter of civilization." The story of Bosnia is one of
> sadness. My discussion with you will focus on the following points: first, the
> Serbian slaughter; second, the slaughter of civilization; third, lessons from
> these events. So lend me your hearts and your ears, for the sermon is long.

Abd al-Hamid Kishk, who pioneered the cassette phenomenon and who has an exemplary status among sermon listeners and preachers alike (see more below), sequentially numbered his sermons, a rhetorical device that further served to shift the sermon from the ritual context of utterance to the abstract seriality of the commodity. Such rhetorical devices signal the sermon's relocation in relation to Egyptian social and political discourse afforded by the cassette's mode of circulation.

The fact that tapes are mass produced and commercially sold has also had an impact on the relationship between the *khatib* and his audience. As *khutaba'* have become "media stars," they have had to engage with a cultural sphere mediated by discourses of consumption, including the norms of public self-presentation governing media contexts. This has resulted in a personalization of these figures, characterized in part by a rhetoric of greater intimacy and proximity. Let me clarify this with an example. In late 1996, Muhammad Hassan put out a rerecording of his most popular sermon, on the death of the Prophet, which is prefaced by an apology for certain errors in *hadith* citation he had made in the original. Addressing himself to his audience of cassette listeners, he acknowledges the seriousness of such errors given the mass circulation of the sermon on tape. After opening with the performative statements of a conventional sermon preamble, Hassan continues:

> I want to bring something to your attention before you listen to this tape.
> When I initially gave this sermon about five years ago, I made a number
> of errors in regard to both the text [*matn*] and ascription [*sanad*] of cer-
> tain *hadiths*. Given the vast circulation of this tape, it was incumbent on
> me [by God] to study the science of *hadith* usage. God rewards with favor
> people who recount *hadith*. So I had to amend this sermon on the death
> of the Prophet, entitled "Death of the Apostle: On His Honors and Death."

I corrected every *hadith* on the tape, God willing, in accord with the books of *hadith* so as to achieve the highest level of accuracy.

He then proceeds with a few supplicatory verses asking forgiveness from God for errors he may have committed, finally closing his prefatory remarks with the words, "Your brother, Muhammad Hassan [*Akhukum*, Muhammad Hasan]."

These remarks are extraordinary in a number of ways. Hassan does not speak here from the *khatib's* usual position of enunciation, as a religious authority enacting his prescribed public role before the collective assembly of Muslims. As a media personality speaking within the space and time defined by cassette media practices, his discourse cannot be authorized by the institutions of the mosque and the Friday sermon. Rather, bridging the distance corresponding to the pastoral relation between the *khatib* and his audience, Hassan speaks directly to his listeners in the privacy of their individual auditions, less as a learned scholar speaking to his disciples than as a fellow traveler engaging in a common endeavor. In this regard, his manner of address is not that of a *khatib*, with the authority that title connotes, but of a *da'iya* and fellow participant in the Islamic Revival movement. This sense of intimacy and fellowship is further heightened by his use of a convention appropriate to a written missive: his closing signature, "Your brother, Muhammad Hassan." Foregoing any formal title, such as "shaykh" or "imam of the Suez mosque," as would generally be found in the introduction to a published collection of sermons or edificatory writings, he presents himself with his bare personal name.

Hassan's rhetoric of personal disclosure—admitting his previous errors, the inadequacy of his learning, and his need to overcome this inadequacy through further study—mediates a relationship to his listeners that is not one of hierarchical authority but of mutuality and pedagogical reciprocity—the principles of relation undergirding the Islamic counterpublic I describe in chapter 4. He speaks to "you," as "your brother" in the common project of self-improvement and moral reform that the institutions of *da'wa* have given rise to. More is involved here than simply the strategies of a media star marketing his public persona. I was always struck by the matter-of-factness with which people in the mosque would approach famous *khutaba'* after the sermon and prayers were completed to ask advice on personal issues. These exchanges took place without any of the sense of social distance we associate with fame or stardom. Rarely would petitioners use honorifics or the sort of gestures of deference or gratitude characteristic of gatherings around Sufi shaykhs (see Gilsenan 1983). During one of my lessons with my preaching instructor, Muhammad Subhi, I received a striking demonstration of this sense of accessibility and familiarity binding *khutaba'* to their audiences. We had been attempting to outline some of the features of Abd al-Hamid Kishk's rhetorical style when Muhammad made what was at least to me a startling suggestion: "Why don't we call him up and ask him?" The idea of dropping a call to Shaykh Kishk, one of the most famous religio-political figures alive at the time in Egypt, seemed well outside the realm of possibility (like deciding to give Billy Graham a ring). The next day, Muhammad had gotten the number from a friend who knew it, and we called. Equally surprising, from my point of view, was the fact that Kishk himself answered and proceeded to respond to our questions without hesitation.

Muhammad Hassan's preface to his *khutba*, which I quoted earlier, also makes evident the extent to which the institutions of *da'wa* have changed the conditions of Islamic argumentation in Egypt. It would have been extremely unusual for an audience member to question the accuracy of a particular *hadith* reference made during the course of a live sermon fifty years ago. As a ceremonial act, the sermon was judged less for its scholarly precision and more for other criteria. Yet as the life of the sermon has been extended through the use of tapes and its spatial and temporal frame expanded, the sermon is now more readily subjected to critical scrutiny on scholarly grounds. More important, the question of an error in a *khatib's* discourse, something that before would have been solely a concern of religious specialists, has now become a topic to be addressed before the mass public of sermon listeners.

QURANIC ECHOES

The sermons of contemporary Egyptian preachers of the *da'wa* movement are characterized by a heterogeneity of rhetorical styles, compositional forms, and idioms. The challenge of crafting an oratorical form adequate to the sermon's new modalities of circulation and to a shifting set of social and political demands has been met through a variety of strategies. Thus, while the *khatib* Wagdi Ghunim, of the Muslim Brotherhood, mines the resources of humor and irony found within Egyptian vernacular with a conversational style reminiscent of a stand-up comedian, Muhammad Hassan privileges the classical language, in a performance that combines a display of scholarly rigor with intense passional expression. While I will explore some of the rhetorics and stylistic innovations pioneered by contemporary Egyptian *khutaba'* below, it is useful to locate this discussion within the context of the slow but relentless change to which the inherited tradition of Arabo-Islamic homiletics has been subjected in the twentieth century. Contemporary sermons need to be seen as part of this longer trend, albeit a trend that was dramatically accelerated and altered through the efforts of a number of *khutaba'* now broadly associated with the revival movement.

In order to elucidate this, let me begin with a short excerpt drawn from a collection of sermons (*diwan*) delivered by a little-known preacher, Abd al-Majid al-Shernubi, who was trained at al-Azhar but preached at various mosques in Cairo during the 1930s and 1940s. This *diwan* is similar to a number of other collections published during the same time period: they are cheaply published collections of sermons targeted toward the growing literate class who were able to afford these publications. Like other collections of this time, the sermons in this *diwan* are organized strictly around the Islamic calendar, the subject of each sermon determined to a certain extent either by the ritual practices occurring during that month, or by a celebrated event within Islamic history having taken place around that part of the year: the battle of Badr, the *hijra* (Muhammad's flight from Mecca to Medina), Muhammad's ascension to paradise (*al-mi'raj*), and so on. Common sermon topics—whether on social matters, such as marriage, the importance of advising those who are in error, the dangers of gossip, the rules of prayer, and almsgiving, or on soteriological concerns about the last days or final judgment—are frequently entwined with religious obligations specific to the month the sermon was given. In other words, the temporal frame that informed the overall organization of the sermon was the calendrical time of the Muslim *umma*, the practices that constituted the rhythm of its progression, the articulation of the successive events that defined its temporal mode of existence. Indeed, as I demonstrate in chapter 2, it is precisely this form of temporality that was increasingly subjected to criticism from the late nineteenth century onward for its failure to incorporate key aspects of a new kind of modern Muslim life and experience. We still find today a class of sermons which, in their form, language, and subject matter, closely resemble the historical examples preserved in the *diwans*: most notably, the sermons given at the state-run al-Azhar mosque and broadcast simultaneously on television and radio. The poetic conceits and rhetorical figures used in these sermons belong to a style of Islamic homiletics that today has few practitioners. This is not to say, however, that this style has been entirely lost. Indeed, many of today's *khutaba'* continue to incorporate elements of this homiletic repertoire into their sermons, though interspersing them with rhetorical forms grounded in modern social and political discourse.

In turning to Abd al-Majid al-Shernubi's sermon, note that he begins by marking the first month of the Islamic calendar, *muharram*, in this manner:

> Thanks be to God who created the worlds with His vast and great wisdom, and renewed the years: their passing is a clear example [*'ibar*] for mankind to contemplate upon; He inaugurated [the yearly cycle] with the holy month of *muharram*, in Islam and before its coming; and He made the passing of days an indication [*dalil*] of the inevitable annihilation of all: this is a sign [*aya*] for humans to reflect upon [*yatafakkarun*]. I praise God and thank him for the succession of the days and years, and I ask Him for forgiveness [*istaghfaruhu*]. I bear witness that there is no God but the One God, the Most Holy. I bear witness that our Lord Muhammad is the Messenger of God, the best of humankind.
>
> (AL-SHERNUBI N.D.:4)

Al-Shernubi marks his opening with a central theme within Islamic thought, one easily linked to the calendrical context of its delivery: the passing of time as a sign from God of the impermanence of life. The preamble has three constitutive elements: the *hamdala* (thanking and praising God), the *shahada* (invocation of God's unity) and *salat 'ala al-nabi* (the calling for prayers upon Muhammad). In enunciating the three requisite speech acts of the preamble, the *khatib* not only fulfills the ritual obligations but also seeks to orient his audience by evoking in them the proper attitude for sermon audition. The primary methods for achieving this are *dhikr* (remembrance of God) and *du'a'* (supplicatory prayer).[4] *Dhikr* and *du'a'* are generally associated with prayer, but are also practiced in all sorts of other daily contexts by many Muslims. *Dhikr* takes many forms, all of which involve a turning away from worldly affairs and focusing on God, a movement of the heart usually achieved through the utterance of certain formulaic phrases, or simply the repetition of the word "Allah," or other names of God.[5] Another practice of *dhikr* centers on calling to mind one's death, the grave, Judgment Day, the punishments of hell—images that produce those sentiments in the heart of the believer that sermon listeners attempt to cultivate: fear (*khawf*), gratitude (*shukr*), humility (*khushu'*). *Du'a'*, or supplication, likewise has practical benefit as a moral exercise: in the act of supplication, one assumes the attitudes, states of the heart, mind, and body appropriate for a slave of God (*'abd allah*), such as humbleness (*khushu'*), submissiveness (*tadaru'*), and trust in God's wisdom (*tawakkul*). As with *dhikr*, *du'a'* usually entails the repetition of traditional prayer formulas. In drawing on these, the supplicant learns both the correct external forms of supplication and the inner attitudes proper to his or her relation with God, attitudes that these prayers gradually mold when practiced consistently over a long period of time. The task of a skillful *khatib* is to use these methods in the sermon preamble to draw his audience away from the daily toils and concerns that distract them from the proper moral and psychological disposition: humble supplication and reverence for God, fear of His power, and love of His greatness.

Al-Shernubi's verse, here and throughout his sermon, is composed in a flexible rhyming style often referred to as *saj'* (the flavor of which is lost, of course, in the English translation of his sermon). The use of *saj'* has been a subject of controversy within Islam from the time of the Prophet Muhammad, who, according to some scholars, forbade its use as inappropriately artificial for pious expression.[6] This criticism is still widely echoed today, though the contemporary critique has been strongly influenced by the modernist condemnation of the artificiality of poetic forms for nonaesthetic purposes. Yet, much as the art of rhetoric survived for well over a millennium within Roman and then Christian societies despite ongoing attacks on its legitimacy, even those who impugn *saj'* frequently take recourse to rhyme. In other words, the term *saj'* has come to mark a kind of illegitimate artificiality, though what is held up as an alternative often involves the use of stylistic conventions that have been classically referred to as *saj'*.[7]

Having delivered the preamble, al-Shernubi then moves to the main body of the sermon, a movement always signaled in Islamic sermons by the expression "now then [*'imma ba'd*]":

O worshippers of God, what is this worldly life except hours which pass, breaths that come and go, moments that return and years that are renewed, and flowers that entice, and bodies that are wasted away; "life in the afterlife is far better for those who fear God, so will you not, then, use your reason" [Surat al-An'am:32], fear God, and be warned of this world, for it deceives its people; "and ward off from yourselves and those who are close to you that fire [of the hereafter] whose fuel is human beings and stones" [Surat al-Tahrim:6]; "and offer up something in charity on each occasion of your consultation" [Surat al-Mujadala:12]; for this is the blessing of commerce with God; "that which is with God is far better" [Surat al-Jumu'a:11] and more enduring; "[it shall be given] to all who attain to faith and in their Sustainer place their trust" [Surat al-Shura:36]; for how long will you remain awed by the inevitability of death.

(AL-SHERNUBI N.D.:4–5)

Here al-Shernubi expands on his theme of worldly dissipation, drawing his listeners to a consideration of hell, fear of which provides a basis for right conduct in this world. This is the rhetorical technique I referred to earlier as *tarhib* (from the verb *rahhab*, to terrify, to frighten), and it is the subject of an extensive literature, both classical and contemporary. In classic rhetorical style, al-Shernubi follows the verses of *tarhib* with those offering the possibility of heaven, in this case through invoking beneficence of God toward His worshippers who practice the virtue of charity. Within Islamic exhortatory styles the latter is referred to as either *targhib* (literally, the act of awakening desire) or *wa'd* (meaning "promise" and, in the context of sermons, referring specifically to God's promise of an eternity in heaven for those who live rightly).

The rhyming structure of the introduction is continued in this excerpt from al-Shernubi's *khutba*, but is joined by another form of parallelism: the verbs "to come and go" (*tataraddad*), "to waste away" (*tatabaddad*), and "to be renewed" (*tatajaddad*) in lines two and three are all passive forms built on a four-consonant base rather than the usual three. As these verbs all end with the doubled "d" followed by a single "d" (in Arabic, the letter "*dal*"), they give to the phrase a marked staccato rhythm that mimics phonically the repetitive motion of time being described. Beyond the extensive utilization of such poetic conceits, however, what is striking about the sermon is its intense reliance on Quranic verses. The sermon is largely composed of small parts of Quranic verses, sometimes placed back to back or separated by joining phrases. The verses are not "cited" per se, as there is no marking in the text to indicate their origin as is customary when verses are used, for example, to provide authoritative evidence for a point being made by a *khatib*.[8] Rather, the verses provide the very material from which the discourse of the *khatib* is formed. Indeed, even where explicit verses are not identifiable, much of the vocabulary itself is Quranic in origin. Thus, a word like "flower" (*zahra*) appears in the Quran to suggest the deceptive pleasures of worldly life and indeed occurs in the chapter Taha (verse 131) right before the clause "this worldly life" (*hayat al-dunya*); in the sermon above, "flowers that entice" are part of the imagery surrounding "this worldly life."

The Arabic term for death in the last line, "*al-manun*," occurs in the chapter al-Tur, and its Quranic origin is obvious to a listener familiar with the Quran.[9] In its language and its rhetorical and poetic devices, the sermon is thoroughly dependent upon and resonant with the revealed word.

Al-Shernubi's sermons demonstrate mastery of a particular art of elegant oratorical composition that over the years has been subjected to a variety of critiques. One of these concerns its comprehensibility: namely, that the rhetorical forms and classical Arabic vocabulary of such sermons presuppose language capacities that few Muslims possess and are thus suitable only for a small elite of religious experts. This critique marks the introduction of a new set of assumptions about the nature of reception and understanding and about the operation of devotional language[10] in relation to the soul more generally—issues I address at some length in the previous chapters. I will limit myself here, therefore, to a few remarks about the tradition to which this critique was directed.

The tradition of sermon giving that al-Shernubi exemplifies takes its model of speech from the Quran, as a text containing multiple levels of meaning, accessible to human beings in proportion to the depth of each person's capacity for understanding as developed over the course of his or her life.[11] The inexhaustibility of the text's meanings is part of its "inimitability," as found in the doctrine of *iʿjaz* (see chapter 2). Indeed, a professor from al-Azhar, who worked with me as I analyzed various sermons, referred specifically to this doctrine in order to explain the richness of al-Shernubi's language, the layeredness of its meaning structure. The value of the divine word is not limited to what is identified by the humanly produced techniques of interpretation, which in Christianity get formulated in terms of the distinction between literal, allegorical, tropological, and anagogical interpretations of the Bible. Rather, the divine word, spoken, read, or heard, has a capacity to influence, to inshine human souls, that is not predicated on such rational procedures and, indeed, is a necessary prerequisite for their proper application. That is, divine speech is a key element in a prerational ordering of the self upon which more rational practices depend. This idea regarding the word's intrinsic value is given doctrinal expression in various ways, including the idea that one accrues a certain quantity of beneficence with God—what is called *hasana* in Arabic—by simply hearing the Quran recited. This accrued beneficence increases further when one recites the Quran oneself. Thus, the men I worked with, after describing the specific excellence of a certain sermon, would frequently add, "and of course one gets *hasanat* for just listening to the sermon, and additional ones for the

Quranic verses cited by the *khatib*." In short, to the extent that the standards of sermon audition were (and continue to be) modeled on the Quran, with the sermon itself incorporating its verses, the benefits that accrue to the listeners (the positive effects on their souls) are not entirely limited to the particular kind of cognitive process we conventionally associate with "understanding."[12] Sermon oratory works itself into the human compound, much like the stories of Benjamin's storyteller worked themselves into the flesh and spirit of their laboring audiences.

THE CINEMATIC IMAGINATION

As I suggest earlier in this chapter, some of the characteristics of early-twentieth-century sermons, captured so well in al-Shernubi's *khutba* quoted above, have been preserved within the homiletic styles of contemporary *khutaba'* of the Islamic Revival movement, albeit in a transmogrified form. The nationalist project and the mass mediatization of the popular imaginary have played a key role in shaping the structure and performative space of today's sermons. While chapter 2 traces the changes effected by the nationalist project, in this section I want to focus on how specific aspects of the mass media—particularly its visual aesthetics—have altered the character of sermon rhetoric and its reception. Quranic imagery and its associated affective and kinesthetic forms, long a constitutive aspect of traditional homiletics, have now come to be configured in new ways under the "regime of visuality" so central to the experience of the modern (Crary 1990; Gay 1984; Jay 1994). A key figure in this reconfiguration is Sayyid Qutb—most commonly known in Western scholarship for his polemical militant tract *Milestones*. Qutb's impact on contemporary *da'wa* preaching, however, owes not only to his polemical writings but also, equally, to his work on aesthetics, in particular his discussion of the aesthetic image in the Quran. In what follows, I want to trace some of the ways in which the sermons of the revival have ushered in a new style of mediatized homiletics, a style already presaged in the writings of Sayyid Qutb.

From the 1940s onward, preachers have faced the challenging task of creating an authoritative Islamic discourse that recognizes and authorizes the discursive conventions and forms of auditory concentration characteristic of popular media. Among the most salient features of the sensory regime that has shaped the sensibilities of contemporary sermon listeners in Cairo is the increasing predominance of the visual. From the vast production of objects for sight to the proliferation of visual media, modern Cairenes are engulfed by images in a way unparalleled in earlier generations. As Timothy Mitchell has explored, a key aspect of the transformations brought about in Egypt under conditions of colonial occupation involved the increasing importance of techniques of order and organization grounded in visuality (T. Mitchell 1988). Even the textbooks used for the religious education of children within Egypt's public schools today are full of images (though the representation of Muhammad and other prophets is still considered unacceptable). Between the 1940s and the 1970s, Egypt developed one of the largest film industries in the world, putting out close to five hundred films per year for domestic consumption and export to other Arab countries (see Armbrust 1996). While it is not my intention here to contribute to the modern history of the visual in Egypt, what I do want to point to is the impact of an expanded visualism on the practices of sermons and on the understanding of the agency of speech in the context of ethical listening.

One place where this impact is registered in a profound and striking manner is in the writings of Sayyid Qutb.[13] Qutb's influence on the ideology of Islamic activist movements within Sunni Islam during the latter half of the twentieth century is unparalleled. Almost without exception, the *khutaba'* I spoke with in Cairo who are part of the Islamic Revival cited Qutb's exegesis of the Quran as having had a profound impact on their moral and intellectual formation.[14] My preaching instructor, Muhammad Subhi, would often recite long sections of this work, for example when explaining a particular point of doctrine to me, and, as with many other *khutaba'*, he would regularly draw on the text when fashioning his sermons. Though Qutb was ultimately executed by the Egyptian government in 1966, his many writings continue to provide a primary source of reference for Muslim activists and preachers.

In two of his works, written during the 1940s, midway through his career, Qutb explores the question of the Quran's aesthetic uniqueness, what previous scholars had addressed in terms of the doctrine of the inimitability of the Quran (*i'jaz al-qur'an;* see chapter 2). In *al-Taswir al-Fanni fi al-Qur'an* (Artistic representation in the Quran), Qutb criticizes the classical grammarians and rhetoricians for remaining trapped within an unproductive debate about whether the text's beauty lies in its wording or its meaning, a problem compounded by the practice of limiting their analyses to short segments of verse, which, according to Qutb, caused them to lose sight of the broader aesthetic principles that give the text its unity.[15] Eschewing the sort of grammatical and syntactical analyses performed by his predecessors, Qutb argues that the inimitable beauty of the Quran is the result of a unique compositional principle he calls *al-taswir al-fanni*, artistic portrayal or representation. *Taswir*, derived from the trilateral root *s.w.r.*, had been employed extensively within Muslim traditions of aesthetic appreciation but never in relation to the doctrine of *i'jaz*. While the most common noun form of *s.w.r.*, *sura*, means "image" or resemblance," the verb form, *saw-wara*, signifies "to form." When supplemented by the addition of the prefix "*ta*" and the doubling of the "*waw*" (*tasawwara*), it encompasses both the sense of "to imagine" and "to conceive."[16]

Qutb exploits the aesthetic and philosophical meanings of the term while extending them in a unique and original manner. He describes *tas-wir* as follows:

> Taswir is the preferred tool in the style of the Quran. By palpable fancied images, it designates intellectual meanings, psychological states, perceptible events, visual scenes, human types, and human nature. It then elevates these images it draws, and grants them living presence or regenerating move-ment; whereupon intellectual meanings become forms or motions, psycho-logical states become tableaux or spectacles, human types become vivid and at hand, and human nature becomes visible and embodied. As for events, scenes, stories, and sights, it renders them actual and immediate, pulsating with life and movement. When it adds dialogue to them, it brings into play all of the elements of imaginative representation in them.
>
> (QUTB 1993:36)[17]

While *taswir* involves more than the strictly visual—Qutb frequently mentions the contributions of Quranic rhythm and musicality and their ability to engage senses of hearing, touch, and taste—it is nonetheless the visual sense that dominates and gives unity to the overall sensory experi-ence. Moreover, the style of visualization he describes bears the imprint of a distinct cultural form: the cinematic image. The Quran's power to influence the hearts of sensitive listeners lies in its presentation of "scenes" that in their sensual intensity, their movement and sequential flow, transcend mere images to become life itself: "There is life there, not the story of life" (Qutb 1993:36). The rhythms and tonalities of the recited verses create a "music" that accompanies and intensifies the sensory-rich imagery (104–9), as does the deployment of dialogue. The scenes unfold at different speeds, some so quickly that "sight [*al-basar*] can barely capture them," some so slowly that "one imagines [*yukhayyil*] at times that they will never finish" (128). Here and throughout the text, the visual imagination that Qutb locates at the heart of the Quran's aesthetic procedures constantly gestures to the cinematic. In Qutb's *taswir*, sound will still reverberate with image, but their interrelation will be conceived on the model of film—a sound *accompanying* an image. One effect of this Qutbian vision on the narrative structure of a sermon is a tendency to disarticulate and alternate between segments with highly visual languages and those with strong phonic associations—a shift from al-Shernubi's thorough integration of the two perceptual modes.

"WORD AS CAMERA"

No single *khatib* has been as important both in shaping contemporary sermon styles and in defining the cassette sermon as a medium of contestation as Shaykh Abd al-Hamid Kishk. Born of humble origins in a small town in Egypt, Kishk lost his sight when he was in his teens but continued to pursue secondary and higher education at Azhari institutions.[18] After his graduation in the early 1960s, he preached in a variety of mosques until he was appointed to one of Cairo's largest, Dayr al-Malak. It was there that Shaykh Kishk's fame skyrocketed and his preaching style, so distinct from the traditional al-Azhar sermons, began to draw ever-larger crowds. His fiery and emotional sermons were often commentaries on current sociopolitical issues, enfolding searing critiques of the Egyptian government. It is widely believed that when Kishk was asked by the Egyptian government in 1965 to declare Sayyid Qutb an apostate, he refused, an insubordination for which he was imprisoned and tortured for three years.

Kishk started a tradition of preaching that garnered a wide following among younger preachers. His sermons were recorded on cassettes and widely distributed all around the Arab world. In 1981, President Anwar Sadat had Kishk put under arrest again as part of his crackdown on Islamists, and when Kishk was finally released following Sadat's assassination, he was banned from preaching. This ban remained in effect for the rest of his life. Despite these obstacles, the popularity of his recorded sermons acquired a status even during his lifetime that few other preachers have experienced.

Among Islamist preachers, Shaykh Kishk has the status of a virtuoso performer whose vocal dynamics could bring an audience to great heights of pathos and yet who, at the same time, remained solidly grounded in the authoritative traditions of Islamic argumentation and exegesis. Kishk had a personal reputation as a deeply learned scholar (*'alim*) and as a man willing to suffer recrimination for the sake of the truth. His skill in masterfully applying traditional Islamic homiletic techniques, while weaving in elements not conventionally within the domain of sermon rhetoric, played a key role in extending the authority of the sermon in new directions. Kishk pioneered what his fans often refer to as a "word as camera" style, which foregrounds a rhetoric of visual realism and a style of representation deeply indebted to cinematic technique (a fact all the more striking given his blindness). In the following sermon, entitled "The Death of the Shah [of Iran]," Kishk begins with a preamble built on Sufi techniques of repetition aimed at evoking the sentiments of humility and fear of God in the audience. In the excerpt below, I use musical notation to give the reader a better sense of the actual performance. The audience's collective responses (captured on the tape) appear in bracketed quotes ([“God!”]).

Thanks be to God, Lord of the worlds; O Lord! [long pause, then *crescendo* and *accelerando*] O God, have mercy for our weaknesses [“Amen”], and guide us in our affairs [“Amen”], lead us to salvation [“Amen”], loose us from what binds us [“Amen”], mend us where we are broken [“Amen”]; O God, heal our sicknesses [“Amen”]; O God heal our sickness [“Amen”]; O God, return those who are absent to their people safe and sound [“Amen”]; O God of the worlds; O God, make the goodness of our actions that which persists [“Amen”], and the goodness of our days, what we bring to you on the day of our meeting [“Amen”]; O God, make our end a good one [“Amen”]; O God, make our end a good one [“Amen”]; O God, gather us into the group of our Prophet [“Amen”], under the banner of our beloved [*habibina*] [“Amen”] . . . [*pianissimo*] Amen . . . Amen.

I bear witness that there is no god but the one God; [*crescendo*] the King [*malik*] sent an angel [*malak*] to Ma'adi Hospital, and he took the soul of a king [*malik*].[19] Who is the King?! [“God!”] [pause, then *accelerando* and *crescendo* until *fortissimo*) Who is the King? [“God!”] Who is the Most Holy? [“God!”] Who is the Flawless? [“God!”] Who is the Faithful? [“God!”] Who is the Guardian? [“God!”] Who is the Guardian? [“God!”] Who is the Guardian? [“God!”] Who is the Eminent? [“God!”] Who is the Compeller? [“God!”] Who is the Proud? [“God!”] . . . [shouting] Who is the Unique? [“God!”] Who is the Unique? [“God!”] Who is the Unique? [“God!”] Who is the Unique? [“God!”] . . . [pause, and then *pianissimo*] God . . . God . . . God. . . .

[*piano*] Sons of Adam! . . . Sons of Adam! [*forte*] remember, my handsome one, since I created you from a drop of sperm, and don't forget, in your innermost being, what I have fashioned and my grace; [now *lento* and

piano] remember, my handsome one; remember, my handsome one; and submit to me, submit to me, and know that I devise my commands and I do what I will.

Sons of Adam: if the world closes around you, say Oh God! ["Oh God!"]; [*accelerando* and *crescendo* until *fortissimo*] if mankind disowns you, all of it, say Oh God! ["Oh God!"]; if you face hardship, say Oh God! ["Oh God!"]; if you sleep on a sickbed, say Oh God! ["Oh God!"]; if you seek help, say Oh God! ["Oh God!"] [continues for twenty more verses, then, lengthening the word "God"], Oh God! Oh God! Oh God! Oh God! [pause, then slowly with breathiness] Oh God! . . . Oh God!

[*forte, lento*] I bear witness that our lord and our Prophet and our Greatness and our beloved Muhammad is the Messenger of God: when death visited him, he wiped his generous cheek with cool water and petitioned God: "O God, lessen upon me the agonies of death"; the beloved, the best of God's creation and his highest creature; I swear, there is no other among mortals such as Muhammad, and nonetheless even he on his death bed says: "Praise be to God, death has its agony!" [now *piano*] Then what are we to do?!

This transcription captures little of the flavor, the rhythmic and tonal intensities, of Kishk's actual performance. Kishk's rhetorical style has a theatricality and a dynamism unmatched by any other contemporary orator in Egypt. His voice moves from the slow, burdened rasp of a dying old bull to the fiercest, most explosive of roars, often following a pulsating rhythm of standard prayer verses with audience response, as occurs three times in the preamble transcribed here. Here we see the skillful sermonic use of *dhikr* (remembrance of God) and *du'a'* (supplicatory prayer) to seize the audience's attention, leading them along with rhythm and repetition, so as to evoke in them the affects and attitudes that will enable them to listen properly and benefit from the sermon. In the taped version of the sermon, one hears audience members emphatically and spontaneously shouting out "God" (Allah), "There is no god but the One God" (*la ilaha illa Allah*), and other exclamations after Kishk has carried them to the end of the *crescendo*.

Note also how Kishk takes the obligatory utterance of Muhammad's apostleship to present an admonitory lesson (*wa'z*) to his listeners, putting before their eyes and ears the vivid image of Muhammad in the throes of death. In some sermons Kishk builds a momentum in his audience by repeating the word "God" as many as fifty times, languorously and breathily running his voice over the word at the beginning, giving vocal embodiment to the sentiments of love and awe, and then gradually increasing the tempo until his body, and the collective body of his audience, is pulsing with the affective and physical intensities propelled by the chant. While in Sufi practice this type of *dhikr* exercise may lead a master of the practice to the experience of *fana'*, a dissolution of one's self in a mystical union with God, in the context of present-day sermons it is used simply to free the listeners from worldly concerns and focus their hearts and minds on God.

As he reaches the second part of the preamble, Kishk introduces a radical shift of reference: having opened with a series of conventional sermon phrases grounded in classical traditions of supplicatory prayer and then, having just uttered the doctrinal formula attesting to the truth of the one God, he shifts to a seemingly incongruous point of reference, a hospital in Ma'adi, a wealthy suburb of Cairo ("the King [*malik*—that is, God] sent an angel [malak] to Ma'adi Hospital, who took the soul of a king [*malik*—that is, the Shah]."). The subject and structure of this phrase locates it, for the audience, in the classical genre of *qisas*, the stock of stories about the lives of the prophets (*qisas al-anbiya'*) and the early Muslims that are standard tools of a *khatib*'s trade. In most sermons, these stories constitute a shared body of well-known references used to clarify, illustrate, and deepen the appreciation of a particular human quality or virtue or to criticize or comment upon contemporary events by means of analogy. Kishk, however, is doing something different. He borrows the authority of the genre to vouchsafe a narrative about a current political issue. In doing so, he effects a particular mode of historicity, a set of assumptions governing the relation of past exempla to present experience.

Two other points should be made in regard to this preamble. The first concerns Kishk's use of direct speech, in this case, the speech of God. Adopting a haunting, grave, foreboding tone, Kishk begins to speak in the voice of God, calling down to the human beings he has created: "Sons of Adam!" Then, he delivers his warning, first with an angry roar, then slowly and methodically tracing over the words again with a tone of forced restraint, barely concealed rage. This sort of theatricality—founded on the dynamic impersonation of God, Muhammad, and other Muslim figures— was pioneered by Kishk but is also used now by other leading *khutaba'*. Its contemporary reference is in popular theater and television drama, and, indeed, Kishk himself refers to the unfolding of the events he describes as a "play" (*masrahiyya*). Kishk's sermons, in this sense, are built on a practice of *taswir*, with strong echoes of Qutb's formulation, a transmutation of image and sound modeled more on film than audition. Echoing Qutb's framework, Kishk's sermons combine two perceptual modes: one based on the old phonic language of the kind al-Shernubi's sermon (referenced earlier) clearly drew upon, and the other based on a form of visuality characteristic of the new media of film and theatre.

Kishk ends his preamble by asking his audience: "Where are we going?"—inviting them to envision the scene of the Shah's death that he lays out before them:

> To a strange place. I will shift with you my respected audience [*hadratikum*] now to the Maʿadi Hospital in order to present to you a detailed description of the funeral of the Shah. But before I obtain the permit to enter the military hospital, let me ask these questions: What did the angel of death say to the Shah at the moment he extracted his soul? What did he say to him as he was sleeping on the table of ritual cleansing? What did the Shah say when he was leaving ʿAbdin Palace? And what did the tomb say to him when he was placed within it? . . . We are now in front of the information office in order to obtain a permit so as to enter the Shah's room. The hospital is surrounded by security of all types, the soldiers of Central Security Agency and various investigators: some belonging to the Department of Criminal Investigations, some to State Security, others to the Secret Service. Who will allow the angel of death to enter without permit? ["God!"] "Now verily it is We who have created man, and We know what his innermost self whispers within him: for we are closer to him than his neck vein. And so, whenever the two demands (of his nature) come face to face, contending from the right and left, not even a word can he utter but there is a watcher with him, ever-present. And then the twilight of death brings with it the full truth, the very thing (O man!) from which thou wouldst look away" [Surat Qaf:16–19]. . . . The angel of death now enters with us into the room of the Shah. I see in front of me thirty doctors, among them an American doctor named Michael Webiky. I see the angel of death dismiss all of them in order to take charge of the last act of the play.

What immediately strikes the listener in this section of the sermon is Kishk's use of the narrative voice of the television news reporter. The audience does not simply witness the events unfolding from a distance, but accompanies the narrator throughout his movements, occupying a shifting set of perspectives in relation to the actions before them. The first-person narrative style, with its grounding in visual perception and movement ("I will shift with you," "I see the angel of death"), heightens the listener's experience of viewing acts upon a stage or screen, one further reinforced by Kishk's employment of the framing device of the theater itself ("last act of the play").[20] By employing the dramatic code of television ("We are now in front of the information office"), in a context where television production remains completely state controlled, Kishk's narrative positions the listener as national public spectator. A national, televisual eye is incorporated into a rhetorical practice geared to evocation of both political opinion and pious sensibility, the constituent elements of the Islamic counterpublic I describe in chapter 4.

The tradition of Islamic homiletics has never lacked a language rich in imagery. The Quranic verses, traditions of the prophet, and stories that provide the *khatib* with his raw materials abound with images, evident, for example, in the sermon of Shaykh Shernubi from the early twentieth century discussed earlier. At the same time, however, Kishk's "word as camera" style signals a radical departure from past practices. Notably, classical sermons demanded of the listener a set of skills cultivated in pedagogical programs of memorization and recitation, in which phonic, rather than iconic, aspects of language took priority (an anti-iconic emphasis that is found throughout Islamic oratorical and plastic arts). In other words, the power of an image, the manner in which it was subjectively experienced, was deeply entwined with both the acoustical sound and the affective-gestural act through which that sound was pronounced or actively heard. While Kishk does not leave that tradition behind—he repeatedly exploits the phonic aspects of the Quranic vocabulary, as well as sermonic usages of rhythm and rhyme—he joins it with a style of visualization characteristic of televisual technique, one that is for his audience necessarily indexical of a national perspective. In this way, Kishk builds the sense of terror and the macabre so important in Islamic exhortation, but does so through a rhetorical form that presupposes a very different kind of "literacy" and concentration from its audience, one tied to modern technologies of the image and a national public sphere.

Note how Kishk interweaves these two styles of *tarhib* (the rhetorical technique of evoking fear of God) when he inserts the Quranic verse on death into his cinematic narrative. To the question, "Who will allow the angel of death to enter without a permit?" he recites from the Quranic chapter entitled Surat Qaf. The political thrust of his message here is fairly obvious: the Egyptian state is fundamentally an instrument of repression, so much so that it even seeks to impede the workings of the divine. The verses respond to this presumption, attesting to God's power and the inescapability of his punishment for those who sin—a warning directed both at the state and at the shah upon whom judgment is about to arrive. When Kishk reaches the verse referring to death, he intensifies the emotional coloring of his voice by shifting to a sonorous recitational mode (*tajwid*). In the Arabic, the verse is far more vivid, the imagery more gripping, than is suggested by the somewhat intellectualist translation of the Quran I have cited. For example, the expression figuratively rendered "the twilight of death" by the translator, literally means "death throes" (*sakarat al-mawt*), a locution dense with moral and eschatological significance within Islam and that, for many of the Egyptians I worked with, elicited a strong sense of physical dread (in order to communicate the meaning of *sakarat al-mawt*, one contorts one's face in an expression of horror and shakes the body). The pious dispositions associated with this language serve to recontextualize the surrounding narrative, to root it in the moral orientations of a Quranically tuned body. In this way, Kishk recruits the particular sensory experiences of "suspense" and "horror" associated with cinematic entertainment and bends them toward ethical (as well as political) aims.

Shaykh Kishk's compositional method needs to be viewed in light of the sermon's overall ethical goals and the notion of subject formation these goals presuppose. His sermons do not impart a knowledge of abstract rules but rather stories, spoken maxims, and other fragments drawn from the textual corpus that constitutes a living body of communally experienced wisdom. Through acts of audition, sermon listeners fashion a memory composed of bits of affectively charged speech, a crowd of voices, attitudinal dispositions, and sensorimotor imprints that together form the basis of one's ethical equipment.[21]

The core of Shaykh Kishk's art lies in his ability to render Islamic textual traditions into drama staged through such rhetorical devices as the theatrical curtain and the on-site investigative reporter. Instead of citing texts, he presents scenes of speech, scenes crafted through a continuous shifting between direct and indirect discourse, between narrative and impersonation. Instead of a corpus and its contemporary interpretation and application, Kishk moves through a set of encounters—drawn from the Quran, *sira* and *qisas* genres, and from recent historical events and daily news—a movement that defines a mode of historical practice characterized by an indifference to the pastness of the past in favor of its exemplary value in the present. That is, through their staging of speech acts of vastly different historical status within a common temporal frame (a uniformly objective present), his dramas effect a particular mode of historicity (a comparable practice of historical poesis is described in Lambek 2000b). Deploying the rhetorical device of the televisual gaze, with its infinite mobility, Kishk distributes the disparate textual elements along a spatial plane, one he traverses, together with his audience, through a succession of imagined displacements: "Let us now shift to . . ."; "Come with me . . ."; "we are now going to enter . . ."—be it the gates of hell or those of a local hospital well known to his listeners.

I want to draw on another of Kishk's sermons in order to further flesh out this narrative method, especially in light of the great impact Kishk has had on other leading *khutaba'* within Egypt and beyond. The sermon is entitled "To the Grand Tribunal of Divine Justice" (number 288 in his series), and it centers on a classical theme of Islamic ethical preaching: the benefits one can expect at the moment of passing into the next world if one has acted rightly in this one. The excerpts presented are drawn from different sections of the sermon, so as to give some sense of its development and thematic coherence. Following the preamble, Kishk begins with his customary opening question, phrased, in this instance, to directly recruit the mediatic imagination of his listeners: "From where will I broadcast the sermon today? [*Min ayna udhi' khutba al-yawm?*]." The answer:

> I go with you to the edge of the Day of Reckoning [*al-qiyama*]. . . . Listen! Life insurance is from God. He did not go to an insurance office on 'Imad id-Din Street; nor did he go to life insurance agencies. Rather, he went to Insurance Office Number Nine, in [the Quranic chapter] Surat an-Nisa'; and he made the payments to God. And the payments for God are two, without a third. Do you know what is the insurance office in Surat an-Nisa'? It is Office Number Nine [that is, verse 9], and it is there that insurance is obtained. He says: "And let those who fear [in their behavior toward orphans], who if they left behind them offspring would be afraid for them" [Surat al-Nisa:9].
>
> What should they do, O God? They must insure their children by making two payments without a third. The first: "Let them mind their duty to God" [Surat al-Nisa:9]. And the second: "And let them speak justly" [Surat al-Nisa:9].

At this point in the sermon, Kishk introduces a shift of scene, inviting his audience to an impromptu encounter with two exemplary Muslim figures— the Prophet Moses and al-Khidr (also referred to as "the Righteous Servant" [*'abd al-salih*]). The description is recited directly from the Quran:

> Come with me and let us spend five minutes with the Prophet of God, Moses, and with the Righteous Servant al-Khidr, may God be pleased with him: "Until they reached the inhabitants of a village; they asked its people

for food, but they refused to feed them; then they found in [the village] a wall about to collapse, and he [al-Khidr] straightened it; [Moses] said, 'If you wish, you could have asked for compensation'; [al-Khidr] said, 'This is the point of separation between you and me, so I will explain to you that which you had no patience over'" [Surat al-Kahf:77–78].

Why? Why did you straighten the wall in a village that refused to feed us? [It] refused to provide us with a meal when we were hungry! Do you straighten this wall when we were treated with miserliness, as an advance reward?! The Righteous Servant [al-Khidr] said to him: "The wall belonged to two young orphans in the town, under which there was a treasure for them" [Surat al-Kahf: 82]. And why these two orphans in particular, O Khidr, while this world is full of orphans? Why these two in particular, O Righteous Servant of God?

He said to him: "And their father was righteous" [Surat al-Kahf:82] [*long pause*] Life insurance. "And their father was righteous" [Surat al-Kahf:82].

Here again Kishk mines the textual tradition for another scene depicting the benefits bequeathed to children by the righteous actions of their parents. The opening reference to "five minutes" frames the scene as a chance encounter within the space of daily life, thereby vernacularizing the Quranic account that follows, while nonetheless remaining faithful to the verses' classical form. Then, momentarily interrupting the recitation, Kishk adopts the indignant voice of Moses to further the interrogation extra-Quranically, finally returning to the Quran at the end to intone the lesson's moral crux.

This brief detour completed, we now move to the site of the divine tribunal, or rather, just outside the tribunal's doors. Here, as in many other places in the sermon, Kishk employs the rhetorical trope of contrasting the divine with its mundane equivalents, juxtaposing, with humorous effect, divine judgment with various earthly tribunals. Within his narrative, the listeners now move from being in the position of witnesses to being themselves subject to the divine court's procedures:

Dear brothers: Get ready to enter the court. But it is not a primary court or an oversight court or a court of appeals. And its Judge is not one of the holders of a law license. Nor is he a normal advising judge, or a head of a district. This court is the Great Court of Divine Justice. And its Judge is the Knower of the unknown, Exalted is He. Be ready to enter this court [*ista'iddu li dukhul al-mahkama*]. And before going to this court, there must be—before the opening of the trial—some preliminaries. After God commands [the angel] Israfil to blow the trumpet, the first blow, all those in the heavens and on earth will die, except for those God wishes [to spare]. God will ask Israfil: "O Israfil! Have all those on earth died?" And He knows more [than anyone]. . . .

Enter the court before the One Who knows the secret and that which is more hidden. The first question: The Lord asks you: Your youth, in which [state] did you spend it? The second question: Your life, in which [acts] did you spend it? The third question: Your money, from where did you gain it? And on what did you spend it? The fourth question: Your knowledge, what did you do with it? Youth, life, money, and knowledge; and there will be no excuse for anyone being questioned!

If you said, "Oh God! Why didn't you send me a notice to attend the trial?" they will say to you, "The notice to attend the trial reached you and you read it seventeen times each day. In every prostration in the prayers you read it once." This notice is God's saying, "The Lord of the Day of Judgment" [Surat al-Fatiha:4]. I am the Lord, and this is the Day of Judgment!

Be ready to answer the questions. Insure the lives of your children through your acts of pious fear [*taqwa*]; pious fear [*taqwa*] insures the lives of your children.

Drawn from *hadith* accounts, the scene of the four questions is a staple of Egyptian preaching. Kishk dialogizes the textual materials he incorporates, both by inserting them into rhetorical contexts in which he himself is an interlocutor and by putting them in relation to situations drawn from quotidian experience. As in the earlier sermon I cited on the death of the Shah of Iran, Kishk here repeatedly defers the moment of entering the court ("Be ready!"), pulling his listeners forward then holding them back (at the door of the divine tribunal or the gates of a hospital) so as to heighten the tension and sense of anticipation among the audience. Note also that, as in most of the other segments cited, the visual scene here is composed almost entirely of dialogue: the scenes' lack of visual complexity is compensated for by their emotional intensity, communicated vocally in Kishk's expressions of surprise, awe, and anger but also grounded in the audience's passional relationship to the exemplary figures that populate the narrative. At this point, and without forewarning, Kishk redirects his hortatory to a leading official in Egypt's government-administered religious bureaucracy, the mufti of Egypt, a figure whose religious edicts (*fatawi*) carry the authority of the state. Kishk first describes what he views as a dangerous error on the part of the mufti and then addresses the mufti directly in an admonitory tone. The shift from morally edifying discourse to personal critique, and from the temporal frame of a universal tradition to a national present, passes without any rhetorical framing, other than his assumption of the first person singular, "I":

I swear by God, other than Whom there is no god. I was surprised by the Mufti of Egypt as he was arguing about the prohibition of wine when it is used for treatment. We were expecting from his Excellency to prohibit wine for the healthy; the country is in no need for your fatwa to make wine a medicine for the ill. Whereas the beloved, Muhammad, says—and his word is the truth—it is an illness and not a medicine. O Your Excellency, the Mufti: the Messenger of God says it is an illness, and you say it is a medicine!? Are you trying to refute the master of the messengers, O Mufti of Egypt? No, by God! No, by God! It was not proper for you to begin your life as a mufti with this fatwa. And know, Your Excellency, the Mufti, that the fatwa is a grave responsibility. Abdullah b. Umar—may God be pleased with him—Abdullah used to be asked for a fatwa and he used to abstain, saying to the one who asked him: "Man, make not our backs bridges to hellfire." And we are tried with the one who gives a fatwa about what!? I wish that you wrote a letter to the ruler asking therein to close down the bars. God says: "Stay away from it, so that you may prosper" [Surat al-Ma'ida:9] and we make headlines in *al-Jumhuriyyah* newspaper, and we say, "treatment by wine." The headline in and of itself declares a war against God. God says "stay away from it" and we say that we treat the ill with it. How then do You command that we stay away from it? Aren't You the Knower of the unknown?

 O Your Excellency, the Mufti: When the Quran speaks, there can be no word after the word of God; and when the *sunna* speaks, there can be no interpretive engagement [*ijtihad*] next to authoritative text. So long as the text is clear, and the *hadith* is clear . . . Would God say this!? And His Messenger says this!? And afterwards we try to make wine a medicine! Besides, have people quit drinking wine, so that you now have to call on them to drink it?

Kishk's moral lesson here directly embraces the political context of its utterance, one wherein religious institutions have been harnessed to the task of authorizing national policy. Although he chastises a specific national figure—the mufti of Egypt—it is the public context of the mufti's fatwa, its necessary appropriation by a collective subject, that is at stake in the critique. The same "we" who are "afflicted" by the dangerous fatwa also participate in its utterance by our status as members of its public: "*We* make headlines in *al-Jumhuriyyah* newspaper, and *we* say, 'treatment by wine.'" The reference to *al-Jumhuriyyah* in this segment of the sermon locates Kishk's speech within a national public sphere. Once we view the segment in relation to the sermon as a whole, however, that ascription becomes problematic. Note that the moral discourses informing the sermon transcend the boundaries of the nation in their universality, and in this sense they are similar to the kind of universalism undergirding the liberal discourse of human rights also in circulation in Egypt today. But what makes the pannationalism of Kishk's discourse distinct is the challenge it throws to the nation-state as the primary site of collective identity and affective investment. It is this complicated and oppositional relation to the public sphere of the nation that has warranted my appellation "counterpublic" in chapter 4.

At the time of the regime of Anwar Sadat (1970–1981), Shaykh Kishk's style of criticizing public figures directly and openly was considered by some to be a violation of the ethics of public criticism within Islam. Echoing these sentiments, Saif, the Cairo University student I knew, said to me once: "In Islam, a *da'iya* should always first approach the wrongdoer ['*asi*] directly and personally, so as to gently encourage him to correct his errors. Only if he then persists in sinning is it allowable to speak openly about his misconduct. Of course, it's fine for *khutaba'* to make general criticisms in their sermons, but naming names, like Kishk did, that just rouses people but serves no good purpose." Saif's opinion of Kishk—and other *khutaba'* for that matter—was not universally shared and, indeed, was often contested by others. The point I wish to emphasize here is that tapes frequently serve as a catalyst for arguments between listeners about the duties and responsibilities of preachers in relation to the nation-state. But to the extent that Kishk occupies a central place within the politico-ethical landscape of Egypt, his homiletics—its content as much as its style—has become a cornerstone in the debate about the responsibilities of the preacher in relation to the protocols of public criticism. Since Kishk's death, this debate has only intensified as more and more preachers have become active in the promotion of the *da'wa* counterpublic.

EXEMPLARY DRAMAS

There are two concepts that have been particularly important in articulating the critical stance toward contemporary social trends put forward by the *khutaba'-du'at* of the Islamic Revival movement: *al-'almaniyya*, one of the terms used to translate "secularism," and *al-ghazwa al-fikri*, which literally means "ideological conquest" but is perhaps best translated as "cultural imperialism." Many of the social critiques put forward by preachers are framed by these notions, and they have thus come to be widely used to refer to a variety of changes associated with the proliferation of Western social, cultural, and political forms. Most of the people I spoke with within the *da'wa* counterpublic identified *al-'almaniyya* as a political system, adopted from the West, whereby religion was restricted to personal matters of belief. *Al-ghazwa al-fikri*, on the other hand, is frequently invoked to describe the ideological operation of mass media, films, secular education, and the increasing hegemony of Western cultural forms more generally. *Khutaba'* often relate the necessity of preaching on basic Islamic practices and doctrines to the fact that *al-ghazwa al-fikri* has led to the dissemination of false or distorted understandings of Islamic principles. As used in sermons, these concepts define a historical and political project that must be engaged with and struggled against by Muslims, especially the vanguards of the Islamic Revival such as the *khutaba'* themselves, if Islam is not to be effaced from Muslim lives.

While these concepts ground the critical analysis of contemporary society proffered by Egyptian *du'at*, individual sermons tend to be organized around one of the following topics or themes: (1) ethical topics that concern the practice of virtues such as modesty (*khushu'*), patience (*sabr*), and faith (*iman*); (2) social topics that focus, for example, on the appropriate role of women in society, the dangers of alcohol, adultery, or the duty to advise other Muslims when they err; (3) soteriological issues, such as the events surrounding death, judgment, and the afterlife; and (4) exemplary histories, such as those centering on accounts of the Prophet, his companions (the *sahaba*), and events in early Islam. In actual practice, of course, a sermon on any one of these topics necessarily cuts across such classifications: a sermon on death, for example, may focus on the death of the Prophet in order to demonstrate the impropriety of contemporary hospital practices, on the one hand, and to highlight the virtues upon which salvation depends, on the other. I explore just such a sermon in chapter 6. A sermon on the life of one of the "Rightly Guided Caliphs"[22] may provide the frame for discussing the failure of the Egyptian government to apply the *shari'a*, the breakdown of communal norms, the injustices faced by Muslim communities beyond Egypt, such as those in Bosnia, Chechnya, or Palestine. It may also provide the occasion to draw attention to erroneous positions put forward by other *khutaba'* or religious scholars; issues of immediate public concern within

Egypt, such as restrictive laws imposed by the government; large public events hosted in Cairo; or international political developments of concern to Muslims.[23]

The most popular sermon tape in Egypt during the mid-1990s was Muhammad Hassan's "Death of the Apostle: Between His Honors and His Death," the tape whose revision and rerelease is discussed in detail at the beginning of this chapter. As I mention there, Muhammad Hassan is one of the leading figures in one of the largest *da'wa* organizations, Ahl al-Sunna, which administers thousands of nongovernmental mosques in Egypt and provides a variety of welfare and preacher-training services. For his vast audience, Hassan's preaching is distinguished by the beauty of his chanting voice and the range and clarity of the emotions he is able to embody with it.[24] Notably, his recitation style is unorthodox and was frequently described to me by his listeners as closer to "singing" (*al-ghina*') than to conventional recitation. In addition, Hassan frequently draws on classical Arabic poetry, especially mystical works, to deepen the emotional textures of his discourse.[25] For example, one of Hassan's most popular tapes, "'Adhab al-qabr" (Torments of the grave), ends with his pathos-laden recitation of a poem on death by the eighth-century Sufi poet Abu Nuwas. Coming at the close of a long sermon describing the list of horrors that await the sinner inside the tomb, the beautiful and macabre poem gives an expressive form to the fears and anxieties evoked by such knowledge, moving the audience to weep unrestrainedly, along with Hassan himself (as one can hear on the tape). The choice of Abu Nuwas, best known for his poetic eulogies on the virtues of wine and the ecstatic experience it affords, is particularly surprising given the condemnation of Sufi forms of Islam by the contemporary *salafi* movement of which Hassan is a part. As I have mentioned in previous chapters, the ongoing recourse to such Sufi genres, even by those who take issue with mystical forms of contemporary Islamic practice, must be understood in light of the broad impact Sufism has had in shaping the sensory underpinnings of the movement I describe in this book. Here, as elsewhere in his sermons, Hassan's limpid and soulful voice carries the sensitive listener along the ethical pathway he charts.

Drawn from numerous *hadiths*, the narration of Muhammad's death has long been a staple of Islamic homiletics and admonitory literature. Today, taped versions of the account are available from most of the contemporary preachers who make use of the cassette medium. In Hassan's case, the death scene occurs in a sermon that emphasizes the uniqueness of Muhammad's prophecy, indicated by the extent to which God accorded Muhammad tributes and honors beyond those conferred on other prophets. Hassan closes the sermon with a number of the themes generally connected with sermons on this topic, including the need to recognize and constantly bring to mind the inescapability of death and to use one's short time in this life to prepare for this event. The sermon also touches on other important themes, reminding listeners of the horrible drama that occurs at death and providing examples of proper behavior on the part of the living who grieve. The pathos of the account, and hence its ability to move an audience, is accentuated by the intense love and respect felt for the Prophet and, to a lesser extent, for the Prophet's companions and family, Ali; Ibn Abbas; Umar al-Khattab; his wife, Aysha; and daughter, Fatima. Thus, the horror associated with the approach of death, the figure of the angel of death, 'Azra'il, and the extraction of the soul from the body are all intensified in the context of Muhammad's death.

Hassan's narrative unfolds through an emotional crescendo that culminates in the moment of the Prophet's death. The funereal cadence of the progression is propelled and marked by the repeated testimony to Muhammad's suffering, "And the Apostle's pain grew stronger! [*wa ishtadda al-waja' bi rasul allah*]." The Prophet's pain intensifies in tandem with Hassan's absorption by his own passional response, as sadness and loss gradually overwhelm him and leave him powerless and stuttering before his convulsions. Collective weeping replaces speech on the tape at a number of junctures, sometimes lasting as long as half a minute.

The affective dynamics created by the sermon also derive from its rich sensory imagery. Muhammad repeatedly cries out from the severity of the ache in his head, the intensity of his rising fever. On his way to visit his wife, Aysha, his legs fail him and he must be carried by his companions, Ali and Abbas. To soothe his fever, he implores them for cold water, which they pour over him. After he cleans his mouth with a tooth-cleaning stick (*siwak*), Aysha takes the stick into her own mouth and, "for the last time," tastes his saliva. On his daughter Fatima's final visit, she kisses him between the eyes with her tears pouring down, until he himself is overcome by weeping.

What follows is an excerpt from the culmination of Hassan's sermon. Note the triple voicing that structures Hassan's closing account, one that alternates between Hassan's own voice, the Prophet's voice, and the voices of those witnessing his death. This inculcates in the audience a participatory mood, one crucially informed by the aural-visual scene that Hassan sketches before them, drawing them into a collective pathos that breaks out in the end in a collective sense of loss and renewal.

Al-Mustafa's pain grew, and his sickness worsened, on that fated day.[26] On the day that al-Mustafa went to God, the people met in the mosque, filling it to its limit. And during the *fajr* [early morning] prayer, Abu Bakr led the congregation. Abu Bakr had led the Muslims in prayer seventeen times since the Apostle of God [Muhammad] had become sick. The Apostle of God was pleased [to see them pray] and felt a spark of power. Something allowed him to see, and he found the mosque full to its limits, and he smiled and praised God. He called out, and spoke, "O Ali, O Abbas!" They went to him and carried him to the mosque. The assembled Muslims rejoiced and raised their voices in praise of God. Abu Bakr al-Sadiq understood that this joy was due only to the appearance of al-Mustafa (SAAS).[27] Al-Sadiq wished to withdraw from the front, but the Apostle of God gestured to him, saying, Be still, Abu Bakr, be still, Abu Bakr. And then the Prophet sat at the side of al-Sadiq and prayed as Abu Bakr led the prayers. This is the ultimate tribute and honor for al-Sadiq. That the lord of creation Muhammad prayed as he [Abu Bakr] led the prayer! And after the prayers were completed, he asked to be lifted up upon the *minbar*. He sat upon its base, and then raised himself up onto the *minbar*. He spoke: "O People, I have been told that you fear the impending death of your Prophet. Has any other prophet before lived eternally?" After that the Apostle of God (SAAS) went down, but before he did he said to them, "O People, all those who have followed me in my deed from this day until the day of final judgment, wish peace upon me." "Peace be upon you [they said]. O Apostle of God! Peace be upon you and God's compassion, O Apostle of God." Then the Prophet (SAAS) descended and went to the house of Aysha, and his sickness increased, and he slept with his head on Aysha's chest, Aysha tells us. . . . Then he reawoke and saw [the angel] Gabriel standing by his side. He said, "Who are you?" He replied, "I am Gabriel, O Apostle of God; God has sent me to you, O Apostle of God. And this is the angel of death. My Lord has sent me to discover if you wish to be conveyed to God. For this is the angel of death, but if you want to remain alive, God will grant you life, O Apostle of God." The Apostle of God (SAAS) looked at Gabriel and said, "I grant permission to the angel of death, O Gabriel." Then the angel of death approached al-Mustafa and said, "Peace be upon you, O Apostle of God. God sent me to you and ordered me to obey you in all that you demand of me, O Apostle of God."

[Muhammad Hassan interjects at this point]: What a tribute and honor, even at the moment of death! The angel of death asked permission as he had done with no one before and no one after the Prophet. The Apostle of God looked at Gabriel, and Gabriel said: "O Apostle of God, perhaps your longing for God has become protracted." The Apostle of God said, "I have long desired to meet my Lord, O Gabriel. Enter, O angel of death." And the angel of death approached the Apostle of God. And now Gabriel wanted to leave and said, "Peace be upon you, O Apostle of God, peace be upon you, members of the Prophet's household. "Every soul tastes death" [Quran 3:187]." And Gabriel left, and the angel of death sat at al-Mustafa's head. And then he called to the most pure of souls, most honorable of souls, and said [to Muhammad]: "O tranquil soul [*nafs mutmin*], return to your Lord willingly and contentedly; Enter my worship, enter my heaven. O goodly soul, come forth into God's forgiveness and satisfaction, for my Lord is content with you." And then the most pure of souls went to God. Al-Mustafa Muhammad died. The Apostle of God died. The best of God's creation, Muhammad died.

As the most exemplary human being, the Prophet Muhammad's death prefigures everyone's death and registers its inescapability. For this reason, it is through the recounting of this event that death, as an existential condition, can best be depicted, explored, and rooted in human experience and knowledge. For both *khatib* and listener, however, the primary challenge centers on the status and agency accorded to such knowledge within the structures of contemporary moral and political life. How does one live the pain and sadness encountered in the passional narration of Muhammad's death? What demands does the fact of human mortality place on us today in our status as men and women, as Egyptian citizens, as Muslims? By what ethical and institutional means do we bridge the differences between the Prophet's exemplary death and our own? These questions, at the heart of the chapter I now turn to, give direction and form to the *da'wa* movement.

[6]

THE ACOUSTICS OF DEATH

Now it behooves him for whom death is his destruction, the earth his bed, the worm his intimate, Munkar and Nakir his companions, the tomb his abode and the belly of the earth his resting-place, the Arising his tryst and Heaven or Hell his destiny, that he should harbor no thought or recollection but of death . . . . It is right that he should account himself among the dead and see himself as one of the people of the graves. For all that comes is certainly near; the distant is what never comes.

—ABU HAMID AL-GHAZALI

IN HER short story "At the Time of the Jasmine," the contemporary Egyptian writer Alifa Rifaat tells the tale of a man who returns from Cairo to the village of his birth in upper Egypt to attend the funeral of his father. In many ways, the story rehearses a modernist return-to-self narrative: a man's rediscovery of spiritual and emotional vitality among the rural peasantry after having been subjected to the alienating experience of the modern metropolis. Hassan has lived in the city ever since, while still a young boy, his mother sent him to study at an English school in Ma'adi, a wealthy suburb of Cairo known for its large foreign population. Over the years, and under the guidance of his "foreign tutors," he has become a "sophisticated man not greatly concerned with emotions," one who lives entirely by "rational standards" and a dutiful compliance to social convention (Rifaat 1983:78–79). His memories of the village of his youth have long been erased, and even his father, long before his recent death, has become "like someone already dead" (78). Upon returning to the village, he finds once again a world of human connection and sentiment, one that contrasts starkly with the emotional poverty and bureaucratic sterility of his Cairene existence.

Beyond this romantic trope, however, there is another narrative tradition operative in the story that I want to draw attention to, one grounded in Muslim thanatology and the homiletic discourses elaborated upon it. Specifically, the village, we find, is not simply dead to Hassan's memory; it is itself permeated by death. Indeed, from the moment of his departure from Cairo, it is clear Hassan is bound for an otherworldly realm. The train carries him with a "doleful rhythm," one that blurs his vision until telephone poles merge into "spectral forms of date palms," which in turn fade into "misty phantoms that were soon erased leaving the yellow surface of the sky" (Rifaat 1983:77). The land around him becomes a "scorching inferno," in which time has ceased its normal flow, remaining "at a standstill" (77). As he arrives in the village, he finds that the comfort and rationality of his Cairene life have been replaced by a different sensory order, one of "burning sands" and "white vapour that made their eyes smart," of "shrill screeches" that jolt his nerves. In this world, the body loses its self-control and integrity: "incense inflamed the sensitivity of his nose" (82), his "eyes became reddened and puffy" (80) from intense coughing, and his legs shook uncontrollably as he approached his father's corpse for the first time (81). The bodies of the men who assist in the funeral take on a frightening, distorted appearance, "their shoulders almost twisted from their bodies" (83) as they "trod across a pool of blood" (83) left from the slaughtered ram on their way to the tomb. Here in the village, the world of the dead merges with that of the living: "The tombs looked similar to the scattered houses in the dusky light of sunset" (84).

Rifaat's narrative bears the imprint of a vast corpus of Islamic ethical, eschatological, and homiletic discourses wherein the overwhelming reality of death and the hereafter continuously imprints itself on mundane existence and where the next world, in its enormity, encompasses the earthly one and subjects it to its tenebrous order. Within this tradition, life doesn't simply precede death: in its immensity and intense reality, death subsumes life within it. (It is notable, in this regard, that Hassan is an accountant, a *hasib*. *Hasib* is one of the names of God, referring to the act of judgment, the *accounting* of souls, that occurs within the eschatological drama. Here again

Rifaat contrasts the sterile bureaucratic activity of the modern professional with the momentous and infinitely consequential one of divine judgment.)

Rifaat's deployment of a thanatological scenography, however, does not serve here to impart an admonitory lesson, as is usually the case in homiletic practice. Rather, what Hassan discovers is not the pious fear that undergirds right conduct but a communal sensibility that brings into relief the poverty of his own personal attachments within the urban milieu. For within their enactment of the prescribed funereal tradition, with its formulaic sayings, gestures, and acts, the villagers reveal a depth of human intimacy and relationship that contrasts starkly with Hassan's perfunctory performance of his filial duty. Their unsophisticated speech startles Hassan for the sensitivity toward his deceased father it encloses. "What was special about him," comments one man, referring to the father, "was that he could put his ear to the ground and say 'So-and-so's going along such-and-such a track and he'll be arriving after such-a-such a time' and his words would ring true like a gold guinnea" (Rifaat 1983:85). Upon reading his father's will and finding his daughter listed among the inheritors—a daughter the father never met due to Hassan's insensitivity to the affective bonds of kinship—Hassan comes to realize that his father possessed a sense of caring and emotional depth he had never imagined. Notably, Rifaat's story follows Islamic ethical discourse in its suggestion that it is only in the shadow of the hereafter, a world permeated by death's signs and sensations, that meaningful human existence flourishes.

As noted earlier, it is easy to understand this story in terms of a common romantic trope, the rediscovery of meaningful human relationship and community in the vanishing realm of simple rural existence. My own reading, however, has instead sought to highlight a particular sensibility around issues of death and the hereafter that infuses the story, a sensibility that, as I explore in this chapter, is also central to ethical practices of sermon audition. For those who cultivate this sensibility, death is recognized—and must be continually remembered—as the fundamental condition of human life. Awareness and certitude of this condition cannot be achieved through the abstract knowledge of the rational mind (al-ʿaql), a faculty whose exercise may actually diminish the possibility of such awareness when given authority over too much of human life, as in Hassan's case. Rather, it must be acquired through what Muslim theologians have called "tasting" (dhawq),[1] a concept indicating a kind of knowledge gained through personal experience rather than rational intellection and embodied as a permanent disposition of the heart (al-qalb), the limbs (al-jawarih), and the tongue (al-lisan).[2]

Not unlike the mimesis that worried Plato, *dhawq* indicates a learning that bypasses one's rational faculties, one, for example, that may be acquired in listening to stories (*qisas*), sermons, or even those *hadiths* of questionable authority but unassailable wisdom.[3] One of the primary tasks of *khutaba'* is to afford listeners such a taste of death, to portray death in its manifold dimensions and ramifications with a vividness and moral depth so as to root it in their sensory experience, to constitute it as a habit of thought, heart, and body.[4] The tasting of death through continual acts of remembrance enables an ethical orientation in this world, a moral-emotional bearing proper to pious human action, as exemplified in Rifaat's depiction of village life.

While fear of the horrors of the grave and the fires of hell serves as a disincentive to immoral conduct, such fear is also a virtue of character, a condition not only for the avoidance of error but for the proper performance of good as practiced in all fields of human endeavor. In this sense, death is less an inescapable future than a present reality, embodied as an ethical sensibility and practiced in the enactment of one's divinely mandated duties. That is to say, an experiential knowledge of death is a condition of moral agency. The qualities of fear and sadness that accompany such knowledge open up a distinct way of living as a human being. According to the participants of the Islamic Revival movement I came to know, the task of acquiring this agency has been rendered increasingly difficult by the gradual effacement of death—in all its sensory dimensions—from public life within the modern metropolis and by the assumption of ever more responsibility for the dying by secular bureaucracies of medical expertise. Within this context, sermon listening represents a technique of remembrance, a way to revivify the awareness and experience of death within daily life or—stated in terms closer to those used by today's *khutaba'*—to "remortify" life within the larger reality of death and the hereafter.

For many in the West today, Muslim discourses on death are taken as evidence of a diseased culture, one frequently epitomized in the figure of the suicide bomber. Many contemporary Egyptians are also critical of the emphasis on death and the afterlife within the rhetorics of the *da'wa* movement. In their view, the plethora of sermons and books on the tortures of hell and the horrors of the grave stimulates a morbid fascination among the popular classes that distracts them from the serious issues that they, as national citizens, must confront. This unhealthy obsession, I was often told, undermines the positive orientation toward life necessary for everything from social progress to a respect for human rights. The attitudes and sensibilities reflected in such judgments bear witness to the modern discourses on life that Foucault saw as central to the constitution of modernity. As I explore in this chapter, however, such judgments are not entirely satisfactory. The acknowledgment of death that animates much of *da'wa* preaching does not preempt worldly engagement but rather gives it direction and purpose. For this reason, Egypt's Islamic counterpublic may be properly understood as a space organized around a collective inquiry into how Muslims should live today in light of (or in the shadow of) the fact of human mortality and its aftermath.

The difficulty we face in understanding the contemporary homiletics of death as something more, or other, than a potentially dangerous distraction owes, of course, to the immense transformation that occurred in Western attitudes toward death from the late nineteenth century (see Ariès 1974; Dollimore 2001). As the French historian Philippe Ariès has described, in the context of an emerging norm of public sociability requiring individuals to avoid modes of self-expression incongruous with the appearance of individual and collective happiness, death becomes an ugliness, a disturbance to society's serene exterior that must be removed from view, relegated to silence and invisibility within the special bureaucracies of medical expertise that now assume responsibility for its administration. Rendered a kind of obscenity, one producing displays of strong emotion in a public arena that now shuns all such display, death must be forbidden from view. In this new situation, not only is the dramatic impact of death highly attenuated, but, in addition, the *danse macabre* loses all the edificatory value it once possessed.

As Ariès notes, moreover, the interdiction on death since the late nineteenth century has also generated a new fascination, often eroticized, with the subject. Evacuated from the space of daily public experience, death now becomes available to the realm of the fictional and fantastic, in cinema, novels, and in mass entertainment, where, stripped of its edificatory powers, it can be consumed as excitement and pleasure.[5] While philosophers, psychologists, and literary writers may continue to plumb the obscure depths offered up by death for bits of wisdom, at the popular level its function within (secular) public discourse has been reduced, for the most part, to pure sensationalism, commodified as mass entertainment. In this light, it is not surprising that for many of the more secularly oriented people I met in Cairo, the danger of sermons on the grave or Judgment Day owed not to their status as escapist entertainment but to the fact that they are taken as real by their audiences, a category mistake often seen to be responsible for social evils ranging from backwardness to terrorism.

SEEING WITH DEAD EYES

While death has always been a privileged site of ethical and theological reflection across the history of Islamic societies, the content of that reflection
has varied from one sociohistorical location to the next.[6] In contexts of militancy and war, for example, Islamic meditations on death have frequently
centered on the theme of martyrdom, emphasizing the moral excellence
and heavenly rewards entailed in the act of giving up one's life while fighting on behalf of Islam. The militant movements of the twentieth century
have not been an exception in this regard. Hassan al-Banna, the founder
of the Muslim Brotherhood, emphasized that if his followers were to suc-
ceed in their struggle, they would have to learn "the art of death" (*fann al-
mawt*)—to come to love death more than life, as the Quran commanded,
and so be willing to sacrifice their lives for their cause (R. Mitchell 1993:207).
This emphasis on death, found within the writings and speeches of Brotherhood members, was further nourished and deepened by the long and
brutal experience in Nasser's prisons during the 1950s and 1960s, a period
when thousands of members were routinely incarcerated and tortured. As a
number of scholars have pointed out, the sensibility that emerged from this
experience found ideological expression in Sayyid Qutb's apocalyptic vision
of revolutionary social change (Abu Rabi' 1996; T. Mitchell 1990).

There can be little doubt that the discourse on human mortality proffered by today's cassette *khutaba'* owes a certain debt to the elaboration of
this topic within more militant Islamic currents. Indeed, for a number of
the *khutaba'* who pioneered the practice of cassette sermons—for example,
Abd al-Hamid Kishk and Ahmad al-Mahlawi—prison was a formative experience, one they often refer to in their writings and sermons. However,
despite the undeniable impact of Islamic militancy on the contemporary
sermon, the themes of martyrdom and violent struggle are marginal to today's *da'wa* movement and the *khutaba'* who now articulate its goals and
ideological directions. For these thinkers, death is first and foremost a concern of ethics, of how one lives.

Contemporary Islamic thinkers in Egypt tend to emphasize the hereafter (*al-akhira*) as one of five articles of faith (*iman*), belief in which is
incumbent upon every Muslim: faith in God, his angels, his messengers,
his books, and the Final Day (*yawm al-akhira*) (Smith and Haddad 1981:27–
28). And while belief in what are called the "events of the grave" (*ahdath al-
qabr*) are not explicitly identified within the prophetic traditions as conditions of faith, insomuch as they are mentioned in the Quran they are often

included among the elements that every Muslim is required to affirm his or her faith in. A recognition and affirmation of human mortality and its consequences also has a salutary effect on human action and thus provides a stable basis for social life. Belief in the hereafter, I was frequently instructed, was necessary in order to counter the human tendency to stray into moral error: knowing that one was going to die and face the possibility of unending torments of the most horrific sort—or, alternatively, the chance of eternal paradise[7]—inclined one toward correct comportment, the performance of one's religious duties, and the avoidance of error and disobedience. As an Egyptian author says in a recent book entitled *al-Qabr: ʿAzabuhu wa naʿimuhu* (The grave: its torments and comforts):

> With a knowledge of the torments of the grave, as well as its comforts, the torments of hell and the comforts of heaven, together with a faith in these [*wa al-iman biha*], thus are the inward aspects [*al-batin*] [of each individual] put into good order, and from this the outward is reformed as well. And from the moral rectitude that follows these transformations, a secure and tranquil society is established.
>
> (TAHTAWI N.D.:3)

The looming threat of hell, as described here, acts as the motor of social reform, such that when a true believer "acts improperly, in a way that is unpleasing to God, he sees the torments of hell and the grave closer to him than the sole of his shoe" (Tahtawi n.d.:4). Moreover, the idea that a knowledge of the hereafter has a therapeutic effect on human action is not one restricted to Islamic pedagogues. Most of the young men I worked with invoked this idea frequently when explaining why a familiarity with Islamic eschatological doctrines was so important. In their view, the fact that images of death and the eschaton were those most able to seize their attention, to shake them violently, and to throw them toward repentance and good works (*al-iʿmal al-saliha*) was in itself a good reason (though not the only reason) why such doctrines should be given credence.[8]

My preaching instructor, Muhammad Subhi, explained to me the importance of death for Islamic preaching in the following terms:

> Shaykh Kishk focuses on the issue of death, and on how an emphasis on this world weakens faith in the heart. Sins multiply until the heart dies, and this in turn leads one to forget death, until everything gets turned upside down.

Kishk uses *wa'z* and *irshad* [guidance] to show people the truth of the world through which they are rushing headlong. Thus, the sermon is not an escape from the world, but rather a view of the world which the *khatib* makes possible by setting himself off at a certain distance from it. As we know, when we get too close to something, we see only a small part of it, but most of it we miss. *Thus, we need to travel to the other world, the world of death, in order to see this world with dead eyes* ['uyun mawta]. Thus we can say that the emphasis on death is not purely a concern for death itself, but more a concern with reformulating life anew, with new criteria. These criteria envelop all that is included in the Islamic creed [al-'aqida al-islamiyya], its comportments, virtues, doctrines.

Muhammad suggests that knowledge of death is an epistemic condition for one to reason and act correctly in this world; that this life only appears in its true perspective when viewed in light of the frightening truth of one's real circumstances, as a being poised on the edge of perdition and eternal suffering. To see with "dead eyes," as he expresses it, means to see with capacities of vision shaped by intense and continuous personal experience of this truth. What is required is not an intellectual knowledge of the Islamic doctrines of death and the hereafter but a refashioning of one's sensory experience until one becomes capable of perceiving this reality. Such a knowledge must, in other words, be an active belief, a honed attitude of recognition, acceptance, and responsibility infused with the appropriate emotions of fear, sadness, and humility.

Ahmad's friend Ibrahim also elaborated on how such "vision" shaped the totality of one's behavior:

> For the issue of the unity of God [*tawhid*] in itself implies comportments [*sulukiyat*], from which feelings toward death are deepened, and then points us to what is after death. Thus we fear God and are not so greatly interested in worldly things [*al-dunya*]. If I affirm the unity of God, I need to know that this affirmation requires [*yaqtadi*] that I pray, give alms, fast, purify my tongue from lies and gossip, because I will die and I'll meet God. *For these comportments to be deepened, in every moment, through every action I take, I must feel that I am dead* [*innani mayyit*]; that if I have lived an hour, I may not live two. Listening to taped sermons helps you remember all of this.

Admonitory sermons on the calamity of death, as Ibrahim suggests, help one maintain the presence of death, to feel as if one were, in a sense, already dead. Through repeated listening, this presence becomes imprinted on one's heart to the point that one no longer needs constant reminding, as the world of the hereafter now permeates one's sensory horizon. Ahmad described this in terms of fear becoming so natural that one no longer has reason to fear:

> You'll see in any sermon, the *khatib* will use both styles, *tarhib and targhib*.[9] Some people's actions are motivated by fear, others by love, so you need both styles. Of course God created humans so that the degree of fear [*khawf*] will be more. Someone with strong faith [*iman*], when he sees a girl on the street, won't look at her. He doesn't need *tarhib* or *targhib*, because he is always doing the two in his mind. What constitutes a true believer [*mu'min*]? He doesn't need that you scare him [*khawwifu*], or promise him reward [*targhibu*], both are always present. Tortures of hell [*'azab*]? He doesn't fear them. He knows them so well he practically lives with them, so why should he fear?

To always be "doing" *tarhib* is to be attuned to death with all its moments and manifestations—to have lingered over and tasted its images and sensations until they have become a part of one's thoughts and actions. Fear of death, in this sense, constitutes an adverbial virtue, one that orients the individual to the world by coloring and shaping all of his or her actions.[10] As an ethical emotion, such fear does not simply inhibit wrong behavior or limit human agency but allows one to achieve excellence in the performance of the moral acts one undertakes.

ESCHATOLOGY IS NOW

During one of our conversations, I asked Muhammad Subhi how he had come to acquire such an active awareness of death. In responding, he referred to his childhood experiences, growing up in a small village in upper Egypt:

> My father served as the imam in our village. He was very learned in religious issues, the doctrines of Islam, and the people in our village relied on him for guidance in many of their affairs. For this reason, and because of his position as imam, death was a constant part of his life. He was always being called upon to lead prayers for the dead, prepare corpses for burial, organize funerals, and so on. In small towns in Egypt, death is always present [*al-mawt da'iman mawguda*], not like here in Cairo. Once when he

was off visiting relatives for a few days in Beni Suef, someone died in the village. Some people decided to bury the body, but they didn't wash it and prepare it like they should have. They just stuck it in the ground. When my father got back the next day, and heard about what had happened, he was furious, and even beat one of the men with his cane. He made them dig up the corpse and then rebury it correctly. They were scared to do it, but my father insisted. Things like that were always happening in the village. In the countryside, one tastes death all of the time.

Although most of the young men I came to know in Cairo had grown up in the city, many of them recounted to me times when they had assisted in the preparation and burial of a deceased relative. Ahmad, for example, spoke to me on a few occasions about the horror he had experienced when asked to help in the washing of the corpse of a deceased cousin. This was the only time in his life that he had participated in the handling of a dead body, but it had left a deep impression on him.

At a certain pause in Muhammad's account, I asked him about how his move from the village to the city had impacted upon his eschatological vision, his ability to see with "dead eyes":

> Don't think that death isn't ever-present here in Cairo. On the contrary! Death is always tied to corruption in the world, and the city is full of it, especially within the institutions and bureaucracies. As I told you before, I used to work for the Ministry of Religious Affairs, a bureaucratic job. My office was full of corruption, lying, backbiting. Wherever this goes on, death is always near. And this was in a place of religion [*din*]! Of pious fear [*taqwa*]! Hell is right beneath their feet, but they go on talking behind the back of so and so. I'll tell you: the tongue is the fastest way to go to hell! Not that everyone in the ministry is that way—remember, Kishk worked as a preacher for the Ministry of Religious Affairs for most of his life! But the place also has its share of hypocrites. That's why I started preaching for [the nongovernmental religious association] al-Jam'iyya al-Shar'iyya. The people in the Jam'iyya don't just work for themselves, but for Islam.

As with most of the people I met who took cassette-sermon audition to be an important part of their lives, Muhammad tended to impute moral motivations to the nongovernmental *da'wa* associations like al-Jam'iyya al-Shar'iyya, while viewing state religious institutions with considerable skepticism. What I want to draw attention to here, however, is the way in which an eschatological sensibility plays itself out within Muhammad's autobiographical narrative. Not satisfied that I fully appreciated the relevance of death to modern life, he continued:

> Yes, everyone ignores death today, you are right about that. The media is largely to blame. Media today work through dazzlement [*ibhar*]; they make you pant after the images, to the point that people don't want to do anything but sit in front of the TV. They just descend into a state of listlessness [*hallat futur*] and indifference [*la mubalat*], until they don't care about anything. Visiting your relatives? Why bother. Prayers? But the soap opera is on! The Quran? Leave me alone, buddy! [Muhammad slumps in his chair to demonstrate the effect] The media just induce this listlessness [*futur*]. That's why Muslims are so weak today. The West doesn't send armies to kill us today; they use their media to attack us, to sap our strength and leave us lifeless. [In a brooding voice] Don't tell me about graves, torments, snakes—I'm free! [Muhammad put his foot up on the table, and further slid his body down into the chair] You see, their end is written all over them! So no one remembers death today—but death remembers them! That is why the *khutaba'* on the tapes we listen to are always talking about the grave, the tortures. How else could they shake people from their torpor [*humud*]?

Like Dorian Grey's portrait, those who ignore death for worldly distraction bear its disfiguring signs in their slumbering, corpselike bodies, their unpleasant demise figured in their slackened sinews and bent posture. In short, for Muhammad, death's instructive shadow was always near, and, indeed, he ran into it with considerable regularity. Often when he would come to visit me, he would tell of some event that had happened shortly before and that had reminded him of death's presence: a close call with a speeding car in the street, a body waiting for burial in the mosque where he just came from praying, news of further Palestinian casualties, or simply a recent fight with his wife that had cast his day into shadow.

In their study of contemporary Islamic eschatological thought, Smith and Haddad have noted how the issue of ethical responsibility and accountability in this life has been a dominant theme within theological treatments of afterlife themes written in Egypt during the twentieth century (1979, 1981). For contemporary interpreters of the Quran (*mufassirin*), they note, "*Eschatology is now* in the immediateness of human ethical responsibility. . . . Here no distinction is made between the immediate after-death period and the eschaton: the point is to see all of life, from the present to eternity, as one continuum" (Smith and Haddad 1981:106–7, emphasis added). Through the practice of sermon audition, listeners seek to adjust and attune themselves to the presentness of this eschatological world through the fashioning of a sensorium that renders that world perceptible. The daily happenstances of human life tend to subvert one's ability to perceive the reality of death and the hereafter. In this context, it is only by developing and practicing the affects and sensibilities that constitute a lived human response to this reality that the true situation of human existence becomes available to human knowledge and practice. By learning to adjust one's life to accord with death, one's actions come to inhabit the temporal plane of eschatological time. In this way, life is undertaken not only as a preparation for death, as action geared toward a telos in the hereafter, but as a task of bringing the future into the present, the next world into this one, through one's ethical actions. One lives as if eschatology were now, not as a Pascalian gamble, but in recognition of the temporality of human life as deeply inflected by the significance of human mortality.

REMEMBERING AGAINST THE WORLD

Death must be remembered. In the face of the human tendency to forget its reality under the distracting sway of material existence, death must be continuously excavated from memory and held before the mind for contemplation. To bring to awareness the fact that one will die and have to face the horrifying moments of the grave and final judgment is painful, both fearsome (*mukhif*) and saddening (*mahzun*), and humans by nature seek to avoid it. Forgetting offers a false sense of comfort, a momentary haven from the burden of this difficult and painful recollection. Human beings bear the responsibility of holding the truth of death forever active in memory in the face of this constant pressure toward its dissolution. Moral action, in this understanding, is a function of the faculty of memory, a product of the conflict between the inclination to forget—rooted in the sensory attachments of the lower soul, or *nafs*[11]—and the disciplined will to remember. Everything one does in one's life, every action or inaction, speech uttered or unspoken, plays itself out within the space of these two opposing processes, fortifying the hold of one on the self while weakening that of the other. Although this conflict takes place within the individual, as the ultimate bearer of moral responsibility, it is mediated socially, by the sensory landscape of daily life.

According to those I worked with, the contemporary dominance of a consumerist ethos and the proliferation of Western cultural forms—dress styles, seductive advertising, popular music, and so on—have skewed the struggle in favor of the side of forgetting. And while the effacement of death from public view has not occurred in Cairo to the same extent as it has in Western countries, progress in that direction has definitely taken place, in the increasing recourse to a class of trained specialists for the performance of death-related tasks, if nowhere else. Evidence of the development of a modern secularist sensibility toward death can also be witnessed in a number of different arenas, including work in Quranic interpretation from early in the twentieth century. In the context of responding to Orientalist stereotypes of Islamic fatalism and an exaggerated concern for the otherworldly, many theologians and religious thinkers over the course of the twentieth century have tended to emphasize a this-worldly orientation. As Smith and Haddad note, recent commentators on the Quran—particularly those the authors refer to as "modernist"—have downplayed the frightening, fear-inducing aspects of Islamic eschatology and instead have framed the issue of death as a transitory phase, one that need not arouse anxieties or strong emotions (1981:105). As should be clear from the discussion in this book, the *khutaba'* at the forefront of the *da'wa* movement represent a contrary trend. For these men, death's loss of its instructive power is one of the primary reasons for a decline of religiosity in today's society: "Death is losing its moral lesson for us with each passing day, and the events that follow death no longer inhabit us in the way that they should," notes Abd al-Latif Ashur in his book on the torments of the grave (n.d.:5). Death should be listened to, attended to with a sensitive heart open to its admonitory lessons—lessons, however, that modern society has made increasingly inaudible. In this context, sermon tapes are a line of defense, infusing the car, the shop, the street, and the home with acoustic conditions that encourage remembrance.

For some of the men I worked with, death was also to be made present through regular reflection on the decay of the body, the furrowing of the face, or the death of loved ones. Sensations such as hunger, physical pain, sickness, or the tiring of the muscles after labor were also signs, opportunities to recognize the approach of death. The narrative of universal dissolution and decay recounted in sermons and eschatological writings, in other words, provides a language, a grid of intelligibility through which bodily sensations can come to be experienced as the workings of death's providential hand. Through repeated practices of reflection and ethical listening, such sensations are refined, their meanings increasingly delineated in terms set by the Islamic discourses on mortality and the beyond. It is not surprising, in this regard, that many of those I met in Cairo who participated in *da'wa* often related their turn toward a more devout life to health crises they had suffered. In their attempt to make sense of such moments of intense physical debility and pain, these men had found succor and strength in the interpretation of their condition provided by such Islamic doctrines of worldly dissolution, a discovery that reoriented their entire lives.

Ahmad's brother-in-law, Yusuf, was someone whose life had been radically reoriented by an episode of pain and debility. Yusuf had studied law at Cairo University and had worked as a lawyer for a number of years. Shortly after a stay in the hospital for the removal of a kidney, he came to the realization that "there was little value in practicing law within a judicial system founded on traditions of European civil law rather than on the Islamic *shari'a.*" Abandoning the legal profession entirely, he decided to dedicate himself to *da'wa* and joined a local mosque association that sent its members on tours around the country to promote pious behavior. During these journeys, he would invite people from the town he was visiting to sit with him in the mosque, where they would spend a number of days collectively analyzing their daily actions to see if they accorded with the Prophet's example. Yusuf was already learned in matters of religious doctrine before his change of heart, but once his new vocation had become clear to him, he dedicated himself with a passion to the study of ethical and exegetical literature. His shelves were not only full of such classical exegetical writings as those of Ibn Kathir, Ibn al-Qayyam, and al-Nawawi, but many of these books had extensive notes written in the margins.[12]

During one of my visits with Yusuf, he recounted how a stay in the hospital had transformed his life:

> I wasn't always pious [*mutadayyin*]. But at one point I got sick, and had to have a kidney removed. While I was there in the hospital, I looked at those around me, some of whom were suffering terribly. I asked myself, why are they made to suffer so? What have they done? I realized it was God's will [*iradat allah*], as a means to bring them close to Him. I also began to see how precious the body was, a treasure [*kanz*]! The eye alone is worth so much. So I asked myself: given that God has granted me this body, how should I use it? I could listen to music with these ears, but was that the way I should treat what God has given me?

In his account, Yusuf makes use of a conventional conversion narrative, one that I often heard both from people I met and on the sermon tapes I listened to. At this point in our conversation, Yusuf's five-year-old daughter,

Shayma, came into the room and sat down with us. Yusuf took the opportunity of her arrival to demonstrate to me the power of God's will to bring
about both life and death:

> It is truly amazing! Shayma's body is made up of seventeen basic chemi-
> cal ingredients—magnesium, calcium, and others—that are all brought
> together by God to form this beautiful human being. And then, when she
> dies, she will decompose yet again into those seventeen chemical elements.
> The power of God is truly wonderful. It makes you think!

The particularity of the sensibility toward death cultivated by men such as
Yusuf is revealed in the openness with which he speaks about the future
death of his own child, a subject that many people would avoid at all costs.
For Yusuf, life offers endless possibilities to reflect upon and achieve an
anticipatory awareness of death.

Yusuf suffered from a particularly severe form of diabetes, which frequently caused him considerable pain. Yet when, on occasion, I asked him
about it, he always responded with the same warm smile he brought to all
of our meetings, telling me that it was a gift from God, as it brought him
closer to God. In one such instance, he went on,

> Hunger and thirst also bring one to God. You see, through the veins flow
> water and blood, and as they move, the devil moves with them. When you
> are hungry, it stops the flow [he put his hand around his wrist like a tour-
> niquet]. You say [looking up in supplication]: O Lord! [*Ya rubb*] When you
> are full, the devil flows through you, and you get lazy; you forget God. God
> reaches out even to those who only make the slightest effort, His mercy
> is so great! Sometimes He sends them difficulties [*masa'ib*] or sickness so
> they will remember and be brought back to Him. This is a testimony to
> his mercy!

Yusuf did not resent his suffering but rather appreciated it for the ethical
benefits it brought. This is not to say that Yusuf was an ascetic in any strong
sense of the word. Rather, he lived his pain with an attitude of acceptance
and appreciation in accord with its ethical significance. His pain was constitutive of a way of life he both endured and valued.[13]

The cultivated sensibility I describe here colors and configures daily experience. It is registered in an attentiveness to death's presence in the bad
smells that inhabit places of questionable repute or that cling to those who

commit acts of disobedience to God. Or it may appear in the sweet aroma that seeps through the floor of a neighborhood shop, perhaps signaling the hidden burial site of a pious man. It is present in the Quranic verses of warning echoing from the tape players of taxis, cafés, and barbershops. Death may loom up dangerously before one as a result of the illicit desires, lusts, and inclinations that rise within the self and threaten to cast one into hell. It can likewise be found in the sensations of hunger, sickness, and pain, or as a shadow accompanying corruption, poverty, or excessive wealth. The abandonment of Islamic social mores and shrinking attendance at Friday worship bear witness to its presence and the approach of "the last days." Or death may simply be glimpsed in the beauty of one's child. These experiences do not pass by in silence but are opportunities for comment and shared reflection, for reminding one's fellows of the brevity of life, the inevitability of death, the power of God, and the torments and rewards of the hereafter. In these myriad ways, human mortality comes to imprint itself on experience, knowledge, and action.

TARHIB

Numerous rhetorical techniques are employed by *khutaba'* to endow their listeners with a memory that holds death ever before the eyes, on the tongue, and as "close to one's next step as the sole of one's own shoe." Through the continual telling and retelling of death in its many apparitions and through the techniques of audition and the processes of speech and gestural mimesis that the sermon promotes, *khutaba'* seek to infuse an awareness of death into the practices of speech, emotion, and reflection—into the modes of perception and proprioception—of their listeners. One narrative technique, for example, involves depicting each type of corruption found in society today in terms of its consequences at the moment of death, in the grave, and throughout the eschatological drama. In this way, a person's every action may be contemplated in light of its telos in death, until the knowledge of death becomes the principle of all action. Every act, decision, habit of thought, or type of social character can be dramatically illuminated in its true moral dimensions once transposed upon the stage of salvational history. Acts of lying or bribery or a failure to perform one's religious duties have distinguishable and unpleasant consequences in each of the tribulations that follow death, whether in the grave, at the weighing of good and bad deeds, in crossing the bridge over hell (*sirat*), in drinking from the heavenly pool of *kawthar*, or otherwise. This is evident in Kishk's theatrical rendering of the encounter of the shah of Iran with the angel of death, where the shah's wickedness and the error of the Egyptian government in providing him refuge are given vivid depiction (see chapter 5). All of the events of life appear in the mirror of death, in the Dantean world that is held up and brought close to the mundane one.[14] In other words, the story of death and what follows it provide a particular intelligibility to one's present actions, a narrative within which they become meaningful as moral acts. It is the continual retelling, refashioning, and audition of these narratives, until they have become an ever-present memory anchored in one's heart, that makes moral action within one's life possible.

One of the most frequently recounted events from the Islamic eschatological narrative is the act of judgment itself, and, in particular, the individual's total isolation from all human contact and support in the moment of coming before God to be judged.[15] It is toward this moment, one in which moral responsibility is radically individualized, that a person's acts in this world are teleologically oriented. For the men I worked with, the solitude of this encounter was one of the most terrifying elements of the eschatological sequence, a sense they would often try to impress on me through comments such as this one made by the taxi driver Beha as he explained a segment of tape to me: "Imagine! Not even your mother, not even your son, no one will be there to help you!" In order to intensify this experience of complete and utter aloneness among their audiences, *khutaba'* frequently deploy a narrative in which each of the human bonds that sustain one within collective life are successively negated and stripped away. The painful emotions shaped by such images form the basis of an experiential, sensory knowledge that helps bind the listener to her eschatological future, such that the significance of that future can be incorporated into her present actions.

A second technique deployed by contemporary *khutaba'* centers around the construction of spatial correspondences, mapping the territories of the hereafter onto those of daily experience. As described in an earlier chapter, the *khatib* Umar Abd al-Kafi likens the pathway one crosses in order to arrive to heaven (*al-sirat*) to the central street in Cairo, Tahrir Street, drawing an analogy between each disaster that awaits the sinner along *al-sirat* and the various exits off of Tahrir. In another sermon, this one entitled "Dar al-akhira" (The realm of the afterlife), al-Kafi admonishes his listeners for their neglect of the hereafter with a figure that connects the abode they inhabit in this life with that they will occupy in the next: "You spend so much time preparing to buy an apartment, saving money, buying furniture, a TV, when what you should really be concerned with is preparing your tomb." *Khutaba'* give eschatological traditions a new vitality and meaning by weaving them into the fabric of contemporary experience, reinterpreting them in terms of the vocabularies and social landscapes of their present-day audiences.

A third narrative style used by *khutaba'* works to establish a temporal relation between this world and the next, wherein the present is seen to foreshadow and continuously be opening up upon the eschatological future. Numerous sermon tapes discuss the cataclysmic events, "the lesser and greater signs" (*al-'alamat al-sughra wa al-kubra*) that precede and anticipate the "Final Day" (*yawm al-akhira*), and *khutaba'* and their audiences often point to evidence that the succession of anticipatory signs has indeed already begun to unfold. Sometimes the signs are discoverable within the common experience of urban life. A man in his late forties, for example, whom I chanced to meet at a café, described to me how he had just come from the Friday mosque sermon where the *khatib* had told the audience that they were living in the time of *al-'alamat al-sughra*, the "lesser signs" that foreshadow the Final Day:

> Today is the period just before the arrival of the Day of Resurrection [*yawm al-qiyama*], the Shaykh said. It is obvious from the way you see women walking in the street. Plus, last night, someone saw a car parked out on the road that runs to the airport, in which there was a couple having sex. This is one of the small signs [*al-'alamat al-sughra*].

When I would listen with others to taped sermons on these premonitory signs, people would often stop the tape after the *khatib* had described one of the aspects of social breakdown that signal the onset of the end and comment to me, "This is exactly the time we are living in."[16] One of the oft-cited signs that elicits this reaction is that which states that a time will come when no one remembers what the practice of *din* (religion) entails any longer. Through the practice of such temporal accounting, the present is always figured as collapsing toward the future, accelerating toward a known eschatological history that itself stretches backward to encompass the present.[17]

A fourth technique for the presencing of death in the lives of today's sermon listeners involves the elaboration of schemata for reorganizing bodily experience, techniques for the formation of what may be called an eschatological body. One of the events of the eschaton most commonly referred to is the testifying of the limbs or body parts (*shahadat al-a'da'*). According to Islamic eschatological traditions, at the time of judgment, all of one's body parts are given the power of speech and made to testify to the good and bad acts they have committed during the individual's life. This event is referred to in the Quran, in the chapter entitled Fussilat (Clearly spelled out): "Hence, [warn all men of] the day when the enemies of God shall be gathered together before the fire, and then shall be driven onward, till, when they come close to it, their hearing and their sight and their [very] skins will bear witness against them, speaking of what they were doing [on earth]" (Surat Fussilat:19). Thus, as it was frequently explained to me, the hands will speak of the illicitly earned money they have handled, the legs will speak of the evil places they have walked, and the tongue will speak of the impious words uttered, lies told, or gossip spread. The popular *khatib* Wagdi Ghunim, in his sermon entitled "Scenes from Judgment Day," weaves the verses from the chapter Fussilat into his own rendition of the story, told in the "man-on-the-street" vernacular style he is well known for:

Their hearing, their sight, their ears, their eyes, their skin, all will testify before God. Their ears will say, "I heard . . ."; their eyes will say, "I saw . . ."; their skin will say, "I did. . . ." "And they will ask their skins, 'Why did you bear witness against us?'" [Fussilat:21]. You, why did you testify against me, oh body members [*ya i'da'ina*], when you also will be tortured with me in hell!? Why did you bear witness against me?! The answer comes: "God who gives speech to all things, has given speech to us as well" [Fussilat:21]. "God has given speech to us . . ."—that is, they didn't do it because they wanted to [*bi iradatihim*], or because they felt like it [*bi mizaghum*]. No! After that, what will their body parts say to them? He—that is, you—were you a good sort ['*anduku damm*]? He . . . were you shy of us when you rebelled against God and acted immorally [*lama bita'mal al-sayyat wa al-ma'asi*]? Huh? Then they say: "God who gives speech to all things, has given speech to us as well; for He [it is who] has created you in the first instance, and unto Him you are [now] brought back. And you did not try to hide your sins" [Fussilat:21–22]. . . . O Brother, I'll tell you what: whenever you find the devil playing with your head [*dimaghak*], egging you on to transgress against God, remember this situation in the hereafter [*fi al-akhira*].

Most of the men I worked with had heard this tale countless times over their lives, though they thoroughly appreciated it when retold in innovative ways, as in Ghunim's humorous rendition of the wrongdoer's complaint to his body parts. Ghunim's personalizing commentary on the Quranic verses, shifting from Quranic Arabic to colloquial, from third person to second, situating the listener within the scene of his or her solitary encounter with judgment and then framing the experience as an object to be instilled in memory—these features of Ghunim's rhetorical style are a staple of contemporary sermon practice.

Importantly, the schematization of the body into individual sites of moral action and responsibility that takes place at the moment of giving witness before God also occurs outside the narration of the eschaton. A similar disaggregation of the body informs a common act of daily life, the ablutions undertaken before each of the daily prayers. As a Muslim child in Egypt, one learns that in cleansing each part of the body during ablutions, one literally washes away the moral errors one has committed during the day. Saif, the Cairo University student introduced in chapter 3, described his own understanding of it this way:

> Let's say perhaps you hit someone during the day, then when you wash your hand, and do so with the right intention [niyya], you remove the error from it. Likewise, when you wash your mouth you cleanse it of all the bad things you may have said over the course of the day. Washing your hair, that is for the evil thoughts you may have had, the lusts [shahawat] you might have felt, or harm you may have wished upon others.

In other words, the body, as organized and acted upon within the context of ablutions, parallels and mirrors that which comes before God at the moment of judgment. In this way, the eschatological body, as narrated within popular sermons, acquires new dimensions of sensory experience from daily devotional practice.[18] Similarly, the common term used for difficulty or hardship, "dayyiq," literally "narrow," carries a strong kinesthetic undertone that finds its paradigmatic image in the tightness of the grave that holds a wrongdoer. Such a metaphorical link binds the experience of "being in a tough strait" to the sensations one anticipates in the hereafter. Through such metaphors, sensory bridges to the hereafter are continuously established.[19] In all of these ways, the rhetorics of death and the hereafter need to be seen as a technique du corps by which the bodily memory of the existential predicament of human mortality becomes inscribed as habit and perception.

MACABRE PLEASURES

While speaking with Ibrahim one day at the Karim Coffee Shop—the same shop in the sprawling lower-class neighborhood of Bulaq Dukrur where

Ibrahim had argued with another client on a previous visit (see chapter 4)—he took out of his bag a Muhammad Hassan sermon that a friend had lent him. With the iconography of a Hollywood B-movie, the cassette box displayed a skeleton figure standing against a burning red sky, with the title "Beware: Death is Coming!" "A great tape," Ibrahim commented with enthusiasm, "Terrifying [*faziʿa*]! A lot of it I had never heard before. This tape will put the door of hell right in front of your eyes the next time you think about disobeying God." Then, with a certain grim delight, Ibrahim went on to recount some of the especially lugubrious facts he had encountered in the sermon: that the skin of those in hell would be stretched to a surface area of seventy thousand square kilometers before being applied with fire; that while still in the grave, wrongdoers are visited by an immense snake, called *tinin*, who pounds on their graves with its tail, sending them tumbling down fifty thousand meters to the depths of hell.

For many of those like Ibrahim who listen to sermon tapes in Cairo, there is an excitement, what we might call a "thrill," afforded by the homiletic discourses on death and the eschaton. People would often express their appreciation for a particular tape in terms of the intensity of fear (*khawf*) it engendered, the terror (*fazaʿ*) produced by its imagery. The images on the covers of tapes and books sold on the sidewalks and outside the mosques also testify to the contemporary pleasure of an Islamic macabre: snakes twisting through empty eye sockets, screaming crowds engulfed in flames, cadaverous figures rising up from the grave, demons towering over the city skyline, blood dripping from walls. This is horror in its most seductive and marketable form.[20] As I describe in chapter 5, commercial tape companies, in their attempt to increase sales, employ the same marketing techniques that are used for other, competing forms of popular media entertainment such as films and cheap fiction. Starting with the sermon recorded live at the mosque, these companies elaborate a media commodity, replete with echo effects and dramatic cover imagery. Some of the most recent and heavily produced tapes go so far as to intersperse segments cut from different sermons with sound effects such as crashing cars, hissing snakes, explosions, and screams and moans. For these commercial enterprises, death sells.[21]

There can be little doubt that the great popularity of such tapes owes in some degree to their ability to compete with non-Islamic entertainment and to offer their consumers the sorts of pleasure that other media products provide. *Khutabaʾ* recognize that their listeners have been brought up in a world of mass media, their tastes and attitudes shaped by its particular forms of seduction, discipline, and pleasure. As I note in chapter 5, the impact of such practices as watching television and listening to recorded music is evident in the styles of narration and argument employed by *khu-taba'* today, as well as the spaces and times within which the practice of audition occurs. The work of the *khatib*, in this regard, involves a reconfig-uring and reorienting of the dispositions, tastes, and modes of appreciation cultivated in such popular media activities in accord with the set of inter-related ethical concepts I have discussed in previous chapters: fear (*khawf*), humility (*khushu'*), regret (*nadam*), tranquility (*itmi'nan*), and the opening of the heart (*inshirah*). That is, through the continuous exercise of ethical listening, the affects and sensations associated with modern media contexts are to be recruited and transformed, given a new function and direction within the self.

It would be a mistake to conclude that the homiletic style of *tarhib* has become nothing more than just another commodified form of popular en-tertainment. For one thing, it is worth recalling that while the commodifi-cation of the sermon as media product is recent, the enjoyment associated with listening to sermons on afterlife themes among popular classes is not. Despite shifting iconographies, themes, and styles of argumentation, the spectacularity of death and its aftermath have for a long time been central to the rhetorics of lay preaching within both Christianity and Islam. Across these traditions, popular preachers have often relied on spectacular thana-tological and eschatological dramas to seize the attention of their unlet-tered audiences, a practice that has frequently drawn censure if not ire from more sober, rationalist religious authorities.

The dismissal of contemporary sermon practices as entertainment, and thus not truly religious, follows a long-standing bias within the literature on religion whereby the religious practices of scholars and elites are viewed as "true religion" while the practices of the popular classes are seen as cor-rupted derivatives, more rooted in the proclivities of the laboring poor than in the structures of thought and practice that constitute religion. Unable to comprehend complex theological arguments, or immunized against the ideological constructs of priests due to their immersion in processes of ma-terial production, the masses draw from religion what can be consumed as entertainment or what serves to distract them from the hardship of their lives. As Peter Brown has argued, this bias represents a failure to explore the extent to which the discourses central to a religion—and, I would add, the practices and sensibilities that ground and contextualize those dis-courses—inform, in variable ways, religious practice *across* the divisions of class (P. Brown 1981:17–22). In this sense, the role of the eschaton and the feelings evoked by the subject of death are not simply concerns restricted to popular classes but are part of a shared set of ideas, practices, and orientations, a common preoccupation of both classically trained Islamic scholars and illiterate Muslim workers.[22] These issues are deeply entwined with Islamic ethical practices and are integral to the cultivation of those sensibilities upon which an Islamic society is understood to rest.

FUNEREAL TONES

In the popular quarters of Cairo, death is far less removed from daily experience than it has come to be in Western societies, or, for that matter, in upper-class Egyptian neighborhoods. Corpses of people recently deceased are commonly found in mosques; neighborhood funerals are quotidian events; and many people, especially those activists committed to *daʿwa*, still play a central role in the washing, wrapping, and burying of the bodies of their relatives. Many of the mosque lesson tapes provide instruction in how to care for the dying, the preparation and washing of the corpse, the wrapping of the body in the burial shroud, and proper comportment during funerals. Indeed, it is common that in the course of a sermon, mosque lesson, or printed work on an eschatological topic, a *khatib* or writer will turn to these more practical issues on the care and handling of the dying and recently deceased. Ashur's book on the torments of the grave, for example, presents, in succession, chapters called "The sayings of the religious scholars about death," "Description of the angel of death," "Raising the dying person's spirits before death," "Doctrinal rules of funerals," and, finally, "What saves one from the torments of the grave" (n.d.:112). The lessons of eschatology, in other words, are thoroughly entwined with issues of practical care for the dying and the deceased.

In Shaykh Kishk's sermon on the death of the shah of Iran, parts of which I analyzed in chapter 5, one of his main concerns is the impropriety of how death is managed by the state. In describing the funeral procession toward the middle of the sermon, he recounts:

> The procession proceeds now to the Abdin Palace. The shah is placed on an artillery car, and this is a heresy [*bidʿa*] and has no basis in Islam. What does it mean for a dead Muslim to be placed on an artillery car? Does he want to announce a war on God after his death?! Does he want to struggle against God while he is dead?! Didn't he wage enough of a war against God while he was alive?! Did we hear of Abu Bakr being placed on an artillery car, or ʿUmar, or ʿUthman, or ʿAli, or Khalid, or Ibn Masʿud, or Saʿad, or Abu

'Ubayda?²³ Evil heresy! In addition, the car is pulled by horses, and this is not Islamic. Horses are for the battle field, "O the chargers that run panting, sparks of fire striking, rushing to assault at morn" [*Surat al-'Adiyat*:1–3]. . . . As far as the horse pulling a coffin, that is a pharaonic funeral with nothing Islamic about it. I am setting the record straight, because the media will carry the funeral throughout the world. In order that Islam not be misunderstood, I am righting the matter here and now: in Islam, horses do not pull the bier of a dead man. The head of a funeral procession does not ride a horse, for a funeral is a place of modesty [*tawadu'*], a place of moral instruction [*wa'z*], a place of guidance [*irshad*]. Worse than that, it was ordered that music be played [at the shah's funeral]. Music playing and the voices of the crowds growing louder! Music playing and voices rising, though the Apostle of God (SAAS) said: "Silence is prescribed on three occasions: when reading the Quran, during a funeral procession, and when sneaking up on an enemy."

Key to Kishk's criticisms is the question of attitude and moral sensibility—what we might more generally call a "funereal sensorium." The military aspect of the event, represented by the artillery car used to carry the bier, the horses, and the playing of music, destroys the moral (and *acoustic*) tone that should pervade the funeral as a place of "modesty," "moral instruction," and "guidance." The martial passions of pride, valor, and glory, along with the gaiety and revelry associated with music, are inappropriate in the presence of death, destructive of the sensibility it demands and instills. Silence and solemnity must be upheld not simply out of respect for the deceased but because they create sensory conditions conducive to the attitude of humility that opens one to the instructive force, the moral lesson, that death holds for human beings. Even the act of supplication interrupts the particular form of attention, the listening of the heart demanded by the funeral. Moreover, the glorification of a ruler contradicts a basic tenet of the ethics of death: in approaching God, there is no distinction between rulers and ordinary men and women.

In this sense, there is more at stake in Kishk's criticisms than theological fastidiousness or political opportunism, an attempt to exploit the shah's unpopularity as a means to impugn the state. The shah's funeral, conducted under the authority of the Egyptian government, is a civil ritual of the modern state, following a protocol derived entirely from European conventions. As such, it does not simply contradict a set of doctrinal rules but, for *da'wa* activists like Kishk, distorts the place and meaning traditionally assigned to death within Islamic societies. Kishk's criticism should be understood in light of this fact and not simply seen as a resistance to Western culture. Other cultural forms of the modern nation-state that have been introduced into Egypt since the nineteenth century have not evoked such a degree of concern. But Kishk recognizes in the European-style funeral something that strikes at the core of Islamic society. In short, Kishk's condemnation of music needs to be seen in light of the passions and sensory conditions that make a recognition of death and its perception in life possible.

THE AFFECTS OF CARE

The care and management of the dying within modern hospitals is also a common sermon topic among *khutaba'* in Egypt. The Egyptian *khatib* Isma'il Humaydi, for example, in a tape entitled "Shiddat sakarat al-mawt" (The calamity of the death throes), vehemently condemns the current administration of death within hospitals in Muslim countries. The sermon's weaving of a rhetoric of admonition and fear—*wa'z* and *tarhib*—together with practical instruction and advice for social reform, is characteristic of many sermons on death-related themes and therefore merits attention.

After a brief preamble, Humaydi introduces his topic, opening with a rather unconventional question:

> What is death [*ma hiya al-mawt*]? What is the meaning [*ta'rif*] of death, the first calamity that awaits all of us? The definition of death, O slaves of God: death is a creature [or created being] [*makhluq*] that God in His power created. For God, the most exalted, said, "Hallowed be He in whose hand all dominion rests, since he has the power to will anything: He who has created death as well as life, so that He might put you to the test [and thus show] which of you is best in conduct, and [make you realize that] He alone is almighty, truly forgiving" [al-Mulk:1] Death. Death is a creature. What does this mean? This means the nonexistence of life prior to its coming into being. And it means the nonexistence of life that follows its having come into being. The interpretation [*tafsir*] of these words is that death stands against life, just as life stands against death.

Humaydi's style here exhibits a number of classic sermon conventions, particularly in its dialectical movement between the citation of a Quranic verse and the verse's elaboration and explanation. Indeed, his progression from definition to Quranic reference to interpretation lends a rather formal or

scholarly flavor to the sermon, one associated more with rational instruction than passionate exhortation. His performance, however, maintains a
strong *wa'zi* (admonitory) aspect, both through the emotive qualities Humaydi gives to his voice, his acoustical modulation of pious sentiments,
and the unconventional and fear-inspiring image of death he manages to
portray. Humaydi takes a Quranic verse extremely familiar to his audience—"*khalaqa al-mawt wa al-hayat* [God created death and life]"—and,
by rephrasing it in the passive form with death now as the subject, imparts
to it a startling and unusual connotation: while the verbal noun *makhluq*,
derived from the verb *khalaqa* (to create), may be glossed as "created," as
the predicate within a simple subject-object sentence, its semantic weight
shifts toward a personification, similar to the English word "creature." Thus
the visually weak figure of God having created death is recast in a striking
and sensorially rich image of death as a living being.[24]

As he continues with the sermon, Humaydi proceeds for a few more
minutes with an account based squarely in Islamic doctrines of the soul
and then turns to the issue of how this conception of death informs the
practices by which we are to care for the dying and the bodily remains of
those who have died. He begins with a series of short vignettes aimed at
demonstrating the inadequacy of modern hospitals in providing proper assistance for the terminally ill.

> I will now present to you a number of scenes [*mashahid*] of the Islamic
> *umma*, from both its eastern and western sides, to show you the level of our
> neglect and forgetfulness of death, of funeral doctrines [*fiqh al-jana'iz*], of
> attending to the dying [*hadarat al-mawt*], that is, our presence at the death
> of others. . . . A man died in a hospital in a Muslim country with no one
> there to attend to him. His family abandoned him and the hospital left him
> on his own, for there was nothing there by the name of *qiblat al-Islam* [the
> niche marking the direction of the Ka'aba in Mecca], even though it was a
> Muslim country. And when his soul was extracted, his right arm was left
> extended outward, and his left leg was bent. They left him in that condition
> for about an hour, and then, with his arm still outward and his leg bent,
> put him in the [morgue] refrigerator, though it was difficult to fit him in
> like that. Later, he was washed [*ghusil*] and wrapped in a shroud [*kafan*],
> you can only imagine how. . . . For, when he meets God, he will complain
> about all of us. . . . The last sad vignette, one I have on good evidence,
> [concerns] a woman in a hospital [who] became deathly ill. So they put an
> apparatus in her mouth. Her daughter was with her . . . and her daughter

knew of her religious duties, so she said to those around her: "My mother is dying. Align her with the *qibla* [prayer niche]." But they refused to listen. And they refused to give the woman water to drink, and told the daughter she could not enter the mother's room and must remain silent. The daughter begged them to align the mother with the *qibla*, but they told her she must leave. And God will testify from this letter that [I have received], the woman died without her daughter being able to give her water to drink. The daughter said, "I want to prompt her [*ulaqqina*] to pronounce the testimony of faith [*al-shahada*]," but she was not allowed to. And the soul of the woman left not in the direction of the *qibla*, and both her mouth and eyes were left open.

Humaydi's vignettes depict the cruelty, neglect, and harsh indifference of the modern, bureaucratized medical institution, highlighting—with macabre imagery of poorly tended cadavers—the violence engendered by the rationalized and technologized administration of care. The hospital remains entirely deaf to the kind of attention demanded by the momentous event of death, its goals, techniques, and protocols not only counter to Muslim doctrinal practice but, more generally, inhumane and brutal. Even a knowledge of the direction of the *qibla*—necessary for orienting the body of the dying person in the direction of Mecca to ensure that the soul's journey may be more easily made—finds no place within hospital organization or design. The drink of cool water to soothe the pain[25] and the elicitation of the testimony of faith that, when uttered just before death, paves the way for one's acceptance into heaven—these key aspects of proper ministration to the dying are denied both by the subordination of the process to technological imperatives—for example, the respirator tube placed in the mouth—and by the monopolization of authority in the hands of a medical staff insensitive to the requirements of Islam.

Humaydi's concern here, however, is not just about the issue of improper procedure. Much of his outrage is directed at the attitude of extreme indifference and lack of respect for the dying he sees as pervasive within hospitals. One of his earlier vignettes describes two nurses laughing together while tending to a patient in the final stages of death. Death for Humaydi—as for Kishk—is an occasion for moral instruction ('*ibra*), admonition (*wa'z*), and modesty (*tawadu'*). It requires an attitude of solemnity and humility, such that one remains open to "taking a moral lesson" (*itta'az*) from the event. As when listening to the recitation of the Quran, one should prepare oneself to accept, to *taste* the reality disclosed by death, a reality that becomes particularly perceptible in moments of sickness and decay, in the last moments of life, and in the bodily remains left once the soul has been taken. It is the complete lack of this sensibility that Humaydi's examples seek to expose.

It is important to point out that Humaydi's sermon does not simply present a blanket critique or total rejection of modern forms of medical practice. Rather, in a reformist tone, he advocates—throughout the latter part of the sermon—the adjustment of hospital procedures to allow for the practice of an Islamic style of death. Humaydi believes that beyond the task of healing and preserving human life, hospitals need to be organized around the particular needs that people face in dying, needs specific to them as Muslims.[26] This requires not only special facilities where the ill may face death undisturbed by the presence of other patients or technical life-saving apparatuses but a medical staff trained in the Islamic prescriptions concerning death (*fiqh al-mawt*), capable of ensuring the conditions of speech and silence that enable a smooth transition to the hereafter. In another sermon tape, Humaydi notes that in preparing the body for burial, the preparer must handle it "softly and gently [*bi rifq wa lin*]," and must care for it with the "correct intention [*bi niyya*]" of ensuring its successful transition to the hereafter. A failure to treat the corpse in this manner will lead the deceased to complain to God about his or her survivors, insomuch as the deceased remains aware and sees and hears those who wash and enshroud him or her.[27]

Insomuch as the sensibility and care shown to the dying has repercussions for the deceased in the hereafter, the events of the grave and the eschaton take on a particular relevance. A knowledge of the angel of death in all its horror, and a pious fear cultivated through the experience of *tasting* this horror, infuses the care one brings to those near death, shaping the practices by which the dying are conveyed to the hereafter. One's fate after death, as Humaydi emphasizes, depends on the sensitivity, care, and knowledge of those who assist one in the passage. In this sense, Humaydi's use of a rhetoric of *tarhib* is not limited to the logic of "do right in this world as you will be judged in the next." Humaydi is not calling on his listeners to reform their treatment of the deathly ill *out of fear* of what will befall them in the hereafter but *with fear*, as one of the emotive conditions that should inform one's attitude and infuse one's actions regarding death and its practical demands. Such fear is not a generic passion but one molded to the contours of a distinct ethical life, with its unique styles of caring, arguing, loving, and listening.

TECHNIQUES FOR THE END

Across the history of Islam, preachers and religious scholars have been ascribed the task of reminding their audiences of the inescapability of death
and the consequences that accompany it.[28] Going beyond simple exhortation, they also developed techniques for fashioning a memory adequate to
the truth of death. Abu Hamid Al-Ghazali, for example, said,

> The most productive method for bringing this [remembrance of death]
> about is for him to make frequent remembrance of those peers and associ-
> ates who have passed away before him: he should contemplate their death
> and dissolution beneath the earth and recall how they appeared in their
> former positions and circumstances, and meditate upon the way in which
> the earth has now obliterated the beauty of their forms, and how their parts
> have been scattered in their tombs. . . . Holding fast to these and other simi-
> lar ideas, and also entering graveyards and seeing ill people, is the way to
> refresh the remembrance of death in the heart until it takes possession of it
> and stands before one's eyes.
>
> (A. H. AL-GHAZALI 1989:13–14)

Such practices of reflecting on death have been central not only to Islam
and Christianity but also to the Greek philosophical and religious traditions that preceded them and influenced their development. The French
historian of antiquity, Pierre Hadot, has argued that we think of the
meditation on death as one of a number of topics (or *topoi*, as the term
was understood within ancient and medieval rhetoric) that have shaped
Western—and, I would add, Islamic—thought. Like the topics, or "com-
monplaces," that classical rhetoricians went to in building an argument,
thinkers in different historical contexts have continually returned to the
practice of reflecting on death, putting it to new uses and imbuing it with
new meanings. To cite a well-known example, for Plato philosophy was
to be considered a "training for death" (Hadot 1995:503–4). Through exercises of meditation on one's death, one gradually detaches oneself from
human particularity, and thus accedes to universality, acquiring a vision
not unlike Muhammad's "dead eyes." Notably, whereas for Plato such a
perspective involves the separation of the body from the soul, and thus a
detachment from the passions, within Islam death instead requires a body,
one passionately attuned to death's reality.

The Epicureans and the Stoics also elaborated exercises of meditating on death. Indeed, the manner of reflecting on death practiced by those I worked with in Cairo bears considerable similarity to the *melete thanatou*—the meditation on and preparation for death encouraged by Seneca and other Stoics. As Foucault notes in commenting on this practice,

> Indeed, it does not consist of the mere reminder, even the insistent reminder, that one is fated to die; it is a way of making death actual in life. . . . By thinking of oneself as being about to die, one can judge each action that one is performing in terms of its own value. . . . And Seneca envisaged the moment of death as one in which an individual would be able to become a sort of judge of himself and assess the moral progress he will have made, up to his final day.
>
> (FOUCAULT 1997:104–5)

In accord with their humanist outlook, the Stoics ascribed the task of final judgment to human beings, rather than to God or eschatological tribulations as did the men I worked with. We might note, in addition, the similarity of al-Ghazali's suggestions to those put forth by writers in the late-medieval Christian *ars moriendi* tradition.[29] In this tradition, the art of dying well required that all of life be lived as a preparation for death. Thus, Jeremy Taylor, in *The Rule and Exercises of Holy Dying* ([1651] 1989), counseled:

> He that would die well must always loook [*sic*] for death, every day knowing at the gates of the grave, and then the gates of the grave shall never prevail upon him to do him mischief. . . . And if we make death present to us, our own death, dwelling and dressed in all its pomp and fancy and proper circumstances, if anything will quench the heats of lust, or the desires of money, or the greedy passionate affections of this world, this must do it.
>
> (314)

Within the tradition Taylor represents, death was to be made present through regular reflection on the body's gradual weakening and decay, the passing away of close friends, on images of the dark solitude of the grave, the body consumed by worms, the rotting bones, and the tortures that await the sinner.

The concern for death shared by Muslims and Christians in different historical epochs, by ancient Greeks and modern Heideggerians, reflects less a shared interpretation of human mortality than a manner of framing a set of questions, of interrogating and responding to diverse aspects of life. The Islamic movement I have explored here follows in this tradition of inquiry, seeking to create social and political conditions wherein viable answers to the predicament of mortality may be elaborated and lived. For my preaching instructor Muhammad Subhi, my friends Ahmad and Ibrahim, and the other men I came to know in Cairo, cassette-recorded sermons have provided a valuable tool in the endeavor to reflect on death and incorporate its significance into their lives. Like other modern modes of self-fashioning, however, a good deal of the reflexive apparatus now has been lodged in a technological form.

SHAYKH KISHK'S FUNERAL

Shaykh Kishk died in early December 1996, at the age of sixty-three, the same age at which the Prophet had died. I heard of his passing the day after, from a taxi driver. "Did you hear Kishk died yesterday?" he asked. "You see this tape," he said, holding up a very worn copy of a Kishk sermon. "It broke yesterday, right as he died."

Two days later, a service (*'aza'*) was to be held at Kishk's mosque in the neighborhood of Hada'iq al-Qubba. By the time I arrived in the late afternoon, there were already ten to twenty thousand people around the mosque, despite the fact that no mention of Kishk's death had been made in any of the state media. It wasn't until almost a week after the event that newspapers were allowed to print an obituary. *Al-Ahram*, the paper of the ruling party and the most widely read daily in Egypt, limited the obituary to two lines, buried in the back pages.

I met up with Muhammad Subhi, who had arrived before me. While we waited for the eulogies and the reading of the Quran to begin, we chatted with some of the people standing next to us. One man exclaimed that the night before he had had a dream in which he had seen Kishk being escorted up to heaven by a group of angels. Two teenagers standing with us said they had never heard Kishk before but had been told he was a great *da'iya*. At about six o'clock, an announcer came up to the podium and made a statement calling on the speakers to not incite people with their words (*'adam ithara bi al-kalam*). Shortly after, the first speaker began: "Where are the masses who used to follow Kishk?! Why are they ignoring him now?! Let us give prayers to him, and to other *du'at* who have recently died, so we can lessen their pains in the grave." He then led a collective prayer, first for Kishk, and then for Muslims suffering throughout the world, in

Jerusalem, in Chechnya, in the Philippines. The next speaker described how he had met Kishk at school years before, and had been immediately struck by the shine (*munawwar*) radiating from his face: "There was no resentment [*hasad*] in him; his heart was white." Next came the dean of the school of *da'wa* at al-Azhar, and thus a government employee: "Everyone who lives will die. No one has power over the soul [*ruh*] except God. When I heard the news of the death of Shaykh Kishk, I felt a deep sadness; then I immediately announced the news over the loudspeakers at the college, so all could share this sadness. . . . We need Kishk as an example to us [*qidwa*], for his truthfulness and sincerity." A succession of scholars and Quran reciters took to the podium to give praise to Kishk. At a certain point, the president of the Engineer's Union [Niqabat al-muhandisin] took the microphone: "Kishk's absence from the field of *da'wa* lasted for sixteen years! For sixteen years he was forced into silence! We were in prison together. Kishk was never someone who could be used by the government to say, 'We have democracy; we have our rights.' No. He always spoke the truth. When some people were selling the country to the U.S., he defended Egypt. He said no. No to Camp David. . . . I know that the security forces are here, and will come to arrest me, but Kishk deserves truthful speech [*sadiq al-kalam*]. That is what we owe him."

The next day I saw Ahmad, who, unbeknownst to me, had also been in the audience at the eulogy, and had tape-recorded the entire proceedings. We sat in his living room and listened.

{ 7 }

EPILOGUE

I N THIS concluding chapter, I want to briefly take up a predictable response my work often elicits from academic and nonacademic audiences: however historically unique and complex the Islamic Revival may be, isn't it nonetheless a *fundamentalist* movement, and therefore a danger to the Middle Eastern societies where it has set root? This response recurs with some regularity despite the fact that a number of scholars, including myself, have pointed to the inadequacy of the term "fundamentalism" for the analysis of contemporary Islam (Goldberg 1989; Esposito 1992; Harris 1994; Hirschkind 1997; Hirschkind and Mahmood 2002). Within both popular and scholarly discourses on Islam, the term "fundamentalism" continues to characterize a wide variety of movements, ideas, and practices—Islamic political parties, pious dress styles, a literalist hermeneutics, conservative social mores and gender relations, and so on. Given the heterogeneity of these diverse social phenomena and the fact that the relation between them is highly contingent, the analytical labor performed by this term is limited to registering little more than a certain moral and political distaste.[1] The judgment encoded in the appellation "fundamentalism" is singular: contemporary Islamic movements, while undeniably of considerable sociological and political significance, are essentially uninteresting and contribute very little to our understanding of human value and creativity, let alone our capacities of moral and political imagination.

Within the explanatory frameworks that continue to dominate the sociology of religion generally, and Islam in particular, movements like the Islamic

Revival in Egypt tend to be viewed as reactive phenomena that can be adequately explained by reference to the sociological conditions under which they arise. Considerable disagreement may exist among analysts about which of these conditions plays a more determining role: whether Islamic reformism should be viewed as a response to the destabilizing effects of rapid modernization, as a defensive maneuver to create stability in a world of accelerating change, or simply as a turn to the comforts of religion by people who have no power to affect the processes of transformation sweeping them along. In each case, however, the uniqueness of the forms of religious thought and action enabled by the Islamic Revival is entirely subsumed within their sociological functions. In stating this, I am not making the common argument that such accounts ignore the role of human agency, only that the style of explanation reflects a judgment deeply lodged within Western intellectual life: namely, that religious humanity is dumb humanity.

Many of the people I worked with in Cairo lived under chronic conditions of economic stress, struggling to get by on very low salaries, delaying marriage for years for lack of resources, living in cramped housing with poor services. Within analyses of Islamic activism in the Middle East, these conditions are generally viewed as an epistemic liability, an impediment to thoughtfulness that at times finds expression in fundamentalist Islam. Scholarly accounts abound in depicting the conditions of poverty and political malaise that are deemed responsible for the ascendance of Islamic movements.[2] It is interesting to note, however, how easily this liability can be interpreted as an asset when the political forms that emerge from such economic conditions take recognizably progressive directions. To give an example, note the following observation by the well known political theorist Sheldon Wolin:

> The possibility of renewal draws on a simple fact that ordinary individuals are capable of creating new cultural patterns of commonality at any moment. Individuals who concert their powers for low income housing, worker ownership of factories, better schools, better health care, safer water, controls over toxic waste disposals, and a thousand other concerns of ordinary lives are experiencing a democratic moment and contributing to the discovery, care, and tending to a commonality of shared concerns. Without necessarily intending it, they are renewing the political by contesting the forms of unequal power that democratic liberty and equality have made possible and that democracy can eliminate only by betraying its own values.
>
> (1996:43)

Wolin emphasizes the capacity of ordinary individuals, including those living under conditions of hardship, to effect democratic change. But when the direction of change happens to be defined by a religious tradition, one not easily mapped onto a progressive teleology or transcribable into the vocabularies of human rights, tolerance, and equality, students of politico-religious movements (such as Islamism) no longer view them as expressions of creative engagement but as the abandonment of this potential for the comforts of the past—in sum, as fundamentalism. In this light, it is not surprising that those who emphasize the positive contributions of the Islamic Revival tend to characterize it as a movement of social protest, one aimed at addressing conditions of social inequality, poverty, and political marginalization.[3] Some of our reluctance to be intellectually challenged by this movement owes, undoubtedly, to the comfort we achieve by having our own viewpoints confirmed.

The Islamic Revival, I have argued in this book, is not a given socio-ideological formation but a contingent and shifting constellation of ideas, practices, and associational forms. Its history has been one of continuous contestation both from within and without. Indeed, my discussion of the public arena articulated by this movement focuses on how this fractured and contestatory character of the movement is embedded in its very institutional forms, in the practices of argument, debate, and disagreement in which its participants routinely engage. The practice of da'wa, as I have described, is founded on a certain discursive openness, understood as a necessary condition for the task of collectively rethinking the contribution of the past to an unfolding future. Even this achievement, however, should be seen as tentative and exploratory, an emerging ethicopolitical institution rather than one already complete. This exploratory, contingent quality of the Islamic Revival is reflected in the biographical trajectories of its supporters and leading figures, many of whom have adopted liberal or leftist viewpoints at other moments of their lives.[4] The shifts within the movement, I have argued, should not be taken as evidence of its lack of seriousness but of its unfinished and tentative character.

A skeptic might counter that however tentative and unfinished the character of this movement, the very attempt to harness politics to a religious tradition necessarily imperils the pluralist framework essential to a multireligious and multiethnic society. Indeed, khutaba' of the Islamic Revival who argue for the reorganization of social and political life along confessional lines are often singled out by critics of this movement for the role they play in both inflaming already existing tensions between Muslims and Copts in Egypt and threatening the fragile accord that for generations linked these communities in relative harmony. While these claims merit our serious attention—and I will turn to them shortly—it is worth remembering that the problem of accommodating religious minorities within the framework of the nation owes to the contradictory character of the nation form itself, as a space defined both in universalist and particularist terms. On one hand, the modern nation form is founded upon a vocabulary of universal rights, in respect to which distinctions of culture, class, ethnicity, or religion are disregarded. Within this framework, public discourse should not be organized on the basis of religious difference. The juridical relegation of organized religion to the sphere of private life helps secure this norm. On the other hand, the nation also incorporates a notion of cultural identity—the values, history, and language through which the unity and particularity of "the people" as a nation is established. "Religion" (however we might understand the term) is deeply entwined with the historical sources from which the idea of a unified national culture is constructed. Insomuch as a national polity is representative of "majoritarian" values (be they religious or cultural), it stands in a necessary relation of tension with the nation's "minority" traditions (see T. Asad 2003). The conflict between universalist and particularist currents of national political life, therefore, cannot be attributed to the rise of religious movements alone precisely because this conflict is integral to the project of secular nationalism itself. For example, the explicitly secular-nationalist project of modern India has from its inception depended on the deployment of a distinctly Hindu symbolism (see Chatterjee 1993; Hansen 1999). In Egypt as well, the national project has from its commencement tended to disfavor and marginalize Coptic Christians in various ways.

The Islamic Revival encompasses a variety of positions and arguments with respect to Egypt's Coptic Christian minority. A number of Islamist political parties have sought to include Copts among their leadership and have also formulated platforms that explicitly address the question of religious minorities living within a Muslim majority state. These platforms have often taken a critical stance in regard to the classical Islamic concept of *wilaya*, a notion conventionally interpreted to mean that non-Muslims should not be in a position of rule over Muslims, and they have instead embraced the idea that qualified Christians are as suitable for political office as their Muslim counterparts (see Baker 2003:178–98).[5] Similarly the Wasat Party, formed in 1996 by a group of young members of the Muslim Brotherhood frustrated with what they considered to be the closed-mindedness of the Brotherhood's older directorship, included a number of Copts among its leadership (see Abdo 2002; Baker 2003). Muslim Brothers have also recently floated Coptic candidates in parliamentary and municipal elections with varying degrees of success.[6] Notable as well is the fact that a number of the leading intellectuals of the Islamic movement in Egypt, among them Fahmi Huwaidi and Tariq al-Bishri, have written extensively on the position of Copts within a self-described Islamic polity, emphasizing the importance of Coptic participation within the institutions of political life (Huwaidi 1985; al-Bishri 2005).

These views, of course, do not represent the entirety of the Islamic Revival movement. Islamic militants, for example, have frequently made Copts the targets of their attacks. Moreover, there are those who argue that Copts should have a subordinate position within Egyptian society, should not be allowed to run for political office, and should have to pay a special tax (*jizya*) in their status as protected minority. Similarly, the Muslim Brotherhood's recent fielding of Coptic candidates is viewed by many Copts with suspicion, and the Brothers' success at the polls in the 2005 parliamentary elections drew mixed reactions from the Coptic community.[7] The fact that these varying Islamist attitudes toward Copts do not fit a singular pattern poses some interesting questions, particularly when viewed against the backdrop of the increasing marginalization of Copts from Egyptian centers of economic and political power in the postcolonial period. These questions include: What forms of religious argumentation can provide the basis for religious coexistence within a democratic political arena that is not beholden to the secular principle of religious indifference? What forms of belonging, collectivity, and reciprocity would such a vision of religious coexistence be based upon? What conceptual resources do we have available to rethink the secular model of democratic politics given the role Islamists are playing in Egypt and other Muslim countries today? These are some of the questions that are important to ask if we want to seriously evaluate the potential and challenges that different currents within the Islamic Revival pose to accustomed ways of thinking about religious politics. The notion of Islamic fundamentalism obscures most of what I have described: its flattening light illuminates only those surfaces upon which liberal anxieties can fix themselves but leaves in darkness all of the surrounding density and complexity.

Let me now turn to the *da'wa* movement that has been the focus of this book and whose political impact lies not so much in its participation in electoral politics but in the changes it effects in the social and moral landscape of Egyptian society. In the *da'wa* movement, too, one finds currents that have clearly sought to intensify the marginalization of Copts from public life and promote anti-Coptic attitudes and comportments, as well as those that have aimed to promote interconfessional harmony. In regard to the former, there are a number of popular cassette sermons that depict Christians as evil conspirers working secretly to retake Egypt from Muslim hands. One of the most widely known tape series, supposedly the testimony of a Coptic priest converted to Islam, claims to give an eyewitness account of the perverse practices involved in secret Christian rites as well as the treacherous strategies of the Coptic Church for destroying Islam. With a certain heightening of tensions between Muslims and Christians in recent years, these tapes must be taken as a further incitement of Christian-Muslim discord and conflict.

Among other sermon tapes that address the question of Christian-Muslim relations, however, one finds a far more complicated or ambiguous stance. One of the tapes that caused considerable public debate on this issue was by the *khatib* Umar Abd al-Kafi, in which he suggests that Muslims should greet Christians not with the standard greeting, "*Salam alaykum* [peace be upon you]," but instead with "*Sabah al-khayr* [good morning]"; that Muslims, in other words, should relate to Christians in a manner distinct from how they relate to other Muslims. Accused of fomenting discord between the two communities, Abd al-Kafi subsequently tried to clarify his position on the issue and distance himself from the anti-Christian positions of some of Egypt's more militant Islamists. During an interview he explained his comments in these terms:

> I said it according to the text [*bil-nas*]: you greet a Christian, you say to him "Good Morning"; you say to him "Good Evening"; you support him when he is sick, and if he is your neighbor, he has the rights of a neighbor and you must not be cruel to him. [The eighth-century scholar] Abu Hanifa said all of this. . . . He said, if you break a bottle of alcohol belonging to a Christian, then you must repay him for it since it has value for him. . . . In any house in Egypt, whether there is a Muslim or a non-Muslim, we don't hear of a Muslim who doesn't go out to felicitate his Christian neighbor on his holy day.
>
> (FAWZI 1993:24)

Although Abd al-Kafi's arguments sit uncomfortably with secular models of friendship and association, particularly with the idea of national identity as transcending religious distinctions, it would be wrong to understand them as simply one more instance of contemporary religio-nationalist hatred directed at a vulnerable minority group. As Abd al-Kafi points out, there exists a considerable body of classical scholarly reflection concerning the forms of address and conduct appropriate to relationships between Christians and Muslims, and even in modern Egypt this topic has never disappeared from public discussion, at least not within religious institutions. Within our modern idea of religion as private belief, distinctions of faith should not produce any fissures upon the social fabric of our common citizenship, or rather, those fissures should remain markers of *private* distinction not mark the boundaries of *public* sociability. Religious affiliation, we tend to feel, should not become a structuring principle within our public settings. This view carries over into the area of friendship insomuch as friendship straddles both public and private, encompassing more intimate or personal aspects as well as public ones.

While some of those I worked with agreed with Abd al-Kafi's position, others did not. Ahmad, for example, told me that while he was a student at the university he had developed close friendships with a number of Christians and that he could not imagine greeting them differently than he did anyone else. Other people I met asserted positions closer to Abd al-Kafi, arguing that mutual respect between Christians and Muslims was obligatory but that there was a qualitative distinction between the kind of friendship possible within one's own confessional community and the kind possible across confessional lines. These discussions are notable both for the plurality of viewpoints expressed on this topic as well as the public arena in which they are discussed and argued by the *khutaba'* and their listeners. The reason liberal and leftist ears remain deaf to the cadences of these various positions is, I believe, because they do not abide by the liberal prescription that we moderns must remain indifferent to people's religious affiliations. This in itself is a moral position and, for many participants in the Islamic Revival, its truth has yet to be demonstrated.

Let me emphasize again that I am not claiming that the Islamic Revival has developed and instituted an ideal model of religious cohabitation. Clearly, certain currents within the revival represent a threat to the form of religious coexistence that has obtained for some time in Egypt. The problem of accommodating religious difference within the framework of the nation-state, however, is not one specific to Islamic societies. Nor is it restricted to postcolonial contexts, for that matter, as is evident in the fact that many Europeans are increasingly finding their Christian heritage incompatible with the practices and values of the Muslim populations within their nations. What I do want to suggest here is that the elaboration of the problem of religious coexistence within Egypt's Islamic movement should not be discounted on the assumption that religious forms of ethical and political thought can only produce interreligious discord and violence. Whether the forms of public debate and ethical reasoning engendered by the *da'wa* movement will give rise to a religio-political vocabulary capable of accommodating the commitments and desires of both religious communities is hard to predict, but it would be premature to assume that such an outcome is impossible.

Since the events of September 11, 2001, the forms of sociability and religiosity promoted by the *da'wa* movement have come under increasing scrutiny. Whereas in the past this movement was viewed as a quietist form of Islam whose dangers were only secondary to the more lethal projects of "political Islam" (Kepel 1993; Roy 1996, 2004) there are those who now view the so-called "traditionalism" of the movement as an even greater threat to the propagation of a liberal, enlightened religiosity commensurate with a modern polity. The dangers of "traditionalism" are said to reside in its backward-looking mentality, one that fetishizes a no longer viable past and promotes a literalist interpretation of scripture that can only result in historical stasis and irrationality. This is not simply a judgment that circulates within academic and popular discourses today, but has been incorporated into planning documents and strategies of the U.S. State Department and other agencies concerned with promoting American interests in the Middle East (see Mahmood 2006).

In contrast to these assessments, as I have argued in the preceding chapters, the aim of the *da'wa* movement is not to stop the movement of history but to render the historical present, in all of its indeterminacy and flux, amenable to ethical deliberation and action and to organize it in ways that give the present purpose and value from the perspective of an inherited tradition. The ethical standpoint from which this challenge is met is drawn from Islamic traditions of argument, reasoning, and listening. ("Tradition" here is used not in a pejorative sense of a regressive attachment to the past but as an attitude that valorizes the past as relevant to the task of living in the present.) As I have emphasized, this project does not take an intellectualist form but is carried out within the sensory fabric of everyday life, through an ongoing effort to achieve what Benjamin, referring to a different context, called the "co-ordination of the soul, the eye, and the hand" (1969:108). This is why the participants of the *da'wa* movement are cautious about the unconditional embrace of everything Western championed by Egypt's elite class. For *da'wa* activists, the ever-more pervasive Western cultural forms—movies, television, music, dress styles, and protocols of sociability—insinuate themselves into the senses most directly, shaping the repertoires of affect, gesture, and sensibility that animate and orient practical reasoning. Proponents of the Islamic Revival recognize this and have sought to develop a politics of the senses in response.

To speak of Islam today, one necessarily encounters a terrain shaped by deeply entrenched presumptions and anxieties. As Edward Said pointed out some time ago, these dispositions toward Islam, sedimented in the Western psyche, have their genesis in a long-standing tradition of scholarly and popular discourse on the inferiority of Muslim practices and doctrines. To dislodge these entrenched attitudes and judgments and to clear a space for a more open-minded inquiry into Islamic societies will, for this reason, require more than a merely intellectual exercise in the narrow sense. The different registers of thought and feeling that give force to these judgments will also require work. The challenge, in other words, is a moral one, especially in light of the current danger of a world increasingly polarized along religious lines.

NOTES

1. INTRODUCTION

1. Michel Foucault, in a series of articles on the Iranian revolution written for the Italian newspaper *Corriere della Sera*, also noted the important role of the cassette in enabling the mass uprising of ordinary Iranians: "If the shah is about to fall, it will be due largely to the cassette tape. It is the tool par excellence of counterinformation" (2005:219).

2. For a discussion of this case and the significance of Abdul Rahman's recorded sermons for the prosecution, see the articles by Joseph Fried (1995) and Chris Hedges (1993) in the *New York Times*.

3. For recent works that address the contingent and contradictory aspects of the unfolding horizon of democratic politics in postcolonial societies, see Partha Chatterjee, *Politics of the Governed* (2004); Dipesh Chakrabarty, *Provincializing Europe* (2000); Thomas Blom Hansen, *The Saffron Wave* (1999); and David Scott, *Conscripts of Western Civilization* (2005).

4. Burchell has pointed to this lacuna within liberal scholarship regarding the place of discipline in preparing the citizen for public life: "What is altogether missing from this kind of controversy [over the conditions of political participation] is a sense of the citizen as a social creation, as an historical persona, whose characteristics have been developed in particular times and places through the activities of social discipline, both externally on the part of governments and internally by techniques of self-discipline and self formation" (1995:549). Burchell's own work focuses on how early-modern forms of civility and public life were understood to depend upon Christian techniques of ethical discipline, enacted through education and institutions of social discipline (e.g., police, schools, factories), as well as through techniques of self-fashioning promoted in manuals and treatises. In this book, I take up Burchell's suggestion through an exploration of the place of

ethical discipline in creating the nondiscursive background of sentiments and habits upon which contemporary forms of Islamic public deliberation depend.

5. Useful discussions of this dimension of the Islamic Revival in Egypt can be found in Baker 2003; Mahmood 2005; Salvatore 2001a, 2001b. For works focusing outside the Egyptian context and relevant to the dimensions of contemporary Islam that I explore here, see T. Asad 1993, 2003; Burgat and Dowell 1997; Bowen 1993; Hefner 2000.

6. Two of the neighborhoods in Cairo where I worked extensively, Imbaba and Bulaq Dukrur, are composed primarily of lower-income families. In contrast, Ain Shams and Zaytun, two other quarters I came to know well, encompass a mix of both middle- and lower-middle-class homes.

7. There is a growing body of literature addressing the contribution of affect to politics. Among the scholars whose insights into the complex relationship between affect and political reasoning have most shaped my own thinking, see Asad 2003; Chakrabarty 2000; Connolly 2002; Deleuze 1988; Massumi 2002; Seremetakis 1994.

8. For anthropological studies focusing on cassette media, see Bull 2000; Greene 1999; Manuel 1993; Miller 2001; Qureshi 1995; Rogers 1986.

9. The most thorough and interesting anthropological works on Islamic sermons in the Middle East are those of Gaffney (1994) and Antoun (1989). Adopting a Weberian framework of analysis, Gaffney provides a richly documented account of three contemporary preaching styles in Egypt in terms of their contrasting ideological perspectives. Antoun, working in a Jordanian context, explores aspects of sermon rhetoric, in particular how preachers use formal structures of sermon oratory to address current issues of practical concern.

10. Since the 1990s, satellite television has extended the media options available to Egyptians, affording them greater access to unofficial viewpoints. The impact of this transformation is discussed in Eickelman and Anderson 1999.

11. Important contributions to this field of inquiry include Crary 1990, 1999; Jameson 1981; Jay 1994; W. Ong 1958, 1982; Schmidt 2000.

12. Howes 2003 provides a very useful account of the anthropological discipline's early concern with the cultural patterning of the senses in the late nineteenth and early twentieth centuries.

13. For a sampling of such nineteenth-century views, see Starrett 1995a.

14. Aspects of this judgment came to be adopted by a number of nineteenth-century Egyptian reformers as well. For example, Ahmed Amin, a prominent reformist author from the period, writes: "If one uses the English language, each assertion leads to the next, concise and to the point. It is very rare that there is any play on words, digression from the subject, or repetition of arguments. . . . However, if one uses the Arabic language, the discussion drags on, becomes more prolix, and ideas often are linked, not with sister-ideas, but with more distant-cousin ideas" (A. Amin 1965:92).

15. All translations from the Arabic are mine unless otherwise indicated.

16. It is interesting to note that this critique of Islamic pedagogical practices occurs at the same time as schools in the United States are being encouraged to place greater emphasis on memorization and collective repetition. American schools have also reembraced the "phonics method" for teaching children to read, while criticizing the "whole-language method" that emphasizes "the meaning of words over their sounds" and that had been heralded earlier as a more progressive replacement for the phonics approach. This emphasis on word sound over meaning, in the American context, has not elicited fears about stunted intellectual development or the inculcation of a "terrorist mentality."

17. It was precisely this fundamentally auditory activity of gathering and sheltering that Heidegger identified as one of the original meanings of the Greek term "*legein*," the verb from which the term "*logos*" was derived. This meaning was already in disuse by the time of Aristotle, as *legein* became reduced to speaking or stating, and listening was left behind. See Corradi Fiumara's interesting discussion of this etymology (1995).

18. Note also how a very different analytical space opens up once we shift to a different kind of site, say a sermon given by a preacher before a silent audience at a mosque in the context of Friday worship. We also find listening, of course, in concert halls or in private living rooms equipped with high-quality stereo equipment, namely, in spaces capable of mediating the aesthetic. It is precisely the relative immunity of such sites from the constellation of elements by which we imagine the modern—those dramatically on display in my urban sketch—that enables aesthetic listening to occur. The more those elements are brought back into the site of audition—say moving from home to car, from concert hall to street corner, from Marantz to Toshiba, from Europe to the Middle East—listening suffers a proportional loss of descriptive force.

19. For a fully developed critique of this position, see Hirschkind 2001c.

20. Seremetakis notes, and criticizes, a similar form of analysis in the context of historical writings on Greece: "The notions of authenticity and inauthenticity are symbiotic concepts that equally repress and silence non-contemporaneous and discordant cultural experiences and sensibilities. Thus the modernist critic would look at Greek society and dismiss any residues and incongruities emanating from the pre-modern as both romantic and invented. In both cases, static impositions of the polarity authentic/inauthentic led to the dismissal of important discontinuous cultural systems and sensibilities that have been repositioned within the modern as non-synchronous elements" (1994:17).

21. See Hobsbawm and Ranger 1992 for one influential account of this kind of reasoning.

22. In *The Names of History: On the Poetics of Knowledge* (1994), Jacques Rancière examines some of the narratives tropes by which forms of religious reasoning are effaced in accord with the precepts of secular history. His specific focus is on some of the classical texts of the historians of the Annales School.

23. Even the objects, methods, and forms of practical reason within the natural sciences, as historians of science have long asserted, are, to a certain extent, incommensurable from one field to the next (Hacking 1983; Rouse 1987; Latour 1993).

24. For studies into modern listening practices, see Bull and Back 2003; Corbin 1998; Drobnick 2004; Erlmann 2004; Kahn 1992; B. Smith 1999.

25. As the historian of media Douglas Kahn notes, the ability of sound to pervade, encompass, and integrate—in contrast to the distance and separation established by vision—made it "the privileged figure of sensory interchange" within romantic thought: "Wherever sound occurred, it was always manifested elsewhere, or other things were manifested through it; a sound had no autonomy but was always relational, being somewhere or something else, a constant deflection that ultimately stretched out to spiritually organize everything from essence to cosmos, always ringing with the voice and music" (1992:15).

26. For works on the role of auditory technologies in extending human capacities of sensory experience and refashioning modern soundscapes, see Corbin 1998; Kahn 1992; B. Smith 1991.

27. This emphasis on the cognitive dimensions of listening owes, in part, to what Derrida identifies as phonocentrism: our image of speech as a site where meaning is rendered transparent to consciousness of both speaker and listener (Derrida 1988). Jean Luc Nancy makes a similar observation when he argues that the question of listening within philosophy (and I would add in the human sciences as well) has often been subsumed under the problem of *understanding*: "La philosophie n'a-t-elle pas d'avance et forcement superpose ou bien substitute à l'écoute queque chose qui serait plutôt de l'ordre de l'entente?" (Nancy 2002, 13).

28. On the conceptual history of experience and its diminishing contribution to the imagination of the future, see Reinhardt Koselleck's *Futures Past* (1985).

29. A useful elaboration of Aristotle's notion of practice is found in MacIntyre 1984.

30. Some of signal publications by anthropologists working in this field (in addition to those I discuss below) include: Classen 1993; Feldman 1991; Howes 2003; Jackson 1989; Scheper-Hughes and Lock 1987; Taussig 1993.

31. One of the central questions addressed by Desjarlais concerns the opacity of bodily experience to analysis. To overcome this epistemological problem, he suggests, anthropologists must learn native ways of using the body through their own bodily participation in the daily activities of their informants (Desjarlais 1992:26). One must seek to acquire, in other words, not only a thorough grasp of native perceptual categories and their use in public life but the habitus of those for whom such categories are meaningful. A similar argument can be heard in Paul Stoller's (1997) call for anthropologists to pay more attention to their own bodies as instruments of sensory knowledge and experience. While I do think there are a number of serious issues to be raised in regard to questions about the communicability of experience, the approach I have adopted addresses concepts of sensory experience in terms of what Wittgenstein calls their "grammar"—namely, the way they are used within specific social practices,

where both interior states (feelings, sensations, etc.) and exterior actions are given expression in publicly available ways (see Wittgenstein 1958; Das 1998).

32. Despite a shared concern for the embodied character of action and perception, the analysis I will present here also departs sharply from the sort of phenomenological approach Csordas has elaborated. Specifically, while Csordas has focused on identifying the preobjective foundations, or habitus, upon which a religious discourse erects its particular discursive architecture, my own work has been concerned with the practical techniques (such as sermon audition) by which the bodily dispositions that underlie virtuous conduct are inculcated. For an ethnographically rich study that draws extensively on Csordas's analytical framework, see Geurts 2003.

33. A growing body of anthropological literature focusing on auditory practices has emerged in the last few years. A fine sampling of this writing can be found in three edited volumes: Bull and Beck 2004; Drobnick 2004; and Erlmann 2004.

2. ISLAM, NATIONALISM, AND AUDITION

1. On the topics of *'ilm al-balagha*, al-Jurjani, and Arabic semantics more generally, see Abu Deeb 1979, Larkin 1995, and Smyth 1992.

2. *Mu'jiz*, an Arabic word from the same root as *i'jaz*, is usually translated into English as "miracle," especially one performed by a prophet. The etymologies of the English and Arabic terms provide a revealing comparison. Lane elaborates the theological meaning of the Arabic term *mu'jiz* as follows: it is "an event at variance with the usual course [of nature], produced by means of one who lays claim to the office of a prophet, in contending with those who disacknowledge [his claim], in such a manner as renders them unable to produce the like thereof" (1984:1961). *Mu'jiz*, in other words, denotes an action performed within the context of an argument. As such, it presupposes a rhetorical situation of debate and contestation. Paradigmatically, this act is one of speech, with the Quran as its primary reference. The English word "miracle," on the other hand, derives from the Latin *mirari*, meaning "to wonder at," an act involving the eyes and the face (the English word "smile" comes from the same root). As a manifestation of divine intervention, its primary mode of perception is visual.

3. Admittedly, there is a tradition of rhetoric, *'ilm al-khataba*, derived directly from Greek sources (particularly Aristotle), which had become a part of the curriculum of advanced studies in institutions of religious learning by the medieval period. Muslim philosophers, informed by Aristotle's work, saw rhetoric as a form of argumentation appropriate for the masses who were incapable of following the philosophical rigor involved in dialectical demonstration. While some of the principles of this discipline undoubtedly found their way into popular oratorical practice, it remained for the most part a topic of philosophical inquiry with little effect on traditions of the sermon. See Goodman 1992 and Smyth 1992.

4. As many scholars have pointed out, Islamic piety combines more rationalistic approaches to the divine text with an attitude of reverential celebration for its miraculous beauty and the grandeur of its eloquence (Denny 1980, 1981; Graham 1985, 1987; Madigan 1995). However, when we speak of Muslim practices as *combining* both rational and aesthetic strands, we must avoid the supposition—embedded in our grammar—that those strands may be conceptually and analytically disarticulated in accord with our own categories. The *art* of Quranic recitation, for instance, stands in a distinct relationship to practices of rational inquiry: its study, according to the fifteenth-century scholar Ibn Khaldun, is as essential to the development of capacities of moral reasoning as are the disciplines of exegesis and theology (Ibn Khaldun 1958:436–47).

5. All translations of the Quran are from M. Asad 1980. Numbers refer to chapter and verse.

6. This active sense of hearing is evident in the range of meanings expressed by the Arabic word "*sam'*." *Sam'* can be translated not only as "to hear," but also as the more explicitly active verbs "to answer," "to comply with," "to accept," and "to obey" (Lane [1863] 1984:1429). The English verb "to hear" also encompasses a similar semantic range.

7. One finds models of active listening within various traditions. The Stoics, for example, developed an art of listening as one of the primary techniques for the cultivation of virtue. Plutarch, among others, wrote extensively on the requirements of a proper and edifying audition, devoting considerable attention to the passions that either impede or facilitate audition of philosophical discourse as well as to the improvement of the soul produced through such exercise. Elaborating on the virtues of a skilled listener, he wrote, "He ought to inspect diligently and try faithfully the state and temper of his mind after hearing, if any of his affections are more moderate, if any afflictions grow lighter, if his constancy and greatness of spirit are confirmed, if he feels any divine emotions or inward workings of virtue and goodness upon his soul" (Plutarch 1881:401). For the Stoics, the edifying discourses of philosophy do not in and of themselves produce the virtuous soul. Rather, the crafting of the enlightened soul falls to the hearer who, through the exercise of perfecting his skills of audition, hones his sensibilities and emotions into their highest form. See Zulick 1992 for a discussion of agentive listening in relation to ancient Hebrew.

8. Key texts within this debate include *Dhamm al-malahi*, by Ibn Abu al-Dunya; *Bawariq al-ilma'*, by Majd al-Din al-Tusi al-Ghazali; *Talbis iblis*, by Ibn al-Jawzi; and a section of Abu Hamid al-Ghazali's famous work, *Ihya' 'ulum al-din*. For useful discussions on the history of the sam' debate, see During 1997; Lewisohn 1997; Shiloah 1963.

9. The theory of emotion underlying the notion of *tarab* bears a resemblance to that which informs the Hindi notion of *bhaw* ("emotion") in Bhatgaon in the Fiji Islands. As Donald Brenneis describes it, *bhaw* "carries the multidimensional meaning of (1) a situation of interpersonal amity, (2) the display of the mutually

respectful and amiable demeanor that embodies this amity, and (3) the experience of that state" (1990:118). *Bhaw* is less an attribute of people than it is a
quality of an event as expressed by those who participate in it.

10. Interestingly, many of the preachers today who are critical of what they perceive
to be the dangers and excesses of mystical Islamic trends are also those who
make the most extensive use of Sufi techniques in their sermons (see chapter 3).
Such seemingly paradoxical practices are not new. As Berkey reminds us, even
Ibn Taymiyya, a fourteenth-century scholar whose attacks on Sufism provide a
point of reference for many Egyptian Muslims today, was himself a member of a
Sufi order (2001:91). This pattern has tended to be the rule more than the exception and points to the inadequacy of considering Sufism as a tradition separate
from orthodox Islam rather than an argument within it.

11. See Calverly 1943 for a useful overview of Islamic understandings of the soul.

12. A similar view can be discerned in Plato. As Iris Murdoch, commenting on
Plato's psychology, succinctly put it: "We cannot escape the causality of sin. We
are told in the *Theaetetus* (176–7) that the inescapable penalty of wickedness is
simply to be the sort of person that one is, and in the *Laws*, that evil-doers are
in Hades in this world" (Murdoch 1977:39).

13. From the earliest preachers to their media-based heirs today, such performers
have been regularly subject to criticism for blurring the boundary between ethics and entertainment. For a discussion of the often tense relationship between
Muslim rulers and popular preachers in the medieval period, see Berkey 2001.

14. A similar psychological model is found in certain strands of Christianity, as
in the work of the nineteenth-century Catholic thinker John Henry Newman.
Newman asserts, for example, that "one important effect of living the religious
life is that it schools the imagination," enhancing our capacity to grasp the truth
of religious arguments (Newman [1870] 1979:415). Living impiously, in contrast,
dulls our sensibilities until we become unable to recognize the error of our
actions.

15. The *sunna* refers to the authoritative example set by Muhammad, as evidenced
in his words and actions, his decisions to not take action, and the attributes of
his character (*sifat*). Daniel Brown's short book (1996) on the history of debates
on the status of the *sunna* provides an excellent introduction to the topic.

16. In *The Calligraphic State* (1993), Brinkley Messick provides a rich account of
how such an aural ethics was embodied in the institutions of learning and jurisprudence in nineteenth-century Yemen. In chapter 4, I explore how this same
tradition has found a very different articulation in relation to the normative
structures of a modern public sphere.

17. On the topic of Augustinian rhetoric, hermeneutics, and language theory, see
Colish [1968] 1983. Todorov (1982) provides a useful discussion of Augustinian
rhetoric and hermeneutics; however, by locating Augustine within a history of
Western skepticism toward rhetoric, he tends to undervalue the contribution of
the discipline throughout the medieval period.

18. Timothy Mitchell (1988) explores the introduction of new forms of moral, political, linguistic, and spatial organization into colonial Egypt. For a critical discussion of Mitchell's original and thoughtful analysis, see Hirschkind 1991.

19. Chatterjee describes a similar transformation in postcolonial India, where the modernizing state has increasingly assigned to itself the role of theologian in order to schematize the heterogeneity of practices now identified as religious in accord with its project of national reform (Chatterjee 1994, 1995).

20. There was considerable debate during the late nineteenth century between liberal and Islamic reformers about what exactly the role of the press should be. In broad terms, liberals promoted bourgeois conceptions of the press as a site for open public debate on issues relevant to the public of national citizens, a debate to which, as they cast it, the knowledges and practices of religion had little to contribute. However, many religious thinkers and other Islamic intellectuals argued that the press should be organized around a pastoral model founded on Islamic modes of authority, and thus should undertake the guidance and correction of the Islamic community, a community, however, now transected by a strong nationalist element. Al-Kumi's two-volume history of the Egyptian press (1992), in Arabic, provides an overview of these debates.

21. See Gasper 2001 on Nadim's contribution to turn-of-the-century reformist thought.

22. For a discussion of Abduh's proposal, and of the professionalization of preaching in Egypt more generally, see Gaffney's extremely well-researched and informative article (1991).

23. In the context of early-twentieth-century Egypt, the term *salafi* refers to the Islamic reform movement centered around Muhammad Abduh, Rashid Rida, and their followers.

24. For information on the institutional reforms of preaching in Egypt, see Abd al-Nabi 1995; Gaffney 1991; Skovgaard-Petersen 1997; and Zeghal 1996

25. In addition to these pedagogical institutions, a variety of administrative bodies concerned with preaching were also established from the 1950s onward, located across a number of different government ministries and agencies. In the 1960s, for example, a General Administration of Preaching (*waʿz*) and Guidance (*irshad*) was established and subsequently renamed the General Administration of Daʿwa and Media. Similarly, a High Council of Islamic Daʿwa was established in 1983, with the head of al-Azhar as its director, to oversee and coordinate a wide variety of state activities now defined as *daʿwa*.

26. We know from medieval documents that the function of *khatib* was generally filled (at least in the larger mosques, for which there are records) by educated men whose primary occupations were as scholars, teachers, notaries, and Quran reciters (Chamberlain 1994; Berkey 1992). The wages paid to these *khutabaʿ* were considerably lower than those of other religious functionaries, and must have served as a supplement to income derived from other more

lucrative occupations. In the smaller mosques and outside of the major cities, the role of *khatib*, to the extent it was enacted at all, was usually performed by some respected member of the local community or neighborhood for little or no remuneration.

27. A *hadith* (pl. *ahadith*) is a prophetic tradition from the authoritative record of the Prophet's exemplary speech and actions. When *hadith* is preceded by the definite article—the *hadith*—it indicates the entire body of prophetic traditions. An explanation of this concept is found in Robson 1999.

28. In the first decade of the twentieth century, Muhammad Abduh, acting on behalf of the Ministry of Religious Affairs (*wizarat al-awqaf*), authorized the first systematic study of the Egyptian mosques that were under the jurisdiction of the ministry (Abduh [1906] 1972). Of note is the fact that in this study less than half of those mosque employees characterized as "*imam-khatib* [prayer-sermon leader]" held any academic degree at all. This was even more likely to be the case in the much larger number of mosques not affiliated with the ministry and consequently not mentioned in Abduh's study.

29. Brinkley Messick's description of the reorganization of the institution of the fatwa in Yemen over the course of the nineteenth and twentieth centuries focuses on a similar process of social disembedding (1993).

30. A summary of different opinions on the *khutba* can be found in Wensinck (1979:74). For sources in Arabic, see al-Sayyid Sabiq, *Fiqh al-sunna*, one of the most popular contemporary reference works on Islamic doctrine, which includes extensive discussion of scholarly views on the performance of *khutba* ([1945] 1994:221–36). Discussions of the doctrinal requirements of the *khutba* are discussed in the works of many medieval scholars. One of the most extensive treatments of this topic can be found in a book by the medieval Jewish scholar al-Attar ([1324] 1996).

31. Among the most popular of these new preaching manuals were *Kayfa takun khatib*, by Ali Rifa'i Muhammad (1972), and *Hidayat al-murshidin ila turuq al-wa'z wa al-khataba*, by Ali Mahfuz (1979). There are scores of books put out every year on the subject of preaching by presses specializing in Islamic topics. Those works I encountered most often in the collections of the *khutaba'* I came to know in Cairo include Bayumi 1988, M. al-Ghazali 1980, Hani'a 1995, Khalif 1986, Kishk 1990, Mahfuz 1984, Abd al-Rahman 1992, and Saqr 1990a.

32. While the shift I have described is most evident in manuals written by state-affiliated authors, its impact is also evident in the writings of figures associated with the Islamic opposition movement. Thus, a recent book entitled *al-Da'wa al-mu'athira* (Effective preaching), written by an author associated with *Hizb al-'amal*, a political party allied with the Muslim Brotherhood, defines the three primary effects of successful preaching: (1) leading the listener to a firm conviction, (2) enabling him or her to develop personal perspective, and (3) helping him or her to choose the right solution to a problem without compulsion (Madi 1995:16). In this regard, we might also note that Egypt's most popular

preacher during the 1990s, Muhammad Hassan, was a graduate of the Department of Communications at Cairo University.

33. This practice was begun under Nasser, but attempts to enforce it have intensified as security concerns have mounted.

34. More recently, in 2003, the Egyptian state attempted to impose a law stipulating that all preachers in Egypt would read the same official sermon throughout the country. In the face of strong opposition from within the state's own religious institutions, coupled with the difficulty of enforcing such a law, the attempt was quickly withdrawn.

35. For the passing of this legislation and the ongoing opposition to it from a range of sources, including the *ʿulamaʾ* from al-Azhar, see *al-Hayat* 1996a, 1996b, 1997a. Useful discussions of this topic in English are found in Moustafa 2000 and Zeghal 1999.

36. For a comprehensive survey of nongovernmental religious organizations in Egypt, see al-Ahram Center for Political and Strategic Studies 1996. A still unequaled study of the early history of the Muslim Brotherhood is that by R. Mitchell (1993).

37. Among them were Abd al-Hamid Kishk, Muhammad al-Ghazali, Wagdi Ghunaim, Muhammad Mitwalli al-Shaʿrawi, and Ahmad al-Mahlawi.

38. The history of this institution is discussed in Aroian 1983.

39. The particular emphasis on the Prophet's exemplary practice common to both of these groups generally leads to their being classified as belonging to the "*salafi*" current. While Muhammad Abduh is an important intellectual figure in their teachings, they also rely heavily on the works of Ibn Taymiyya and Ibn al-Qayyim, and thus diverge considerably from the *salafiyya* movement earlier in the century that was led most prominently by Abduh and Rashid Rida. For a history of the *salafi* movement in Egypt, see Hourani 1983; Skovgaard-Petersen 1997.

40. These two associations combined administer over ten thousand mosques in Egypt today.

41. At the time of my fieldwork in the late 1990s, there were six licensed companies in operation in Cairo that produced and distributed taped sermons, the largest three of these having additional distribution centers outside of Cairo, primarily in the cities of Alexandria, Mansura, and Suez. These same three companies also exported tapes abroad. In addition to sermon tapes, many of these companies also sold other items often associated with Islamist social trends, such as headscarves and modest dress styles for women, the long white shirts (*jallabiyya*) commonly worn by Egyptian men, perfumes and scented oils, incense, and books and pamphlets from Islamist publishers. The tapes were purchased at wholesale prices by retailers and resold either in small stores located in popular neighborhoods or from stalls set up around the medium-sized and larger mosques on Fridays. Wholesale prices were around 2 Egyptian pounds per tape ($0.78) and the retail price averaged around 3 pounds ($1.17). Tapes were also

bought directly by mosques and Islamic welfare and pedagogical associations, which then lent them out to patrons or used them as teaching tools.

42. Kepel (1993), among others, has emphasized the role of income generated from labor in the Gulf as an important economic condition enabling the cassette-sermon phenomenon in Egypt. As I elaborate later in this chapter, I find the economic determinism of this argument unconvincing in light of the limited role of commercial sales relative to total tape circulation.

43. For a description of Kishk's political impact during these years, see Esposito 1992; Gaffney 1994; Kepel 1993; and Zeghal 1996.

44. One of the most frequently cited and well known stories from the autobiography of Shaykh Kishk refers to an instance when, during one of the periods of his imprisonment, his guards placed a German shepherd in his cell that had been trained to attack prisoners. The dog, according to the account, lay down next to Kishk, who was prostrate in prayer, as if to join him in praying. See Kishk 1986.

45. Among popular *khutaba'* in Egypt, Shaykh Sha'rawi was, until his death a few years ago, the only one who was allowed to give lessons and sermons on television, where he also frequently showed up in the company of President Mubarak. Despite this official approval, Sha'rawi has at times supported positions contrary to those of the government. For example, during the early 1990s he and a group of other prominent religious figures called for the opening of some form of dialogue with militant Islamist groups, a suggestion flatly rejected by the government. For a discussion of Sha'rawi's career, see Quijano-Gonzalez 1997.

46. Statistics on the actual number of tapes sold in Egypt are generally unavailable, and those figures sometimes suggested by journalists are extremely unreliable. My own rough estimate, based on data collected in interviews with company owners, is that approximately one million tapes are produced commercially each year, with another one to two million being produced and sold illegally. That being said, the fact that most of the tapes in circulation are fourth-generation copies, reproduced noncommercially, makes any real approximation practically impossible.

47. For example, when the government submitted new legislation to the Egyptian parliament restricting press freedoms, Abd al-Sabbur Shahin strongly condemned it. He was finally barred from preaching in early 1997, though he has retained his professorship at Cairo University's Dar al-Ulum.

48. Admittedly, the degree of representation afforded to contestatory movements has at times been extremely restricted, and television, the most widely popular form of media, has remained entirely off-limits to the Islamists.

49. The response to Kishk is an obvious example of such calculations. Although Kishk's popularity during the 1970s was clearly seen as a danger by the state, there was also the ongoing risk that his removal might provoke protest demonstrations or impel his followers toward a more radical activism—beyond what Kishk himself advocated. In addition, as is well known, in the mid-1970s the

Sadat regime attempted to defuse Islamist opposition by letting up on some of the repressive measures that had been applied to them under Nasser. For discussions of Egyptian state policies in regard to Islamist movements, see Baker 2003, Moustafa 2000, Mustafa 1995, Voll 1991.

50. For discussions of the changing role of the *'ulama'* of al-Azhar in contemporary Egyptian society, see Babeair 1993, Eccel 1988, Moustafa 2000, and Zeghal 1996.

51. While differences between these two distinct ideologies of language inform contemporary debates over the role and proper interpretation of Islamic traditions within Egyptian society, actual practices often incorporate aspects of both views. Webb Keane has explored how tensions between contrasting concepts of self and language shape the ritual practices of Protestant Christians in Sumba, Indonesia (2002). On the one hand, Sumbanese Christianity incorporates a referential notion of language emphasizing the transparency of words to thought; on the other hand, formal interactions continue to rely on long-standing traditions of performance with their distinct speech pragmatics. As Keane observes: "The apparent disjuncture between the idea of sincere belief and the formality with which it is expressed is not simply a matter of an incomplete or 'syncretic' transition from 'traditional' to 'modern' in Sumba. Given this semiotic overdetermination, it may be impossible to fully disarticulate these two sources for this performance style" (2002:82).

3. THE ETHICS OF LISTENING

1. By "godly speech," I refer not only to the Quran but to a vast range of locutions. As Padwick (1996) shows in her analysis of popular Islamic devotional sayings drawn from both Middle Eastern and South Asian materials, many of the expressions used in ordinary speech (prayers, supplications, and other pious locutions) are commonly understood to bestow ethical benefit to both speakers and listeners.

2. The first verse of "al-Sharh" ("The Opening-Up of the Heart," Quran 94) begins: "Have we not opened up thy heart, and lifted from thee the burden that had weighed so heavily on thy back?"

3. My argument here bears a certain similarity to that put forward by a number of cognitive linguists. In *Metaphors We Live By* (1980), Lakoff and Johnson suggest that metaphor, as a process by which we characterize one domain of meaning in terms of another, is fundamental to much of our everyday discourse and not simply a creative literary device. In later writings, these authors argue that such cross-domain mapping involves what they refer to as "image schemata," cognitive constructs grounded in repeated patterns of bodily experience that are then applied to other regions of discourse and experience (Lakoff and Johnson 1999; Johnson 1987). Our sense of verticality, for example, rooted in myriad activities and perceptions such as the feeling of standing upright, the activity of climbing

stairs, viewing tall objects such as trees, and so on, provides a conceptual metaphor for other domains, such as emotions (as when we say we are feeling "up" or "down"), health (e.g., being in "top shape"), or music (e.g., a "high note," an "ascending scale"). A useful summary of this work as it relates to the audition of music is found in Zbikowski 1998. Where my argument here departs from these authors is in its focus on the specific methods of inculcation through which such perceptual patterning is learned.

4. Published in 1925, Jousse's work, *Le style oral rhythmique et mnemotechnique chez les verbo-moteurs*, strongly influenced Milman Parry in his innovative reassessment of Homeric poetry. For a brief discussion of Jousse's contribution to the study of oral traditions, see Sienaert 1990.

5. Jousse composed, in medieval fashion, by citing extensively from a vast library of memorized texts, inserting his own connecting phrases in the sections marked off in brackets. His references, in this case, are Ribot (1914:10) and Draghiesco (1928:333), though his text does not indicate which part of the quotation derives from which author.

6. In his *Opticks*, Newton argued that vibrations in the ether acted on the organs of the ear and brain to produce the sensation of light. He then went on to extend his idea of sensory vibrations to motor processes as well. For a discussion of the impact of Newtonian mechanics on eighteenth-century vitalist theories and notions of sensibility, see Riskin 2002; Roach 1993:93–115.

7. Jousse's ideas on memory bear an obvious debt to Henri Bergson ([1896] 1990), and he cites from Bergson at numerous points in his text.

8. R. G. Collingwood, in *The Principles of Art* (1966), describes aesthetic appreciation in terms very reminiscent of Jousse. For example: "What we get from looking at a picture is not merely the experience of seeing, or even partly seeing and partly imagining; it is also, and in Mr. Berenson's opinion more importantly, the imaginary experience of certain complicated muscular movements" (Collingwood 1966:148). Collingwood understood speech as one specialized form of bodily gesture, distinguished from others in that it may be perceived by both eye and ear. Much as speech must be understood as an action performed by the body in its entirety, so also must our responses to sensation, as when we listen to music or view a painting.

9. Jousse's vision has a distinct resemblance to ideas of memory in the practices of medieval Christian monks and scholars, in which memory was managed gesturally and acoustically. Thomas Aquinas, for instance, subscribing to an Aristotelian notion of the unity of the body and soul, insisted that all knowledge had a somatic component, including an emotional charge acquired in the ruminative process that turned sense impressions into memory. As Mary Carruthers notes in her description of Aquinas's psychology of human knowledge, "Thus all stages and varieties of knowledge for human beings, from the most concrete to the most abstract, occur in some way within a physical matrix. The phantasms are produced by *imaginatio*, the image-making power, which, like memory, is an

'affection' (to use Aristotle's term) or 'motion' (to use that of Averroes) of the soul, motions which are physiological although not simply that, in the way that a house is bricks but not 'simply bricks'" (1996:54). Indeed, some of the Islamic ethical practices I describe in the following chapters can be traced through medieval traditions common to both European and Arab contexts.

10. While these schools had declined in number and attendance with the rise of obligatory secular education for children in Egypt, they have experienced something of a comeback, especially in poorer neighborhoods, in the context of the Islamic Revival of recent decades. See Starrett 1998:118–19.

11. The most interesting works in English on this topic are Denny 1980, 1981; Gade 2004; Graham 1985, 1987; Nelson 1985; and Sells 1999. Among the most influential classical Muslim treatments of this topic are those of A. H. al-Ghazali (1984), from the eleventh century, and Abu Zakariya Yahya al-Nawawi (n.d.), from the thirteenth.

12. The verse cited is from "Surat al-Isra'" (Quran 17:109). The bracketed sections are in the original translation.

13. The exercises of ethical attunement described by al-Ghazali continue to inform the practice of recitation today. A recent rector of al-Azhar University, Abd al-Halim Mahmud, echoes al-Ghazali's commentary in a fatwa advising people that they should, while reading the Quran, "pause and respond to words by enacting what is called for, asking forgiveness, regretting their misdeeds, imploring salvation when reading verses of warning or retribution ['adhab], and so on" (Mahmud 1986).

14. Bourdieu's notion of habitus has obvious resonances with aspects of the approach I have outlined here. However, insomuch as Bourdieu grounds his discussion of this notion in relation to structures of socioeconomic power, he leaves unaddressed the extent to which habitus is also generated and molded by other histories, whether those embodied in a community's existing modes of practice and association, or those fashioned as contingent assemblages from sensory materials submerged beneath the dominant forms of public memory. A habitus may outlive the material conditions that gave rise to it by renewing, reinforcing, and adapting the practices of social and individual discipline that sustain and anchor it. Such continuity does not reflect the durability of embodied dispositions, as Bourdieu suggests (1990:62), but the variety of community-grounded resources that a group is able to bring to the task of maintaining socially valued traditions. These traditions, of course, are continually revised as they adjust to changing sets of material conditions, but the direction of those adjustments is also determined from within those traditions by, among other things, the disciplinary practices through which culturally valued modes of perception, appraisal, and action are inculcated and self-reflexively renewed. On this point, see Cantwell 1999 and Hirschkind 2001b.

15. This is frequently marked grammatically through use of the collective plural, as in, "We praise Him, and we rely on Him, we ask His forgiveness," one of the more common sermon openings.

16. My use of the term "soma-ethical" is inspired in Shusterman's essay on "somaes-thetics" (2002). In this essay, Shusterman explores Wittgenstein's understanding of emotion and bodily sensation, and particularly Wittgenstein's critique of the idea (attributed by Wittgenstein to William James) that mental concepts like will, emotion, or aesthetic judgment can be explained by reference to somatic feelings or private experience. In accord with his broader view of language, Witt-genstein argues that the meaning of such concepts lies in the specific behavioral contexts—the language games—in which they are used and publicly assessed (see Wittgenstein 1958). In his careful reading of Wittgenstein's later writings, Shusterman shows that contrary to what has often been assumed, Wittgenstein's argument is not that bodily sensations are cognitively insignificant. While somatic experiences are not the object of our aesthetic judgments, and thus cannot be said to cause or explain those judgments, they can according to Witt-genstein sharpen our ability to attend to and appreciate works of art. Attention to what Shusterman calls our somaesthetic feelings, in other words, may enable us to shape our (aesthetic) responses, hone our skills until these become part of our unreflective cognitive equipment.

17. Padwick, in her study of Islamic devotional practices, describes *itmi'nan* (or *tumanina*) as the state of physical and spiritual stillness that is achieved by way of repentance. As she notes: "*Tumanina*, then, for all its stillness, *tranquillus tranquillans*, is no drowsy peace, but a gift of grace that can only come to hearts ready to make the response of faith and costly discipline" (1996:123).

18. Modern theater audiences who go to Shakespearean plays or concert audiences already thoroughly familiar with the compositions they choose to see or hear performed participate in a similar manner: despite a foreknowledge of the story or musical score, the audience evaluates the quality of the performance in terms of its ability to evoke in them a range of emotional and intellectual experiences. For two insightful approaches to the analysis of storytelling, see Tedlock 1983 and Zumthor 1990.

19. One of the most popular is a series of mosque lessons by Umar Abd al-Kafi entitled "Dar al-Akhira" (The hereafter), consisting of thirty-three tapes.

20. In this regard, the ambivalence that Stokes (in press) describes in relation to the singer Abd al-Halim Hafiz is registered in the moniker given to him by his fans: "Mr. Tape Recorder."

21. For anthropological analyses of emotion in relation to poetic practice in Arabic contexts, see Abu Lughod 1986 and Caton 1990.

22. Such an understanding of the unity of thought, emotion, and action has deep roots in the Hellenic and Judeo-Christian traditions that preceded and influ-enced the development of Islam. As Onians notes in his exploration of the Greek concepts of mind, body, and soul, for the early Greeks: "Perception or cogni-tion is associated with or immediately followed by an emotion and a tendency to action varying in degree and kind according to the nature of the object. . . . Where cognition and thought are so bound up with feeling and a tendency to act, the relation of moral character, of virtue to knowledge, is closer than where

cognition is more 'pure'" (1951:16–18). Onians argues that for the Greeks of Homer's time, the verb "to know" did not refer to something purely intellectual or cognitive; nor was it simply used, as some translators of Homer have argued, to express disposition and character. These interpretations fail to grasp the way the ancient Greeks understood the relation of knowledge to emotion and conation, a relation predicated upon a notion of the self as a unity of body and soul. Such an understanding is evident in the tendency of the early Greeks to explain cognitive functions in terms of physiological processes. In this way, the body and the soul are understood in accord with a common conceptual field.

23. A graduate in communication studies from Cairo University, Hassan produced some of the most popular sermons in Egypt during the 1990s. He worked as a preacher in Saudi Arabia for several years, and upon his return to Egypt attained his popularity under the auspices of one of the largest non-governmental *da'wa* organizations, Ahl al-Sunna al-Muhammadiyya. The Egyptian government banned Hassan from preaching in 1997 at the peak of his popularity, on the charge that his sharply critical views of the Egyptian government posed a threat to national security. A few years later this ban was dropped and Hassan returned to preaching.

24. See chapter 5 for a more in-depth discussion of this rhetorical technique.

25. There is a vast body of literature on the impact of alphabetic systems on language. Those I have found most useful include W. Ong 1982; Havelock 1986; Illich and Sanders 1988.

26. An extensive discussion of Greek and Roman ideas about the interrelations of the body, the mind, and the soul is found in Onians 1951.

27. I borrow the expression from Dreyfus who, commenting on Heidegger, notes: "Heidegger wants to show that we are not normally thematically conscious of our ongoing everyday activity, and that where thematic self-referential consciousness does arise, it presupposes a non-thematic, non-self-referential mode of awareness" (1994:58).

28. The other categories are *inventio, dispositio, elocutio*, and *memoria*. See McKeon 1942, 1987.

29. It is interesting to compare this model of language with Derrida's critique of phonocentrism, the metaphysical suppositions of transparent communication he links to voice (1988). His reversal of the precedence of speech over writing, a hierarchy central to modern linguists, and his assimilation of the former to the category of the latter have been useful in highlighting one thread of Western reflection on language. But what can the metaphysics of presence tell us about the speech situation described here? How can Derrida's expanded notion of "writing" embrace *this kind* of linguistic performance? The paralinguistic, phonetic, affective, and gestural qualities of this performance are not simply the material anchors for an ideology vouchsafing the transparency and authority of the act. To a large extent, they are the act. They don't secure the presence of that which is actually only *represented* in discourse, only their own presence

as integral components of a total performance. Moreover, this is not simply a time-honored stipulation of the ritual but rather is grounded in the quality and character of a specific form of speech act. If we follow Collingwood's insight that "dance is the mother of all languages" insofar as language is a system of gestures (laryngeal, labial, and otherwise) produced by a human body in its unity and entirety (1966:243–44), we are then drawn to investigate how the linguistic conventions governing a particular speech situation determine which elements from this dance are essential to the success of the speech act.

30. As Augustine argued: "If, however, the hearers require to be roused rather than instructed, in order that they may be diligent to do what they already know, and to bring their feelings into harmony with the truths they admit, greater vigor of speech is needed. Here entreaties and reproaches, exhortations and upbraidings, and all other means of rousing the emotions, are necessary" (1973:496).

31. Thus, early-modern Christian preachers, informed by a moral psychology that saw reason alone as incapable of producing action without the assistance of the passions, geared much of their preaching to the governance of the passions, a task that included not just the modulation of emotional intensities but also the linking of those emotions to their proper objects. See Brinton 1992 for a discussion of this issue in relation to eighteenth-century British sermons.

32. Collingwood makes a distinction between "imaginary motor sensations" and "actual motor sensations" that I do not think is useful for the context of sermon audition (1966:147). As I have described, the responses of the people I worked with to sermon speech fell along a continuum from those without any perceivable component to those easily noted by an observer. At one time fear would be visible in an informant's posture and expression and at other times not, despite his claim to be feeling fear. This may be usefully understood, I would argue, not through a distinction between actual and imaginary experiences but between different kinds of intensities, degrees of experiential involvement.

33. This affinity owes primarily to the privileging of oral verse, a form that, for Jousse and also many Sufi thinkers, bore a more natural relation to the order of the cosmos than did more prosaic forms. As Jousse notes in a characteristic remark: "naturally too, as we have just seen, 'the only ordinary language of these supposedly inferior people is spoken poetry, every part of which is filled with tender living metaphors' (Marius-Ary Leblond: 408). 'By the very constitution of human nature' (Saint Thomas) 'this physical sensual character' is, psycho-physiologically, bound to 'the main feature' of these genuinely living manual and oral languages" (Jousse [1925] 1990:44).

34. This point should not be confused with a more common argument of modern Christian origin. Christian thinkers like Kierkegaard and William James claimed that reason alone was not enough to compel someone to believe in Scripture and that it thus fell to the passions to bridge this gap. Today when Christians speak about religious belief as a practice of the heart more than the rational mind, it is usually this modern view they are expressing.

35. For scholars who have explored this issue with great acuity, see T. Asad 1993; Chakrabarty 2000; Seremetakis 1994.

4. CASSETTES AND COUNTERPUBLICS

1. This progressivist account is most frequently associated with the work of W. Ong (1982) and Goody (1986, 1987), but also played a role in the work of such theorists of modernization as Lerner (1958). Habermas's (1989) influential discussion of the role of print and new reading practices in constituting the bourgeois public sphere has also become a key point of reference for anthropologists interested in media. For recent work on the Middle East emphasizing the deliberative aspect of Islamic media, see Eickelman 1992, 1997; and Eickelman and Anderson 1997; as well as some of the contributions to the volume edited by Augustus Norton (1995) addressing civil society in the Middle East.

2. For scholars focusing on the ideological or disciplinary aspects of Islamic media, see al-Azmeh 1993; Etienne 1983; Kepel 1993; Mohammedi and Mohammedi 1994; Roy 1996; Sivan 1990. For more complicated approaches to the entwining of dialogue and discipline in different media contexts, see Bowen 1993; Street 1993; and Warner 1990.

3. My use of the term "counterpublic" diverges from that of Nancy Fraser, whose 1992 article on "subaltern counterpublics" provides an important and influential elaboration of the notion. For Fraser, counterpublics are those discursive arenas where subordinate groups articulate viewpoints, interests, and identities that stand opposed to the hegemonic discourses of bourgeois society. Their status as counterpublics owes to the oppositional content of their claims, not to any fundamental difference in ideas of what a public is and what it does. In contrast, I use the term "counterpublic" to interrogate a set of discursive practices founded on a very different conceptual articulation of the public than that provided by liberal-democratic traditions.

4. Scholars of the public sphere have tended to dismiss the role of the virtues as inessential or irrelevant to processes of public debate. To predicate public deliberation and participation upon the prior cultivation of a set of virtues, it is argued, only makes sense in the context of an Aristotelian notion that we as human beings have certain definable ends which those virtues enable us to achieve—a notion that has no place in a liberal society committed to value pluralism and individual autonomy. On the view of theorists of liberty from Hobbes to Isaiah Berlin, to root political participation in civic virtue is to impose a demand on the citizen that necessarily restricts his or her individual freedom. Truly rational deliberation, it is claimed, must be grounded in the autonomy of individuals and, hence, their independence from the kind of structures of discipline and authority within which virtues are learned and practiced. One of the most interesting challenges to this view is that of Skinner 1997.

5. Warner suggests that publics thematizing their own embodied and expressive dimensions—their own styles of speech, affect, and gesture—are unable

to "transpose themselves to the generality of the state" (2002:116). Such publics remain rooted in their expressive conditions and therefore cannot extend their agency beyond their own confines. What I explore in this chapter is how such styles of expressivity may themselves constitute the agency whereby those confines are continuously enlarged, such that the public may gradually "generalize" itself via its own expressive activities, without the mediation of the state.

6. For the primary Quranic reference for this interpretation, see Quran 14:46.

7. On the history of the concept and practice of *da'wa* in the modern period, see S. Amin n.d.; Canard 1999; al-Faruqi 1976; Mahmood 2005; Mendel 1995; Waardenburg 1995. Michael Cook's book (2000) on the Islamic principle of *amr bi'l-ma'aruf* (enjoining the righteous) also sheds light on the development of the concept of *da'wa*.

8. According to prominent *du'at*, this transference of the responsibility to enact *da'wa* from collective agents to individuals has a doctrinal basis in the twin concepts of *fard al-kifaya* and *fard al-'ayn*. Briefly, the term *fard al-kifaya* refers to an obligation that falls on the moral community (*umma*) as a whole, though one whose satisfaction only requires that some members of the collective undertake it. *Da'wa* is just such an obligation. *Fard al-'ayn*, on the other hand, refers to an obligation that every Muslim individual must perform, such as praying, the paying of alms, the hajj, and so on. Importantly, when those entrusted to perform a duty designated *fard al-kifaya* fail to, that duty is understood to then revert to all members. In other words, the dispersion of the duty of *da'wa* across the social realm finds its doctrinal justification in a context where the nationalized religious institutions remain silent in the face of erroneous social and legal innovations.

9. This viewpoint is not universal. In other national contexts, such as in Indonesia, no such prohibition exists.

10. For discussion of these aspects of the revival movement, see Armbrust 2000; Baker 2003; Eickelman and Anderson 1999; Salvatore 1997, 2001a; Starrett 1995b, 1998.

11. The most comprehensive discussion of the history of the Muslim Brotherhood remains that of R. Mitchell (1993).

12. The title "khedive" refers to the rulers of Egypt who governed as viceroys of the Ottoman sultan between 1867 and 1914.

13. Al-Banna understood the nation-state as a legitimate object of political loyalty and identity but one secondary to and subsumed within a broader community based on adherence to Islamic practice: "The bone of contention between us [the Muslim Brotherhood] and them [Egyptian nationalists] is that we define patriotism according to the standard of credal belief, while they define it according to territorial borders and geographical boundaries" (al-Banna 1978:50).

14. Throughout the history of Islam, mosques have often served as the locus for a variety of practices and modes of discourse beyond those strictly devotional, including seeking and offering advice, settling disputes, and various types of instruction. Over the course of the twentieth century, the Egyptian state has

sought to limit the use of the mosque to activities of worship alone. Thus, the practice of *isti'dhan*, for example, has been largely curtailed during the last fifteen years by new legislation that prohibits all but state-authorized personnel from addressing the mosque attendees, particularly in state-controlled mosques. The *da'wa* movement that I describe here presents an ongoing challenge to these trends.

15. See Berkey 2001 for a discussion of this tradition as it relates to medieval preaching.

16. Analysts of modern Islam have also adopted a similar perspective, viewing contemporary transformations and relocations of authority as a break from the authentic traditions of Islam (see, for example, Roy 1996 and al-Azmeh 1993). There are many interesting parallels between the *da'wa* movement and early-nineteenth-century evangelism in the United States in regard to this issue. Challenging the institutions of ecclesial authority, the evangelists argued that even those without formal ministerial training could receive a "spiritual calling," that the experience of being summoned by God to take up the Bible and preach was grounds enough for someone to abandon his former occupation and turn to a life of ministry. Church authorities, on the other hand, strongly criticized the validity of such "immediate calls," insisting that a proper calling was one carried out within the ecclesial frameworks. See Schmidt 2000: 38–77.

17. Despite the official ban on Brotherhood activities, the organization continues to exist, and even manages to float candidates in local and national elections through the cooperation of already licensed political parties, in particular the Labor Party (Hizb al-'amal).

18. Zeghal's (1996) work on the institutional and intellectual evolution of al-Azhar University over the course of the twentieth century provides an excellent account of the emergence of *da'wa* as a sphere of religious activism outside the purview of the state; see especially chapter 4. On the topic of Islamic publishing in Egypt, the most thorough discussion to date is found in Quijano-Gonzalez 1994.

19. In this regard it is worth noting that the state has long given up any attempt to promote its views via cassette and instead, only seeks to limit the impact of cassette sermons through censorship and licensing policies, regulation of the *khutaba'* themselves, and the promotion and broadcast of state-approved preachers on radio and television.

20. For a discussion of the concept of *umma* as articulated within both contemporary Islamist and nationalist discourses, see T. Asad 1999:189–92.

21. In this sense, the contemporary *da'wa* movement is grounded in a narrative mode quite distinct from the nationalist press (or for that matter, the novel), the genre that Benedict Anderson (1991) identified as a key enabling condition for the imaginary community of the nation. In chapter 5 I discuss the narrative structure of the Islamic sermons that are central to the *da'wa* movement.

22. For a useful discussion of the notion of renewal within Muslim historical thought, see Voll 1993.

23. In recent years, there have been a number of studies addressing the transnational dimensions of contemporary Islam. See, for example, Beinin and Stork 1997; Fischer and Abedi 1990; Turner 1994.

24. On Sufism in the context of modern Egypt, see Frishkopf 1999; Gilsenan 1983; Hoffman-Ladd 1995; J. Johansen 1996.

25. Michael Sells (2001) provides an excellent introduction to the acoustic and affective dynamics of Quranic narrative.

26. This can be contrasted with the rhetoric of sentimentality that Lauren Berlant (1997, 2000) has shown to play a significant role in structuring contemporary political debate in the United States.

27. For anthropological writings on this notion, see Feld 1982, 1996, 2000; and Seremetakis 1994. See also the studies of Corbin (1998) and B. Smith (1999) on early-modern European soundscapes.

28. See Ghannam's (2002) discussion of the role of sermon tapes in structuring space within public transportation in Cairo.

29. On the role of affect in the shaping of public space, see Connolly 2002; Deleuze 1995; Massumi 2002.

30. Here it is useful to refer to what Gumbrecht, in addressing the phenomenon of rhythmic speech, calls a "constitutive tension" between the creation of semantic forms and kinesthetic perception (1994:177). As Gumbrecht suggests: "If in the perception of rhythm, both the object of distance perception and the perception of one's own body have a form quality, that is, if observation and perception can be monothetically comprehended on both levels, then external observation and kinesthetic perception can enter into a reciprocal relation representing each other" (1994:178). Within this relationship, rhythm (or, in broader terms, embodied form) is not subordinated to the dimension of representation: the two are linked in a constitutive oscillation. Rhythm and language remain in a productive though irreducible tension (cf. Meschonnic 1989). While Gumbrecht's concern is with poetic discourse, his argument can be usefully extended to other genres of rhythmically structured oratory, including the sermons addressed here.

31. A comparison can be drawn here to the Turkish government's decision to forbid the reading of the Quran in schools: the worry is that such a training will orient students favorably to projects that would challenge the secular basis of the state and its goals of Europeanization.

32. In a recent sociological study of the opinions, attitudes, and oratorical styles of preachers in Egypt carried out by the Egyptian researcher Abdul-Fatah Abd al-Nabi (1995), the majority of preachers surveyed identified television as the primary cause for the decline of religiosity in Egypt. The solution to this problem most often recommended by these men was to increase the time allotted for the broadcast of religious programs and for the creation of more popular television serials that gave expression to Muslim ideals and lifestyles.

33. Owing to the overcrowded conditions and a lack of resources at most public schools, private lessons have become an almost ineluctable component of

secondary school education in Egypt. Teachers augment their meager salaries by offering these lessons to their students. For the majority of families, however, this represents a heavy burden on their resources. On public education in Egypt, see Baker 2003 and Starrett 1998.

34. As spaces of political opposition, some of these neighborhoods became radicalized to the extent that they sought to forcibly eject the state from what they defined as "their territories." The most striking case of this occurred in Imbaba, a neighborhood of over one million people where a self-proclaimed Islamic government attempted to oversee the administration of the area. In 1992, the state sent a military contingent of fourteen thousand soldiers to "retake" the neighborhood. While this is an extreme example, forms of neighborhood solidarity in opposition to the state have been widespread in Egypt in recent decades.

35. See Mahmood 2001 and 2004 for a critique of the idea that such sartorial trends are necessarily an expression of identity politics.

36. I should clarify that in speaking of "virtue" I am not making a moral judgment about the participants in the *da'wa* movement or endorsing their actions as "admirable." I make use of a Aristotelian vocabulary simply as a means to talk about a moral psychology tied to traditions of Islamic discipline in which valued forms of behavior are inculcated. See Michael Lambek's insightful discussion of the importance of and resistance to Aristotelian concepts with anthropology (2000a).

37. The number of books on the practice of *da'wa* offered by bookstores and sidewalk vendors in Cairo is vast, with scores of new titles coming out every year. Some of the more popular of these include Hassan 1995, 1996; Jarisha 1985; al-Qaradawi 1991; Saqr 1990b.

38. On the evolution of the concept of *"adab"* in Egypt from the late nineteenth century to the present, see Farag 2002.

39. All of the men I worked with and many of the people I met in Cairo who considered *da'wa* an important aspect of their lives demonstrated the latter virtue at all times, never appearing in public without freshly washed and pressed clothing, carefully groomed hair and beard, perfectly trimmed nails, and so on.

40. My discussion of the distinction between the internal and external goods of practices follows MacIntyre 1984:181–203.

41. Lane, in his *Arabic-English Lexicon*, defines *"amana"* as "becoming true to the trust with respect to which God has confided in one, by a firm believing with the heart; not by profession of belief with the tongue only, without the assent of the heart; for he who does not firmly believe with his heart is either a hypocrite or an ignorant person" ([1863] 1984).

42. The notion of "grammar" suggested here is taken from Wittgenstein 1958.

43. While the decision to deny tenure was eventually overturned, a subsequent court case ended in a ruling that Abu Zayd's work did indeed show him to be an apostate and that, in the interest of the community, his marriage to a Muslim woman should therefore be annulled. For reasons of personal safety, Abu Zayd

has chosen to remain outside of Egypt since this decision was made. An appeal of his case is currently pending. An excellent discussion of the legal dimensions of this case is found in B. Johansen 2003.

44. Said Ashmawi, whose views I allude to in chapter 2, is another influential proponent of such an interpretive stance. In a recent article, Mahmood situates the modernist hermeneutics promoted by Muslim thinkers like al-Ashmawi and Abu Zayd in relation to contemporary projects of secularization in the Middle East, and particularly those projects directly promoted by the United States (Mahmood 2006). Within recent policy reports of such conservative think tanks as the Rand Corporation, these Muslim thinkers have been singled out as strategic allies of the United States for their calls to limit the scope of religious authority to the private sphere. Secularization, from this perspective, should be promoted for its strategic value in relation to U.S. interests in the region. This is not to suggest, of course, that scholars like Ashmawi would appreciate such an interpretation of their intellectual contribution to Middle Eastern societies. On the contrary, they would most likely be appalled by it.

45. Stout (2004) makes a similar argument about the possible contribution of Christianity to American democracy in his analysis of the ideas of Whitman and Emerson.

46. In *Buddha is Hiding* (2003), Aihwa Ong explores how the techniques of moral and political discipline through which Cambodian refugees are shaped and adjusted to the norms of American citizenship often come to be deflected or modified by the actions of refugees themselves. As she notes in her closing remarks, "By discussing how service workers and their clients enacted these everyday instances of discipline and deflection, rules and ruses, conformity and chaos, my analysis shows that such fluid power relations produced not only ongoing norms but also their perpetual undoing, and creating possibilities for alternative expressions, conduct, and notions of what it means to be human, not merely citizen" (A. Ong 2003:276).

47. I am deeply indebted here to T. Asad's (1986) elaboration of Islam as a discursive tradition.

5. RHETORICS OF THE *DA'IYA*

1. Patrick Gaffney (1994), in his study of Egyptian sermons, analyzes three styles of sermon found in contemporary Egyptian preaching: what might be called classical, modernist, and Islamist. While his three categories overlap at certain points with some of the distinctions I make here, his treatment departs significantly from mine in its adoption of a Weberian framework of analysis.

2. Sermons reprinted in books today are often reproduced in accord with the conventions of print media, including the use of titles, subtitles, punctuation, and footnotes with references.

3. Through the first half of the twentieth century, collections of sermons published in print form, in what are called *diwanat* (sing. *diwan*), generally included

headings describing for which occasion within the ritual calendar the sermon was intended.

4. On the practice of dhikr, see Schimmel (1994:119–21) and Padwick (1996:13–20).

5. Among the constellation of terms that were used during the medieval period to designate Muslim orators was *"mudhakkir,"* a nominative form of the verb *dhakkara*, meaning, literally, one who reminds others of God. Often, but not exclusively, associated with more mystical currents in Islam (*tasawwuf*), the *mudhakkir*, like the *wa'iz* (admonitory preacher), preached for the rejection of worldly attachments. In its Sufi form, the session (also termed *"dhikr"*) over which this figure presides involves ecstatic practices of repetitive chanting of the names of God. For a discussion of the role of *mudhakkir*, see Athmina 1992. I examine *dhikr* in relation to death in chapter 6.

6. The term *saj'* has been used by some scholars to describe verses of the Quran itself, though these scholars represent a minority on this point. In one of the most popular reference books used by *khutaba'*, Ali Mahfuz's *Hidayat al-murshidin ila turuq al-wa'z wa al-khataba* (1979), the author warns of all the improper forms of *saj'* but maintains that if these are avoided, it can still be of benefit. A correct use of *saj'*, he argues, must comply with three conditions: "It must avoid all affectation [*takalluf*] and linguistic inaccuracies; second, every use of *saj'* must indicate a precise meaning; and third, the *saj'* verse must be pleasantly tasteful" (1979:132). In other words, the aesthetic aspect must be totally adequate to the rational one.

7. One of the *khutaba'* I worked with would frequently denounce the use of *saj'* by *khutaba'* whose sermons he didn't like but then point out the excellence of rhyme in the sermons of others he appreciated. In the latter case, however, he would not refer to the style with the term *saj'*, which he reserved for those he wished to condemn. The only *khatib* I know who used this term in a positive sense was a professor from al-Azhar who disapproved of most modern styles of preaching.

8. I have inserted references to chapters and verses in the Quran to aid the analysis. In the actual vocal performance of this sermon, the *khatib* often marks the verses with a particular vocal quality.

9. It is important to note that it is not only religiously devout Egyptians who exhibit this familiarity with the Quran; many Egyptians who regard themselves as secular know this tradition well, an indication of their grounding in classical Arabic.

10. I avoid the term "sacred language," much used in anthropology, as it is poorly suited to the case of Arabic, a language which, in its entirety, could be considered in some sense "sacred."

11. The idea that a sermon should provide something for all members of an audience despite differences in their intellectual abilities is also, of course, a tenet of Christian rhetoric. Sermon tracts from medieval times to the present often express this in terms of a distinction between those people who can only grasp the literal sense of a sermon, versus those who are able to accede to the deeper, allegorical one (see Blench 1964 and Pollard 1963 for a discussion of these issues). While a

similar emphasis is found within contemporary Islamic preaching manuals, my point here is to note how this problem faced by all orators is mediated, in the tradition I describe here, by a particular notion of the universal accessibility of divine speech.

12. A comparison could be drawn here with medieval Christian notions of reading. For Christian scholars and monks, *lectio divina* was as much an activity of the hand, the eye, the mouth, the emotions, and the heart as it was one of the rational mind. Moreover, the medieval reader did not seek to extract an objective meaning from a text through a critical reading but sought instead to be possessed by the writing, to be surprised and embraced by it in such a way that it would nourish his or her faith. Achieving this required more than one's cognitive faculties. On the subject of *lectio divina* in the medieval context, see Carruthers 1990:156–88; Illich 1993:51–73; Leclercq 1961; W. Ong 1958.

13. On Qutb's contribution to contemporary Islamic activism, see Abu-Rabiʿ 1996 and Moussalli 1992.

14. Entitled *Fi zilal al-Qurʾan* (In the shadow of the Quran), this work is more a compilation of the author's impressions upon reading the Quran than it is an exegesis in the traditional mold. In a study of preaching in Egypt undertaken by a sociologist at Zaqaziq University, preachers identified Qutb's *tafsir* (explication of the Quran) as one of their primary resources in finding material for preaching (Abd al-Nabi 1995). In contrast, those I spoke to from al-Azhar university generally acknowledged the importance of his *tafsir* but saw it as far less authoritative than the exegetical works of Ibn Kathir (d. 1373) and Ibn al-Qayyim (d. 1350).

15. Qutb's work on Quranic aesthetics has been discussed by Larkin (1995) and Boullata (2000).

16. As Boullata (1991) notes, although *s.w.r.* finds its primary reference in visual perception, it also refers to auditory experience. Among the different derivations of this term found in the Quran is "*sur*," the term designating the trumpet that announces the arrival of final judgment. And while the primary usages of *s.w.r.* today center on vision and image, as used in the vernacular, one derivation of the verb can still be used in the sense of "to hear a deafening noise," that is, to auditory experience (Boullata 1991:100–101).

17. This translation is from Issa Boullata (2000:356).

18. Shaykh Kishk's own autobiography (1986) offers an interesting account of his moral and political formation. He also published a number of works on the art of preaching and the practice of *daʿwa*; see, for example, his *Kayfa takun khatiban* (How to become a preacher) (n.d.). Some aspects of Kishk's life and preaching style are explored by Kepel (1986). I discuss Kishk's complex relationship with the Egyptian state in chapter 2.

19. The reference here is to the Shah of Iran, who was given refuge in Egypt following the Iranian revolution in 1979. He died in Egypt at the Maʾadi Hospital.

20. Qutb also made extensive use of theatrical metaphors in his works on Quranic aesthetics, describing the end of each Quranic "scene" as the curtain having gone down on the play.

21. It is worth comparing the model of subject formation I describe here to medieval understandings of rhetorical memory. As Mary Carruthers has noted, the sayings, parables, and bits of text that medieval Christians learned in the course of their ethical formation did not contain sets of rules or norms to be applied to situations of moral judgment. Rather, such textual fragments were part of a common stock of publicly shared and recognized images, images that, in being incorporated into the self (through processes that medieval scholars called "digestion" or "rumination"), constituted who one was: "memory makes our reading into our own ethical equipment and we express that 'character' in situations that are also rhetorical in nature, in the expressive gestures and performances which we construct from our remembered experience" (Carruthers 1990: 182).

22. The "Rightly Guided Caliphs" (*al-khulafa' al-rashidun*) refers to the first four caliphs who ruled Muslim lands immediately after the death of Muhammad in 631: Abu Bakr, Umar, Uthman, and Ali.

23. For example, the United Nation's international conference on population, held in Cairo in 1995, provoked widespread discussion both in the Islamist press and in the mosques.

24. Few people I knew could listen to his tape on the death of the Prophet and not shed at least a few tears. Some, however, felt that Hassan's "*uslub buka'i*" (weepy style), as they derogatorily referred to it, manipulated their emotions to the detriment of the sermon's ethical aims. "He is too weepy," noted Ibrahim after he, Ahmad, and I had listened to the tape. "Now I understand why he is so popular among the less educated." Ahmad, a long-standing follower of Hassan, countered: "You say that because you don't know anything about him. He has dedicated his whole life to *da'wa* and has always spoken truthfully and sincerely." "I heard the Saudis gave him a lot of money, and that he drives around in a big Mercedes," Ibrahim responded. "How can you do *da'wa* in a Mercedes?" "Those are lies," Ahmad retorted, "lies spread by people who are jealous of the fact that he is beloved among the people."

25. Like Shaykh Kishk, Muhammad Hassan also has numerous publications to his name. These include collections of his sermons, as well as writings on doctrinal issues, the practice of *da'wa*, and preaching techniques. Among his most well known works are, *Haqiqat al-tawhid* (1995), and *Qawa'id al-mujtami' al-muslim* (1996).

26. Al-Mustafa is one of the names used to refer to Muhammad. Literally it means "the clearest" or "the most pure."

27. SAAS is a typographical abbreviation of "*salla allah 'alaihi wa salim*," an expression conventionally used after any occasion when the Prophet's name is uttered or written.

6. THE ACOUSTICS OF DEATH

1. Puritan thinkers also invoked taste as the sense appropriate to a knowledge of spiritual things. According to the Puritan mystic Francis Rous: "After we have

tasted those heavenly things whereof we were possessed, from this taste their ariseth a new, but a true, lively, and experimental knowledge of the things so tasted. And indeed this is a knowledge which no art, eloquence or expression of man can teach us. For even in natural fruits there are certain relishes, and, as I may call them, Idaea's and character's of tastes, which nothing but the tast it self can truly represent and shew unto us. The West Indian Piney [pineapple] cannot be so expressed in words, even by him who hath tasted it, that he can deliver over the true shape and character of that taste to another that hath not tasted it" (cited in Nuttall 1992:139).

2. The concept of *dhawq*, as a nonrationalist mode of acquiring knowledge, was the subject of considerable debate among medieval theologians, and was frequently rejected by some of the more rationalist currents within Islam (see Winter 1989: xx). The term also had a technical use in Arabic linguistics and poetics, referring to an eloquence grounded in habit, as opposed to one resulting from a knowledge of grammatical rules. See Ibn Khaldun's discussion of this point in the *Muqaddimah*, chapter 6, section 50 (1958:358–62), as well as Kamal Abu Deeb's work on the medieval Muslim linguist al-Jurjani (1979). Among twentieth-century Muslim thinkers who have asserted the epistemic importance of *dhawq*, Sayyid Qutb, one of the intellectual leaders of the Muslim Brotherhood, is perhaps the most well known (see Qutb 1993).

3. Scholarly debates among medieval theologians over the acceptability of religious knowledge based on *dhawq* frequently focused on the usage of prophetic traditions (*hadith*) of weak authority—those classified as *da'if*—for the purpose of inspiring hope or fear. See Winter for a discussion of these debates as they relate to A. H. al-Ghazali's writing (Winter 1989:xx).

4. Notably, the notion of taste (*dhawq*) is found in the Quran in a verse expressing the inescapability of death: "Kullu nafs dha'iq al-mawt [Every soul tastes death]" (*Surat al-'Imran*:185).

5. Of course, there is an ongoing concern in contemporary societies about the way the fascination with death, violence, and the macabre within mass entertainment sometimes loops back into the social, whether in the form of mimetic gesture or socialized response. The debates prompted by the Columbine school shooting that took place in 1999 are a recent example.

6. For discussions of Islamic conceptions of death, see Anawati 1982; J. MacDonald 1965; Mew 1892; J. Smith 1980; Smith and Haddad 1979, 1981; W. C. Smith 1981.

7. I was told on various occasions that while the hope of acceptance into heaven may encourage one to mind one's actions, it is the fear of death and hell that has the greatest moral effect on behavior.

8. This assertion may strike a secular reader as a rather paradoxical argument for a "believer," its logic, so it seems, being entirely utilitarian. The argument would appear to resonate with a modern, "disenchanted" understanding of the function of hell within structures of religious authority, an understanding that can be traced back as far as Plato. As Arendt (1976) points out, Plato (in *The Republic*) came to the conclusion that the idea of a world of inescapable punishment

waiting on the other side of this life was a necessary fiction, constructed in order to induce the masses to obey the laws. Thus, the assertion that a belief in the torments of the hereafter is necessary for the government of human conduct appears to present a good case for the need to believe but not for the existence of the object of belief itself. A common interpretation of this conundrum has been to say that in a context where the ability of religious authority to demonstrate the truth of its doctrines has been undermined by the presence of competing theories and rationalities, it will then seek to justify those doctrines on other, pragmatic or utilitarian grounds.

I want to suggest that there is more in the position expressed here than simply the accommodation of the religious mind to a secular age. If we take this claim seriously, we see that what is suggested is that human needs are relevant to knowledge and that just as it is only through disciplined emotions that the more profound truths of sermonic discourse may be digested and embodied, needs also have epistemic value. John Henry Newman argued similarly. Writing to a friend, he noted: "It seems to me you mean to say that the same considerations which make you wish to believe are among the reasons which, when you actually do inquire, lead you prudently to believe, thus serving a double purpose. Do you bring this out anywhere? On the contrary, are you not shy of calling these considerations reasons? Why?" (cited in Wainwright 1995:73). As Wainwright concludes, drawing out the implications of Newman's argument: "To simply assume that our wishes and needs are not 'reasons' begs the question at issue, 'Do wishes, needs, emotions, acts of imagination, and the like sometimes have a positive epistemic value?'" (73).

9. *Targhib*, the rhetorical counterpart to *tarhib*, involves the invocation of the rewards that await the pious believer in heaven.

10. On adverbial virtues, see Oakeshott 1975. The virtues, for Oakeshott, instruct us in *how* we should act but not in *what* we should do. In other words, morality may entail that we act in a courageous manner but does not dictate the actions that should be done in this manner.

11. On the concept of *nafs* (soul or spirit) in Islam, see Calverly 1943; D. MacDonald 1932; J. Smith 1979; Tritton 1971.

12. Messick's discussion of reading practices among nonscholars in contemporary Yemen reveals a similar pattern of engagement with classical Islamic texts (1997).

13. In his insightful exploration of pain as it relates to forms of moral agency within diverse traditions, Talal Asad notes: "My concern is to point to the way in which certain traditions use pain to create a space for moral action that articulates this-world-in-the-next. Thus pain is used and justified by modern state law (including the law of war) to uphold order and attain security. Muslim and Christian princes have also used pain for this purpose. But in addition, Christian and Islamic traditions have, in their different ways, regarded suffering as the working through of worldly evil. For the suffering subject, not all pain is to be avoided; some pain is to be actively endured if evil is to be transcended" (2003:91–92).

14. The relevance of Dante to Islamic ideas on death goes beyond simple analogy. As Miguel Asin Palacios documents in his brilliant exploration of the Islamic roots of Dante's imaginary, the Dantean universe is grounded directly in Islamic eschatological traditions. See Palacios 1943.

15. Martin Luther, in his preaching, placed a similar emphasis on the terrifying solitude of the encounter with God at the moment of judgment. A description of Luther's preaching style is found in Wicks 1998 .

16. As Smith and Haddad note in regard to contemporary eschatological scholarship, "The attempt to see the traditional signs of the Hour realized in events and characteristics of the present is common to much contemporary interpretation" (1981:129–30).

17. See Harding's (2000:228–46) account of a similar temporalizing practice among American fundamentalist and evangelical Christians.

18. The sense of smell also often provides a link to death. Men, particularly young men today, often put on scents, especially musk, before going to the mosque to pray on Fridays. Musk, however, is also frequently put onto a corpse as it is being wrapped in the shroud. Thus, while the scent of musk carries evocations of holiness, it also carries with it an evocation of death, which leads some to shun its use.

19. See Lakoff and Johnson's discussions of such mappings across conceptual domains of experience (1980, 1999).

20. Harding (2000) describes a somewhat similar borrowing of commercialized forms of horror for the sake of religious instruction in fundamentalist Christianity in the United States. For example, every year around the time of Halloween, a Baptist church in Lynchburg, Virginia, sets up a Christian haunted house, called "Scaremare." Scaremare has many of the traditional props of a house of horrors, including scenes of car crashes with mangled bodies and gallons of fake blood, bodies hanging from meat hooks, others writhing in agony at an airplane crash site, complemented by screams, moans, twisting floors, and flashing lights. At the conclusion of the tour, the audience is presented with a short sermon on the saving power of Jesus Christ. According to the organizers, Harding notes, Scaremare "took harvest time back from the devil and replaced the demon-filled message of Halloween with the biblical message 'man dies, Christ saves'" (2000:4).

21. While tapes that explicitly address thanatological and eschatological themes do not constitute the majority of tapes produced, they do tend to be the best selling.

22. As the lives of elites today in Egypt are largely shaped by Western-dominated circuits of capital and culture, these classes have adopted attitudes toward death closer to those prevalent in the West.

23. Those mentioned include the four rightly guided caliphs and other beloved companions of the Prophet known for the leadership role they have played in the history of Islam.

24. Death also appears in other animate forms within Islamic eschatological traditions. According to one tradition, once all souls have been assigned their fate in heaven or hell, God's final action will be to bring death in the form of a spotted ram out onto the divide separating the two domains. In the act of slaughtering the ram, God closes the eschatological progression, thereby ushering in eternity.

25. The provisioning of water shortly before death also appears in prophetic traditions on the Prophet's death, where it is said that Aysha, one of the Prophet's wives, gave him water in his final moments of life.

26. These ideas are not unlike those underlying the hospice movement in the United States.

27. In another tape in the series entitled "al-Ghusl wa al-takfin" (The preparation and enshrouding of the corpse), Humaydi criticizes the professionalization of the tasks of ritual washing and the preparation of the body for burial. Insomuch as the washing of the body is a Muslim duty and therefore part of one's devotional obligations (*ibada*), it should not be performed for monetary gain. Moreover, only those closest to the deceased are capable of showing the required sort of respect for the corpse and are able to treat the body with the care and concern necessary to make the passage from this life to the next easier. Yet, despite these observations, Humaydi recognizes that the social conditions that enable families to enact this role no longer exist. Recognizing the difficulty involved in acquiring the necessary expertise in *fiqh al-mawt*, Humaydi suggests that an examination system be established under the supervision of *fuqaha'* from al-Azhar in order to ensure that those who wash the bodies of the dead possess the required knowledge.

28. The twelfth-century theologian Ibn al-Jawzi, for example, described the function of rhetoric concerning the inescapability of death through a hydraulic metaphor, as holding back the flow of water—or human nature—from its natural tendency to move downward: "It should be observed that when the natural disposition was created, possessing as it did an inborn love for corroding pleasures and frivolous preoccupations which distract from those things that bring profit, it stood in need of a reformer, a teacher and a warner to restrain it. Metaphorically speaking [the natural disposition] is like water which flows [toward the lowest point]. However, when it is held back by a dam its flowing ceases but then continues again with the opening of the passage. Now just as it is necessary that one give meticulous attention to the dam in the way of taking effective measures to fortify it, so likewise it is necessary that one give diligent attention to [the control of] the natural disposition by means of constraining exhortations" (1971:106–7).

29. On the *ars moriendi* tradition, see Atkinson 1992 and Wicks 1998.

7. EPILOGUE

1. A number of scholars have attempted to provide more substantive definitions of Islamic fundamentalism. See, for example, Marty and Appleby 1994. Even in these

cases, I would contend, what gives the term its utility has less to do with similarities between contemporary Islamic movements and those Christian fundamentalist movements in relation to which the term was first developed and more to do with the denunciatory standpoint of which the term is an expression.

2. This approach dominates the literature produced on the topic of Islamism. Some well known examples include, al-Azmeh 1993; Beinin and Stork 1997; Kepel 1993; Roy 1996. For an eloquent critique of the reductionism this literature enacts, see Euben 1999.

3. See, for example, Burgat and Dowell 1997, and Esposito 1992.

4. For biographical accounts of some of the leading Islamic Revival figures, see Baker 2003; Burgat and Dowell 1997; Salvatore 1997.

5. For a recent statement issued by the Muslim Brothers espousing this stance, see Abul-Fotouh 2005.

6. The Muslim Brothers fielded a Coptic candidate in the 1987 election (in alliance with Labor and Liberal Parties), and later in 2000. For a discussion of this relatively new trend within the Muslim Brotherhood, see Abdel-Latif 2000 and Howeidy 2000.

7. The Muslim Brothers won almost a quarter of the seats in the Egyptian parliament in the 2005 elections. For a range of Coptic reactions to both the Muslim Brothers' attempts to build bridges with the Coptic community, and the Brothers' unexpected success in the parliamentary elections, see Shahine 2005. Notably, only one Copt was elected to the People's Assembly in 2005, an imbalance President Mubarak tried to rectify by appointing five Copts (and five women) to the Assembly.

WORKS CITED

Abd al-Nabi, Abdul-Fatah. 1995. *Al-Mu'athirun: dirasat namudhij a'immat al-masa-jid*. Zaqaziq: Maktabat al-nahda al-misriyya.

Abd al-Rahman. 1992. *Risala 'ila khatib masjidina*. Cairo: Dar al- i'tisam.

Abdel-Latif, Omayma. 2000. "The Demise of Politics?" *Al-Ahram Weekly On-line*. November 16–22.

Abdo, Geneive. 2002. *No God but God: Egypt and the Triumph of Islam*. New York: Oxford University Press.

Abduh, Muhammad. [1906] 1972. *Al-A' mal al-kamila li al-imam Muhammad 'Abdu*. Beirut: al-Mu'assasa al-'arabiyya li al-dirasat wa al-nashr.

Abu Deeb, Kamal. 1979. *Al-Jurjani's Theory of Poetic Imaginary*. Warminster: Aris and Phillips.

Abul-Fotouh, Abdel-Moneim. 2005. "One God, One Nation." *Al-Ahram Weekly*. December 15–21.

Abu Lughod, Lila. 1986. *Veiled Sentiments: Honor and Poetry in a Bedouin Society*. Berkeley: University of California Press.

——. 2005. *Dramas of Nationhood: The Politics of Television in Egypt*. Chicago: University of Chicago Press.

Abu Rabi', Ibrahim. 1996. *Intellectual Origins of Islamic Resurgence in the Modern Arab World*. New York: SUNY Press.

Abu Samak, Mustafa Ahmed. 1995. *Al-Madkhal li-dirasat al-khataba wa turuq al-tabligh fi al-Islam*. Cairo: Dar al-taba' al-muhamidiyya.

al-Ahram. 1993. Untitled article. June 27.

al-Ahram Center for Political and Strategic Studies. 1996. *Taqrir al-hala al-diniyya fi misr*. Cairo: Center for Political and Strategic Studies.

al-Ahram Weekly, Apr. 15–21, 1993.

Amin, Ahmed. 1965. "Logique et Langage." In *Anthologie de la littérature Arabe contemporaine*, ed. Anouar Abdel-Malek, 91–95. Paris: Éditions du Seuil.

Amin, Said. n.d. *Al-Daʿwa al-islamiyya: farida sharaʿiyya wa darura bashariyya.* Cairo: Dar al-tauziʿa wa al-nashr al-islamiyya.

Anawati, G. C. 1982. "La Mort en Islam." In *Meaning of Death in Christianity and Other Religions*, ed. Mariasusai Dhavamony, 187–208. Rome: Gregorian University Press.

Anderson, Benedict. 1991. *Imagined Communities: Reflections on the Origin and Spread of Nationalism.* New York: Verso.

Antoun, Richard. 1989. *Muslim Preacher in the Modern World: A Jordanian Case Study in Contemporary Perspective.* Princeton, N.J.: Princeton University Press.

ʿAqidati. 1995. *Istafadna kathiran min al-dawrat al-siyasiyya wa al-ijtimaʿiyya.* April 25.

——. 1996. *Al-Islam laysa subermarket nakhudh minhu ma nashaʾ wa natruk ma la nuhib.* October 29.

Arendt, Hannah. 1958. *The Human Condition.* Chicago: University of Chicago Press

——. 1976. *Between Past and Future.* New York: Viking.

Ariès, Philippe. 1974. *Western Attitudes Toward Death: From the Middle Ages to the Present.* Trans. Patricia M. Ranum. Baltimore, Md.: Johns Hopkins University Press.

Aristotle. 1991. *The Art of Rhetoric.* Trans. H. C. Lawson-Tancred. London: Penguin Books.

Armbrust, Walter. 1996. *Mass Culture and Modernism in Egypt.* Cambridge: Cambridge University Press.

——, ed. 2000. *Mass Mediations: New Approaches to Popular Culture in the Middle East and Beyond.* Berkeley: University of California Press.

Aroian, Lois A. 1983. "The Nationalization of Arabic and Islamic Education in Egypt: Dar al-Ulum and al-Azhar." *Cairo Papers in Social Science* 5 (4): 12–64.

Asad, Muhammed. 1980. *The Message of the Quran.* Gibraltar: Dar al-Andalus.

Asad, Talal. 1986. *The Idea of an Anthropology of Islam.* Occasional Paper Series. Washington, D.C.: Georgetown University Center for Contemporary Arab Studies.

——. 1993. *Genealogies of Religion: Discipline and Reasons of Power in Christianity and Islam.* Baltimore, Md.: Johns Hopkins University Press.

——. 1999. "Religion, Nation State, Secularism." In *The Religious Morality of the Nation State*, ed. H. Lehmann and P. van der Veer, 178–96. Princeton, N.J.: Princeton University Press.

——. 2003. *Formations of the Secular: Christianity, Islam, Modernity.* Stanford, Calif.: Stanford University Press.

Ashur, Abd al-Latif. N.d. *ʿAzab al-qabr wa naʿimihi.* Cairo: Maktaba al-Qurʾan.

Athmina, Khalil. 1992. "*Al-Qasas*: Its Emergence, Religious Origin and its Sociopolitical Impact on Early Muslim Society." *Studia Islamica* 76:53–74.

Atkinson, David. 1992. "The Rule and Exercises of Holy Dying: Jeremy Taylor." In *The English Ars Moriendi.* New York: Peter Lang.

al-Attar, Ala Addin Ali Ibn Ibrahim Ibn. [1324] 1996. *Kitab adab al-khatib.* Beirut: Dar al-ʿarab al-islami.

Augustine, Saint. 1973. *An Augustine Reader*. Ed. John J. O'Meara. New York: Image Books.

Austin, J. L. 1994. *How to Do Things with Words*. Cambridge, Mass.: Harvard University Press.

al-Azmeh, Aziz. 1993. *Islams and Modernities*. New York: Verso.

Babeair, Abdulwahab Saleh. 1993. "The Role of the ʿUlamaʾ in Modern Islamic Society: An Historical Perspective." *The Islamic Quarterly* 37 (2): 80–94.

Badawi, Abdul Nazim. 1996a. "Shurut al-Intifaʿ bil-Quran." *Al-Tawhid* 25 (4): 10–13.

———. 1996b. "Al-Quran wa atharihi fi al-qulub." *Al- Tawhid*. 25 (3): 9–12.

Baker, Raymond. 2003. *Islam Without Fear: Egypt and the New Islamists*. Cambridge, Mass.: Harvard University Press.

al-Banna, Hasan. 1978. *Five Tracts of Hasan al-Banna: A Selection from the Majmuʿat Rasaʾil al-Imam al-Shahid Hasan al-Banna*. Trans. Charles Wendell. Berkeley: University of California Press.

Baxandall, Michael. 1988. *Painting and Experience in Fifteenth-Century Italy: A Primer in the Social History of Pictorial Style*. New York: Oxford University Press.

Bayumi, Masah Sayyid. 1988. *Al-Khataba fi al-Islam wa iʿdad al-khatib al-daʿiya*. Cairo: Maktabat al-majalid al-ʿarabi.

Beinin, Joel, and Joe Stork. 1997. "On the Modernity, Historical Specificity, and International Context of Political Islam." In *Political Islam*, ed. Joel Beinin and Joe Stork, 3–28. Berkeley: University of California Press.

Benjamin, Walter. 1969. *Illuminations*. Ed. Hannah Arendt. Trans. Harry Zohn. New York: Schocken Books.

Bergson, Henri. [1896] 1990. *Matter and Memory*. New York: Zone Books.

Berkey, Jonathan. 1992. *The Transmission of Knowledge in Medieval Cairo: A Social History of Islamic Education*. Princeton, N.J.: Princeton University Press.

———. 2001. *Popular Preaching and Religious Authority in the Medieval Islamic Near East*. Seattle: University of Washington Press.

Berlant, Lauren. 1997. *The Queen of America Goes to Washington City: Essays on Sex and Citizenship*. Durham, N.C.: Duke University Press.

———, ed. 2000. *Intimacy*. Chicago: University of Chicago Press.

al-Bishri, Tariq. 2005. *Al-Jamaʿa al-wataniyya: al-ʿuzla wa al-indimaj*. Cairo: Kitab al-hilal.

Blench, J. W. 1964. *Preaching in England in the Late Fifteenth and Sixteenth Centuries: A Study of English Sermons, 1450 c.–1600*. Oxford: Basil Blackwell Press.

Boullata, Issa. 1991. "La pensée visuelle et la mémoire sémantique arabe." *Science Sociales, Societés Arabes: Peuples mediterranées* 54–55:93–110.

———. 2000. "Sayyid Qutb's Literary Appreciation of the Qurʾan." In *Literary Structures of Religious Meaning in the Qurʾan*, ed. Issa Boullata, 354–71. Richmond, U.K.: Curzon Press.

Bourdieu, Pierre. 1990. *The Logic of Practice*. Trans. Richard Nice. Stanford, Calif.: Stanford University Press.

Bowen, John. 1993. *Muslims Through Discourse: Religion and Ritual in Gayo Society*. Princeton, N.J.: Princeton University Press.

Brenneis, Donald. 2000. "Shared and Solitary Sentiments: The Discourse of Friendship, Play, and Anger in Bhatgaon." In *Language and the Politics of Emotion*, ed. C. Lutz and L. Abu-Lughod, 113–25. New York: Cambridge University Press.

Brinton, Alan. 1992. "The Passions as Subject Matter in Early-Eighteenth-Century British Sermons." *Rhetorica* 10 (1):51–69.

Brown, Daniel. 1996. *Rethinking Tradition in Modern Islamic Thought*. Cambridge: Cambridge University Press.

Brown, Peter. 1981. *The Cult of the Saints: Its Rise and Function in Latin Christianity*. Chicago: University of Chicago Press.

Buck-Morss, Susan. 1989. *The Dialectics of Seeing: Walter Benjamin and the Arcades Project*. Cambridge, Mass.: MIT Press.

Bull, Michael. 2000. *Sounding Out the City: Personal Stereos and the Management of Everyday Life*. Oxford: Berg Publishers.

Bull, Michael, and Les Back. 2003. *The Auditory Cultures Reader*. Oxford: Berg Press.

Burchell, David. 1995. "The Attributes of Citizens: Virtue, Manners, and the Activity of Citizenship." *Economy and Society* 24 (4): 540–58

Burgat, Francois, and William Dowell. 1997. *The Islamic Movement in North Africa*. New ed. Austin: University of Texas at Austin Press.

Burnyeat, M. F. 1998. "Art and Mimesis in Plato's 'Republic.'" *London Review of Books*, May 21.

Calhoun, Craig. 1992. *Habermas and the Public Sphere*. Cambridge, Mass.: MIT Press.

Calverly, Edwin. 1943. "Doctrines of the Soul (*Nafs* and *Ruh*) in Islam." *The Moslem World* 33 (4): 254–64.

Canard, M. 1999. "Daʿwa." In *The Encyclopedia of Islam*. CD-ROM, version 1.0. Leiden: Brill.

Cantwell, Robert. 1999. "Habitus, Ethnomimesis: A Note on the Logic of Practice." *Journal of Folklore Research* 36 (2/3): 219–34.

Carruthers, Mary. 1990. *The Book of Memory: A Study of Memory in Medieval Culture*. Cambridge: Cambridge University Press.

Caton, Steven. 1990. *"Peaks of Yemen I Summon": Poetry as Cultural Practice in a North Yemeni Tribe*. Berkeley: University of California Press.

Chakrabarty, Dipesh. 2000. *Provincializing Europe: Postcolonial Thought and Historical Difference*. Princeton, N.J.: Princeton University Press.

Chamberlain, Michael. 1994. *Knowledge and Social Practice in Medieval Damascus, 1190–1350*. Cambridge: Cambridge University Press.

Chatterjee, Partha. 1993. *The Nation and Its Fragments: Colonial and Postcolonial Histories*. New Jersey: Princeton University Press.

——. 1994. "Secularism and Toleration." *Economic and Political Weekly* (July 9): 1768–77.

——. 1995. "Religious Minorities and the Secular State: Reflections on an Indian Impasse." *Public Culture* 8 (1): 11–39.

——. 2004. *The Politics of the Governed : Reflections on Popular Politics in Most of the World*. New York: Columbia University Press.

Chittick, William. 1989. *The Sufi Path of Knowledge*. Albany: State University of New York Press

Christiansen, Nancy. 1997. "Rhetoric as Character-Fashioning: The Implications of Delivery's 'Places' in the British Renaissance Paideia." *Rhetorica* 15 (3): 297–334.

Classen, Constance. 1993. *Worlds of Sense: Exploring the Senses in History and Across Cultures*. London: Routledge

Colish, Marcia L. [1968] 1983. *The Mirror of Language: A Study in the Medieval Theory of Knowledge*. Lincoln: University of Nebraska Press

Collingwood, R. G. 1966. *The Principles of Art*. Oxford: Oxford University Press.

Connolly, William. 1999. *Why I Am Not a Secularist*. Minneapolis: University of Minnesota Press.

——. 2002. *Neuropolitics: Thinking, Culture, Speed*. Minneapolis: University of Minnesota Press.

Connor, Steven. 1997. "The Modern Auditory 'I.'" In *Rewriting the Self: Histories from the Renaissance to the Present*, ed. Roy Porter, 203–23. New York: Routledge.

Cook, Michael. 2000. *Commanding Right and Forbidding Wrong in Islamic Thought*. Cambridge: Cambridge University Press.

Corbin, Alain. 1998. *Village Bells: Sound and Meaning in the Nineteenth-Century French Countryside*. New York: Columbia University Press.

Corradi Fiumara, Gemma. 1995. *The Other Side of Language: A Philosophy of Listening*. New York : Routledge.

Crary, Jonathan. 1990. *Techniques of the Observer: On Vision and Modernity in the Nineteenth Century*. Cambridge, Mass.: MIT Press.

——. 1999. *Suspensions of Perception: Attention, Spectacle, and Modern Culture*. Cambridge, Mass.: MIT Press.

Crecelius, Daniel. 1966. "Al-Azhar in Revolution." *The Middle East Journal* 20:31–49.

Csordas, Thomas J. 1999. "Embodiment and Cultural Phenomenology." In *Perspectives on Embodiment: The Intersections of Nature and Culture*, ed. G. Weiss and H. F. Haber, 143–62. New York: Routledge.

Danielson, Virginia. 1997. *The Voice of Egypt: Umm Kulthum, Arabic Song, and Egyptian Society in the Twentieth Century*. Chicago: University of Chicago Press.

Das, Veena. 1998. "Wittgenstein and Anthropology." *Annual Review of Anthropology* 27:171–95.

de Certeau, Michel. 1982. *The Mystic Fable*. Vol. 1. Chicago: University of Chicago Press.

Deleuze, Gilles. 1988. *Bergsonism*. Trans. Hugh Tomlinson and Barbara Habberjam. New York: Zone Books.

——. 1995. *Negotiations*. Trans. Martin Joughin. New York: Columbia University Press.

Denny, Frederick. 1980. "Exegesis and Recitation: Their Development as Classical Forms of Quranic Piety." In *Transitions and Transformations in the History of Religions*, ed. Frank E. Reynolds and Theodore M. Ludwig, 91–123. Leiden: E. J. Brill.

——. 1981. "The *Adab* of Quran Recitation: Text and Context." In *International Congress for the Study of the Quran*, ed. A. H. Johns. Canberra: Australian National University.

Derrida, Jacques. 1988. *Limited Inc.* Chicago: Northwestern University Press.

Desjarlais, R. 1992. *Body and Emotion: The Aesthetics of Illness and Healing in the Nepal Himalayas.* Philadelphia: University of Pennsylvania Press.

Diyab, Mirfat. 1996. "Al-Kasit al-dini fi misr: nasf milyun sharit yad'aw 'ila al-tatarruf." *Al-Majala* 874 (November 10–16): 20–23.

Dollimore, Jonathan. 2001. *Death, Desire, and Loss in Western Culture.* New York: Routledge.

Draghiesco, D. 1928. *La réalité de l'esprit. Essais de sociologie subjective.* Intro. L. Lévy-Bruhl. Paris: Félix Alcan.

Dreyfus, Hubert. 1994. *Being-in-the-World: A Commentary on Heidegger's* Being and Time, *Division 1.* Cambridge, Mass.: MIT Press.

Drobnick, James, ed. 2004. *Aural Cultures: Sound Art.* Toronto: YYZ Books.

Dupret, Baudouin, and Jean-Noël Ferrié. 2001. "Inner Self and Public Order." In *Muslim Traditions and Modern Techniques of Power*, ed. Armando Salvatore, 141–62. Münster: Lit Verlag.

During, Jean. 1997. "Hearing and Understanding in Islamic Gnosis." *The World of Music* 39 (2): 127–37.

Eccel, A. Chris. 1988. "'Alim and Mujahid in Egypt: Orthodoxy Versus Subculture, or Division of Labor?" *The Muslim World* 88 (3–4): 189–208.

Eickelman, Dale. 1992. "Mass Higher Education and the Religious Imagination in Contemporary Arab Societies." *American Ethnologist* 19 (4): 643–55.

——. 1997. "Reconstructing Islamic Thought in the Late Twentieth Century: Mass Education and the Mass Media." Paper presented at the Conference on Mass Media and the Transformation of Islamic Discourse, International Institute of Asian Studies, Leiden, The Netherlands.

Eickelman, Dale, and Jon Anderson. 1997. "Print, Islam, and the Prospects for Civic Pluralism: New Religious Writings and their Audiences." *The Journal of Islamic Studies* 8 (1): 43–62.

——, eds. 1999. *New Media in the Muslim World: The Emerging Public Sphere.* Bloomington: Indiana University Press.

Erlmann, Veit. 2004. *Hearing Cultures: Essays on Sound, Listening, and Modernity.* Oxford: Berg Press.

Esposito, John. 1992. *The Islamic Threat: Myth or Reality.* Oxford: Oxford University Press.

Etienne, Bruno. 1983. "La Moëlle de la prédication. Essai sur le prône politique dans l'Islam comtemporain." *Sommaire* 33 (4): 706–20.

Euben, Roxanne. 1999. *Enemy in the Mirror.* Princeton, N.J.: Princeton University Press.

Fakhry, Majid. 1983. *A History of Islamic Philosophy.* New York: Columbia University Press.

Farag, Iman. 2001. "Private Lives, Public Affairs: The Uses of Adab." In *Muslim Traditions and Modern Techniques of Power*, ed. Armando Salvatore, 93–120. Münster: Lit Verlag.

Al-Faruqi, Isma'il. 1976. "On the Nature of the Islamic Da'wah." *International Review of Missions* 65:391–409.

Fawzi, Mahmud. 1993. *ʿUmar ʿAbd al-Kafi wa fatawa sakhina: fi al-din wa al-siyasa wa al-fann*. Cairo: al-Badawi lil-nashr.

Feld, Steven. 1982. *Sound and Sentiment: Birds, Weeping, Poetics, and Song in Kaluli Expression*. Philadelphia: University of Pennsylvania Press.

——. 1996. "Waterfalls of Song: An Acoustemology of Place Resounding in Bosavi, Papua New Guinea." In *Senses of Place*, ed. Steven Feld and Keith Basso, 91–135. Santa Fe, N.M.: School of American Research Press.

——. 2000. "A Sweet Lullaby for World Music." *Public Culture* 12 (1): 145–71.

Feldman, Allen. 1991. *Formations of Violence: The Narrative of the Body and Political Terror in Northern Ireland*. Chicago: University of Chicago Press.

Fischer, Michael, and Mehdi Abedi. 1990. *Debating Muslims: Cultural Dialogues in Postmodernity and Tradition*. Madison: University of Wisconsin Press.

Foucault, Michel. 1983. "The Subject and Power." In *Michel Foucault: Beyond Structuralism and Hermeneutics*, ed. and trans. H. Dreyfus and P. Rabinow, 208–26. Chicago: University of Chicago Press.

——. 1984. "On the Genealogy of Ethics: An Overview of Work in Progress." In *The Foucault Reader*, ed. Paul Rabinow, 340–72. New York: Pantheon.

——. 1988. "Technologies of the Self." In *Technologies of the Self: A Seminar with Michel Foucault*, ed. and trans. Luther Martin, Huck Gutman, and Patrick Hutton, 16–49. Amherst: University of Massachusetts Press.

——. 1990. *The Use of Pleasure*. Vol. 2 of *The History of Sexuality*. Trans. R. Hurley. New York: Vintage Books.

——. 1991. "Governmentality." In *The Foucault Effect: Studies in Governmentality*, ed. G. Burchell, C. Gordon, and P. Miller, 87–104. Chicago: University of Chicago Press.

——. 1997. "The Ethics of the Concern of the Self as a Practice of Freedom." In *Ethics: Subjectivity and Truth*, vol. 1 of *Essential Works of Foucault, 1954–1984*, ed. P. Rabinow and trans. R. Hurley et al., 281–301. New York: New Press.

——. 2005. "The Challenge of the Opposition." In *Foucault and the Iranian Revolution: Gender and the Seductions of Islam*, by Janet Afary and Kevin B. Anderson, 213–20. Chicago: University of Chicago Press.

Fraser, Nancy. 1992. "Rethinking the Public Sphere: A Contribution to the Critique of Actually Existing Democracy." In *Habermas and the Public Sphere*, ed. Craig Calhoun, 109–42. Cambridge, Mass.: MIT Press.

Freud, S. [1912] 1958. "Recommendations to Physicians Practising Psychoanalysis." In *Complete Psychological Works*. Standard ed. 12:109–20. London: Hogarth Press.

Fried, Joseph P. 1995. "Closing Arguments Start Tuesday in Terror Bomb Trial." *New York Times*, September 3.

Frishkopf, Michael. 1999. "Sufism, Ritual, and Modernity in Egypt: Language Performance as an Adaptive Strategy." Ph.D. diss., University of California, Los Angeles.

———. 2001. "Tarab in the Mystic Sufi Chant of Egypt." In *Colors of Enchantment: Visual and Performing Arts in the Middle East*, ed. Sherifa Zuhur, 223–69. Cairo: American University in Cairo Press.

Gabler, Neal. 2001. "Fundamentalism: An Eternal War of Mind-Sets." *Los Angeles Times*, October 7.

Gade, Anna. 2004. *Perfection Makes Practice: Learning, Emotion, and the Recited Quran in Indonesia*. Honolulu: University of Hawaii Press.

Gaffney, Patrick D. 1991. "The Changing Voices of Islam: The Emergence of Professional Preachers in Contemporary Egypt." *The Muslim World* 81 (1): 27–47.

———. 1994. *The Prophet's Pulpit: Islamic Preaching in Contemporary Egypt*. Berkeley: University of California Press.

Gasper, Michael. 2001. "Islamic Reform, and 'Ignorant' Peasants: State-Building in Egypt?" In *Muslim Traditions and Modern Techniques of Power*, ed. Armando Salvatore, 75–92. Münster: Lit Verlag.

Gay, Peter. 1984. *The Bourgeois Experience: Victoria to Freud*. Oxford: Oxford University Press.

Geurts, Kathryn Linn. 2003. *Culture and the Senses: Embodiment, Identity, and Well-being in an African Community*. Berkeley: University of California Press.

Ghannam, Farha. 2002. *Remaking the Modern: Space, Relocation, and the Politics of Identity in a Global Cairo*. Berkeley: University of California Press.

al-Ghazali, Abu Hamid. 1984. *The Recitation and Interpretation of the Qur'an: al-Ghazali's Theory*. Trans. Muhammad Abul Quasem. London: KPI Press.

———. 1989. *Al-Ghazali: The Remembrance of Death and the Afterlife: Book Forty of the Revival of the Religious Sciences*. Trans. T. J. Winter. Cambridge: The Islamic Books Society.

———. 1990. *Mukashafat al-qulub*. al-Haram, Saudi Arabia: Matbaʿ al-irshad.

al-Ghazali, Muhammed. 1980. *Fann al-dhikr wa al-duʿaʾ*. Cairo: Dar al-iʿtisam.

Gilsenan, Michael. 1983. *Recognizing Islam: Religion and Society in the Arab World*. New York: Pantheon Press.

Goldberg, Ellis. 1989. "Smashing Idols and the State: Protestant Ethic and Egyptian Sunni Radicalism." *Comparative Studies in Society and History* 33 (1): 3–35.

Goodman, Lenn E. 1992. *Avicenna*. London: Routledge.

Goody, Jack. 1986. *The Interface between the Written and the Oral*. Cambridge: Cambridge University Press.

———. 1987. *The Logic of Writing and the Organization of Society*. Cambridge: Cambridge University Press.

Gordon, Joel. 1992. *Nasser's Blessed Movement: Egypt's Free Officers and the July Revolution*. New York: Oxford University Press.

Graham, William A. 1985. "Quran as Spoken Word: An Islamic Contribution to the Understanding of Scripture." In *Approaches to Islam in Religious Studies*, ed. Richard C. Martin, 23–40. Tucson: University of Arizona Press.

———. 1987. *Beyond the Written Word: Oral Aspects of Scripture in the History of Religion*. Cambridge: Cambridge University Press.

Greene, Paul D. 1999. "Sound Engineering in a Tamil Village: Playing Audio Cassettes as Devotional Performance." *Ethnomusicology* 43 (3): 459–89.

Gumbrecht, Hans. 1994. "Rhythm and Meaning." In *Materialities of Communication*, ed. Hans Gumbrecht and K. Ludwig Pfeiffer, 170–82. Stanford, Calif.: Stanford University Press.

Habermas, Jurgen. 1989. *The Structural Transformation of the Public Sphere.* Cambridge, Mass.: MIT Press.

Hacking, Ian. 1983. *Representing and Intervening: Introductory Topics in the Philosophy of Natural Science.* New York: Cambridge University Press.

Hadot, Pierre. 1995. *Philosophy as a Way of Life: Spiritual Exercises from Socrates to Foucault.* Ed. A. Davidson. Trans. M. Chase. Oxford: Blackwell.

Hani'a, Yusri Muhammad. 1995. *Irshad al-labib ʾila fann al-khataba wa iʿdad al-khatib.* Mansura, Egypt: Dar nur al-Islam.

Hansen, Thomas Blom. 1999. *The Saffron Wave: Democracy and Hindu Nationalism in Modern India.* Princeton, N.J.: Princeton University Press.

Harding, Susan. 2000. *The Book of Jerry Falwell: Fundamentalist Language and Politics.* Princeton, N.J.: Princeton University Press.

Harris, Jay, 1994. "'Fundamentalism': Objections from a Modern Jewish Historian." In *Fundamentalism and Gender*, ed. John Stratton Hawley, 137–73. New York: Oxford University Press.

Hassan, Muhammad. 1995. *Haqiqat al-tawhid.* Mansura, Egypt: Dar nur al-Islam.

———. 1996. *Qawaʿid al-mujtamiʿ al-muslim.* Mansura, Egypt: Dar Ibn Rajab.

Havelock, Eric. 1986. *The Muse Learns to Write.* New Haven, Conn.: Yale University Press.

Al-Hayat. 1996a. "Jabhat ʿulamaʾ al-Azhar tutalib Tantawi bil-tadakhul li aʿtdil mashruʿ qanun al-duʿat." May 11.

———. 1996b. "Misr: tattajih nahu tasʿaid al-ʿazma bayn wazir al-awqaf wa jabhat ʿulamaʾ al-Azhar." September 6.

———. 1997a. "Daʿwa qadaʾiyya did qanun tanzim al-khataba fi al-masajid al-misriyya." January 3.

———. 1997b. "Wazir al-awqaf al-misri lil-hayat: muʾassasat al-Azhar tuzayyid tanzim al-khataba fi al-masajid." January 25.

Hedges, Christopher. 1993. "A Cry of Islamic Fury, Taped in Brooklyn for Cairo." *New York Times*, January 7.

———. 1995. "A Language Divided Against Itself." *New York Times.* January 24.

Hefner, Robert W. 2000. *Civil Islam: Muslims and Democratization in Indonesia.* Princeton, N.J.: Princeton University Press.

Hertz, Robert. 1909. *Death and the Right Hand.* Glencoe, Ill.: The Free Press.

Hirschkind, Charles. 1991. "The Optics of Colonialism: Egypt at the Exhibition." *Critique of Anthropology* 11 (3): 279–98.

———. 1995. "Heresy or Hermeneutics: The Case of Nasr Hamid Abu Zayd." *Stanford Humanities Review* 5 (1): 35–48.

———. 1997. "What is Political Islam?" *Middle East Research and Information Project* 27 (4): 12–15.

——. 2001b. "The Ethics of Listening: Cassette-Sermon Audition in Contemporary Cairo." *American Ethnologist* 28 (3): 623–649.

——. 2001c. "Tradition, Myth, and Historical Fact in Contemporary Islam." *ISIM Newsletter* 8:18.

Hirschkind, Charles, and Saba Mahmood. 2002. "Feminism, the Taliban, and the Politics of Counter-Insurgency." *Anthropological Quarterly* (Spring): 107–22.

Hobsbawm, Eric, and Terence Ranger, eds. 1992. *The Invention of Tradition*. Cambridge: Cambridge University Press.

Hoffman-Ladd, Valerie. 1995. *Sufism, Mystics, and Saints in Modern Egypt*. Columbia: University of South Carolina Press.

Hourani, Albert. 1983. *Arabic Thought in the Liberal Age, 1798–1939*. Cambridge: Cambridge University Press.

Howeidy, Amira. 2000. "Brothers Forward a New Image, and a Sister." *Al-Ahram Weekly* 497, 31 August–6 September.

Huwaidi, Fahmi. 1985. *Muwatinun la Dhimmiyyun*. Beirut: N.p.

Howes, David. 2003. *Sensual Relations: Engaging the Senses in Culture and Social Theory*. Ann Arbor: University of Michigan Press.

Ibn al-Jawzi, Abi al-Faraj. 1971. *Kitab al-qussas wa-al-mudhakkirin*. Ed. and trans. Merlin Swartz. Beirut: Dar al Mashriq.

Ibn Khaldun. 1958. *The Muqaddimah: An Introduction to History*. Bollingen Series 43. Trans. Franz Rosenthal. Princeton, N.J.: Princeton University Press.

Ibn Taymiyya. n.d. *al-'Ubudiyya fi al-islam*. Cairo: al-Matbaʿ al-salafiyya.

Illich, Ivan. 1993. *In the Vineyard of the Text: A Commentary to Hugh's Didascalion*. Chicago: University of Chicago Press.

Illich, Ivan, and Barry Sanders. 1988. *ABC: The Alphabeticization of the Popular Mind*. San Francisco: North Point Press.

Izutsu, Toshihiko. 1966. *Ethico-Religious Concepts in the Quran*. Montreal: McGill University Press.

——. 1988. *The Concept of Belief in Islamic Theology*. Salem, N.H.: Ayer.

Jackson, Michael. 1989. *Paths Toward a Clearing: Radical Empiricism and Ethnographic Inquiry*. Bloomington: University of Indiana Press.

Jameson, Fredric. 1981. *The Political Unconscious: Narrative as a Socially Symbolic Act*. Ithaca, N.Y.: Cornell University Press.

Jarisha, Ali Muhammad. 1985. *al-Daʿwa wa al-daʿiya*. Cairo: Dar al-tibaʿa wa al-nashr al-islamiyya.

Jay, Martin. 1994. *Downcast Eyes: The Denigration of Vision in Twentieth-Century French Thought*. Berkeley: University of California Press.

Johansen, Baber. 2003. "Apostasy as Objective and Depersonalized Fact: Two Recent Egyptian Court Judgements." *Social Research* 70 (3): 687–710.

Johansen, Julian. 1996. *Sufism and Islamic Reform in Egypt: The Battle for Islamic Tradition*. Oxford: Clarendon Press.

Johnson, Mark. 1987. *The Body in the Mind: The Bodily Basis of Meaning, Imagination, and Reason*. Chicago: University of Chicago Press.

Jousse, Marcel. [1925] 1990. *The Oral Style*. Trans. Edgard Sienaert and Richard Whitaker. New York: Garland Publishing Inc.

Kahn, Douglas. 1992. "Introduction: Histories of Sound Once Removed." In *Wireless Imagination*, ed. Douglas Kahn and Gregory Whitehead, 2–29. Cambridge, Mass.: MIT Press.

Kant, Immanuel. [1790] 1955. *The Critique of Judgement*. In *The Critique of Pure Reason; The Critique of Practical Reason; and Other Ethical Treatises*. Trans. James Creed Meridith. Chicago: University of Chicago Press.

———. [1792] 1998. *Religion Within the Boundaries of Mere Reason and Other Writings*. Ed. and trans. by A. Wood and G. Di Giovanni. Cambridge: Cambridge University Press.

Keane, Webb. 1997. *Signs of Recognition: Powers and Hazards of Representation in an Indonesian Society*. Berkeley: University of California Press.

———. 2002. "Sincerity, 'Modernity,' and the Protestants." *Cultural Anthropology* 17 (1): 65–92.

Kepel, Gilles. 1993. *Muslim Extremism in Egypt: The Prophet and the Pharaoh*. Berkeley: University of California Press.

Khalif, Abdul-Rahman. 1986. *Kayfa takun khatiban*. Mecca: Da'wat al-haqq.

Kishk, Abu al-Hamid. n.d. *Kayfa takun khatiban*. Cairo: Dar al-bashir.

———. 1986. *Qisat ayyami: mudhakkirat al-Shaykh Kishk*. Cairo: al-Mukhtar al-islami Press.

———. 1990. *'Ila fursan al-manabir*. Cairo: Maktabat al-sihafa.

Koselleck, Reinhart. 1985. *Futures Past: On the Semantics of Historical Time*. Trans. Keith Tribe. Cambridge, Mass.: MIT Press.

al-Kumi, Shami Abdul Aziz. 1992. *Al-Sihafa al-islamiyya fi misr fi al-qarn al-tasi'a 'ashar*. Cairo: Dar al-wafa'.

Lakoff, George, and Mark Johnson. 1980. *Metaphors We Live By*. Chicago: University of Chicago Press.

———.1999. *Philosophy in the Flesh: The Embodied Mind and Its Challenge to Western Thought*. New York: Basic Books.

Lambek, Michael. 2000a. "The Anthropology of Religion and the Quarrel Between Poetry and Philosophy." *Current Anthropology* 41 (3): 309–20.

———. 2000b. "Nuriaty, the Saint, and the Sultan." *Anthropology Today* 16 (2): 7–12.

Lane, E.W. [1863] 1984. *Arabic-English Lexicon*. Vols. 1–2. Reprint, Cambridge: The Islamic Texts Society.

Larkin, Margaret. 1995. *The Theology of Meaning : 'Abd al-Qahir al-Jurjani's Theory of Discourse*. New Haven, Conn.: American Oriental Society.

Latour, Bruno. 1993. *We Have Never Been Modern*. Cambridge, Mass.: Harvard University Press.

Leclercq, Jean. 1961. *Love of Learning and the Desire for God*. New York: Fordham University Press.

Lee, Tong Soon. 2003. "Technology and the Production of Islamic Space: The Call to Prayer in Singapore." In *Music and Technoculture*, ed. Rene Lysloff and Leslie Gay, 109–24. Middletown, Conn.: Wesleyan University Press.

Lerner, Daniel. 1958. *The Passing of Traditional Society: Modernizing the Middle East.* New York: Free Press.

Lewisohn, Leonard. 1997. "The Sacred Music of Islam: Sama' in the Persian Sufi Tradition." *British Journal of Ethnomusicology* 6:1–33.

al-Liwa' al-Islami. 1996. "Ma ibtalait al-'umma bi-'abkhath min bala'iha bi-rijal ad'u al-'ilm faddalu wa addalu." September 12.

MacDonald, Duncan B. 1932. "The Development of the Idea of Spirit in Islam." *The Moslem World* 22:25–42.

MacDonald, John. 1965. "The Twilight of the Dead." *Islamic Studies* 4 (1): 54–102.

MacIntyre, Alasdair. 1984. *After Virtue.* Notre Dame, Ind.: University of Notre Dame Press.

Madi, Jamal. 1995. *al-Da'wa al-mu'athira.* Mansura, Egypt: Mutabi' al-wafa'.

Madigan, Daniel. 1995. "Reflections on Some Current Directions in Quranic Studies." *The Muslim World* 85 (3/4): 345–62.

Mahfuz, 'Ali. 1979. *Hidayat al-murshidin 'ila turuq al-wa'z wa al-khataba.* Cairo: Dar al-i'tisam.

——. 1984. *Fann al-khataba wa i'dad al-khatib.* Cairo: Dar al-i'tisam.

al-Mahlawi, Ahmed. n.d. *Khutab al-Shaykh Ahmed al-Mahlawi, juz' al-thani.* Cairo: Dar al-i'tisam.

Mahmood, Saba. 2001. "Feminist Theory, Embodiment, and the Docile Agent: Some Reflections on the Egyptian Islamic Revival." *Cultural Anthropology* 6 (2): 202–36.

——. 2004. *Politics of Piety: The Islamic Revival and the Feminist Subject.* Princeton, N.J.: Princeton University Press.

——. 2006. "Secularism, Hermeneutics, Empire: The Politics of Islamic Reformation." *Public Culture* 18 (2): 323–47.

Mahmud, Abd al-Halim. 1986. *Fatawa al-Imam 'Abd al-Halim Mahmud.* Cairo: Dar al-ma'rif.

Makhluf, Shaykh Hasnain Muhammed. 1950. "Salat al-jum'a khalf al-mudhia' ghayr ja'iza." In *al-Fatawa al-islamiyya.* al-Azhar. Cairo: al-Majlis al-a'la li al-shu'un al-islamiyya, wizarat al-awqaf.

Manuel, Peter. 1993. *Cassette Culture: Popular Music and Technology in North India.* Chicago: University of Chicago Press.

Marsot, Afaf Lutfi al-Sayyid. 1968. "The Beginnings of Modernization Among the Rectors of al-Azhar, 1798–1879." In *Beginnings of Modernization in the Middle East,* ed. Williams Polk and Richard Chambers. Chicago: University of Chicago Press.

Marty, Martin, and Scott Appleby, eds. 1994. *Fundamentalisms Observed.* Chicago: University of Chicago Press

Massumi, Brian. 2002. *Parables for the Virtual: Movement, Affect, Sensation.* Durham, N.C.: Duke University Press.

McKeon, Richard. 1942. "Rhetoric in the Middle Ages." *Speculum: A Journal of Mediaeval Studies* 17 (1): 1–32.

——. 1987. *Rhetoric: Essay in Invention and Discovery.* Ed. Mark Backman. Woodbridge, Conn.: Ox Bow Press.

Mendel, Miloš. 1995. "The Concept of 'ad-Daʿwa al-Islamiyya': Towards a Discussion of the Islamic Reformist Religio-Political Terminology." *Archiv Orientalni* 63:286–304.

Meschonnic, Henri. 1989. *La Rime et la vie*. Paris: Editions Verdier.

Messick, Brinkley. 1993. *The Calligraphic State: Textual Domination and History in a Muslim Society*. Berkeley: University of California Press.

——. 1997. "Genealogies of Reading and the Scholarly Cultures of Islam." In *Cultures of Scholarship*, ed. S. Humphreys, 387–412. Ann Arbor: University of Michigan Press.

Mew, James. 1892. "The Muslim Hell." *The Nineteenth Century: A Monthly Review* 31:433–54.

Miller, W. Flagg. 2001. "Inscribing the Muse: Political Poetry and the Discourse of Circulation in the Yemeni Cassette Industry." Ph.D. diss., University of Michigan, Ann Arbor.

Mitchell, Richard. 1993. *The Society of the Muslim Brothers*. Oxford: Oxford University Press.

Mitchell, Timothy. 1988. *Colonising Egypt*. New York: Cambridge University Press.

——. 1990. "L'experience de l'emprisonnement dans le discourse islamiste." In *Intellectuels et militants de l'Islam contemporain*, ed. Gilles Kepel and Yann Richard, 193–212. Paris: Editions de Seuil.

——. 2002. *Rule of Experts: Egypt, Technopolitics, Modernity*. Berkeley: University of California Press.

Mohammedi, Annabelle, and Ali Mohammedi. 1994. *Small Media, Big Revolution*. Minneapolis: University of Minnesota Press.

Moussalli, Aḥmad. 1992. *Radical Islamic Fundamentalism: The Ideological and Political Discourse of Sayyid Qutb*. Beirut: American University of Beirut.

Moustafa, Tamir. 2000. "Conflict and Cooperation Between the State and Religious Institutions in Contemporary Egypt." *International Journal of Middle East Studies* 32:3–22.

Muhammad, Ali Rifaʾi. 1972. *Kayfa takun khatib*. Cairo: Maktabat wa matbʿat Muhammed Ali Sabih.

Murdoch, Iris. 1977. *The Fire and the Sun: Why Plato Banished the Artists*. Oxford: Clarendon Press.

Mustafa, Hala. 1995. *Al-Dawla wa al-haraka al-islamiyya al-muʿarida: bayna al-muhadana wa al-muwajaha fi ʿahda al-Sadat wa Mubarak*. Cairo: Markaz al-mahrusa.

Nadim, Abdallah. 1881. "al-Tankit wa al-takbit." *Sihafa wataniyya usbuʿiyya* (Cairo), September 15.

Nancy, Jean-Luc. 2002. *A l'écoute*. Paris: Editions Galilée.

al-Nawawi, Abu Zakariyya Yahya. n.d. *Riyad al-salihin*. Cairo: Dar al-fatha lil-ʿalam al-ʿarabi.

Needham, Rodney, ed. 1973. *Right and Left: Essays on Dual Symbolic Classification*. Chicago: University of Chicago Press.

Nelson, Kristina. 1985. *The Art of Reciting the Quran*. Austin: University of Texas Press.

Newman, John Henry. [1870] 1979. *An Essay in Aid of a Grammar of Assent*. Reprint, Notre Dame, Ind.: University of Notre Dame Press.

Norton, Augustus Richard, ed. 1995. *Civil Society in the Middle East*. Vol. 1. Leiden: E. J. Brill.

Nunberg, Geoffrey. 2004. "Bin Laden's Low-Tech Weapon." *New York Times*, April 18.

Nuttall, Geoffrey. 1992. *The Holy Spirit in Puritan Faith and Experience*. Chicago: University of Chicago Press.

Oakeshott, Michael. 1975. *On Human Conduct*. Oxford: Clarendon Press.

Ong, Aihwa. 2003. *Buddha is Hiding: Refugees, Citizenship, the New America*. Berkeley: University of California Press.

Ong, Walter. 1958. *Ramus, Method, and the Decay of Dialogue*. Cambridge, Mass.: Harvard University Press.

——. 1982. *Orality and Literacy: The Technologization of the Word*. London: Methuen Press.

Onians, Richard. 1951. *The Origins of European Thought: About the Body, the Mind, the Soul, the World, Time, and Fate*. Cambridge: The University Press.

Padwick, Constance. 1996. *Muslim Devotions: A Study of Prayer-Manuals in Common Use*. Oxford: Oneworld Publications.

Palacios, Miguel Asin. 1943. *Escatología Musulmana en la Divina Comedia*. Madrid-Granada: Consejo Superior de Investigaciones Cientificas.

Pandey, Gyanendra. 1998. *Constructions of Communalism in Colonial India*. Oxford: Oxford University Press.

Plutarch. *Plutarch's Essays*. ca. 1881. Troy, N.Y.: Nims and Knight.

Pollard, Arthur. 1963. *English Sermons*. London: Longmans, Green and Co.

al-Qaradawi, Yusuf. 1991. *Thaqafat al-daʿiya*. Cairo: Maktabat al-wahba.

Quijano-Gonzalez, Yves. 1994. "Les Gens du livre, champ intellectuel et édition dans l'Egypte républicaine (1952–1993)." Ph.D. diss., Institut d'études politiques de Paris.

——. 1997. "Une 'Star' islamique des années 1990: Fadilat al-Shaykh Mitwalli al-Shaʿrawi." Paper presented at the conference "Mass Media and the Transformation of Islamic Discourse," International Institute of Asian Studies, Leiden, The Netherlands.

Quintilian. 1963. *Institutio Oratoria of Quintillian*. Trans. H. E. Butler. Cambridge, Mass.: Harvard University Press.

Qureshi, Regula Burckhardt. 1995. "Recorded Sound and Religious Music: The Case of Qawwali." In *Media and the Transformation of Religion in South Asia*, ed. Lawrence A. Babb and Susan S. Wadley, 139–66. Philadelphia: University of Pennsylvania Press.

Qutb, Sayyid. 1993. *al-Taswir al-fanni fi al-Qurʾan*. Cairo: Dar al-maʿarif.

Racy, Ali Jihad. 1982. "Musical Aesthetics in Present-Day Cairo." *Ethnomusicology* 26 (3): 391–406.

——. 1998. "Improvisation, Ecstasy, and Performance Dynamics in Arabic Music." In *In the Course of Performance: Studies in the World of Musical Improvisation*, ed. B. Nettl and M. Russell, 95–112. Chicago: University of Chicago Press.

——. 2003. *Making Music in the Arab World: The Culture and Artistry of Tarab*. Cambridge: Cambridge University Press.

Rajagopal, Arvind. 2001. *Politics After Television: Hindu Nationalism and the Reshaping of the Public in India*. Cambridge: Cambridge University Press.

Rancière, Jacques. 1994. *The Names of History: On the Poetics of Knowledge*. Trans. H. Melehy. Minneapolis: University of Minnesota Press.

Ribot, Th. 1914. *La Vie inconsciente et les mouvements*. Paris: F. Alcon.

Rifaat, Alifa. 1983. *Distant View of a Minaret, and Other Stories*. Trans. Denys Johnson-Davies. New York: Quartet Books.

Riskin, Jessica. 2002. *Science in the Age of Sensibility: The Sentimental Empiricists of the French Enlightenment*. Chicago: University of Chicago Press.

Roach, Joseph. 1993. *The Player's Passion: Studies in the Science of Acting*. Ann Arbor: University of Michigan Press.

Robson, J. 1999. "Hadith." In *The Encyclopedia of Islam*. CD-ROM, version 1.0. Leiden: Brill.

Rogers, Susan. 1986. "Batak Tape Cassette Kinship: Constructing Kinship through the Indonesian National Mass Media." *American Ethnologist* 13 (1): 23–42.

Rouse, Joseph. 1987. *Knowledge and Power: Toward a Political Philosophy of Science*. Ithaca, N.Y.: Cornell University Press.

Roy, Olivier. 1996. *The Failure of Political Islam*. Cambridge, Mass.: Harvard University Press.

——. 2004. *Globalized Islam: The Search for a New Ummah*. New York: Columbia University Press.

Sabiq, al-Sayyid. [1945] 1994. *Fiqh al-sunna*. Vol. 1. Reprint, Cairo: Maktabat al-qahira.

Salvatore, Armando, 1997. *Islam and the Political Discourse of Modernity*. Berkshire, U.K.: Ithaca Press.

——. 1998. "Staging Virtue: The Disembodiment of Self-Correctness and the Making of Islam as Public Norm." In *Bielefeld Yearbook of the Sociology of Islam* 1:87–119.

——. ed. 2001a. *Muslim Traditions and Modern Techniques of Power*. Münster: Lit Verlag.

——. 2001b. "Mustafa Mahmud: A Paradigm of Public Islamic Entrepreneurship?" In *Muslim Traditions and Modern Techniques of Power*, ed. A. Salvatore, 211–23. Münster: Lit Verlag.

Saqr, Abd al-Badi'. 1990a. *Al-Irshad li-l a'ima wa khutaba' wa al-'ubbad*. Cairo: Dar al-i'tisam.

——. 1990b. *Kayfa nad'aw al-nas*. Cairo: Maktabat al-wahba.

——. 1994. *Deciphering the Signs of God: A Phenomenological Approach to Islam*. Albany: State University of New York Press.

Scheper-Hughes, Nancy, and Margaret M. Lock. 1987. "The Mindful Body: A Prolegomenon to Future Work in Medical Anthropology." *Medical Anthropological Quarterly* 1:6–41.

Schmidt, Leigh Eric. 2000. *Hearing Things: Religion, Illusion, and the American Enlightenment.* Cambridge, Mass.: Harvard University Press.

Schulze, Reinhard. 1987. "Mass Culture and Islamic Cultural Production in Nine-
teenth-Century Middle East." In *Mass Culture, Popular Culture, and Social Life in the Middle East*, ed. G. Stauth and S. Zubaida. Boulder, Colo.: Westview Press.

Scott, David. 2005. *Conscripts of Modernity: The Tragedy of Colonial Enlightenment.* Durham, N.C.: Duke University Press.

Sells, Michael. 1999. *Approaching the Qur'an: The Early Revelations.* Ashland, Ore.: White Cloud Press.

Seremetakis, C. Nadia, ed. 1994. *The Senses Still: Perception and Memory as Material Culture in Modernity.* Boulder, Colo.: Westview Press.

Shahine, Gihan. 2005. "What Copts Fear?" *Al-Ahram Weekly.* December 8–14.

Shannon, Jonathan. 2003. "Emotion, Performance, and Temporality in Arab Music: Reflections on Tarab." *Cultural Anthropology* 18 (1): 72–98.

Sherif, Mohamed Ahmed. 1975. *Ghazali's Theory of Virtue.* Albany: State University of New York Press.

al-Shernubi, Abd al-Majid. n.d. *Diwan khutab al-shernubi.* Cairo: Maktabat al-
qahira.

Shiloah, Amnon. 1963. *Charactéristiques de l'art vocale arabe au moyen age.* Tel Aviv: Israeli Music Institute.

Shusterman, Richard. 2002. "Wittgenstein's Somaesthetics: Body Feeling in Philosophy of Mind, Art, and Ethics." *Revue internationale de philosophie* 219:91–108.

Sienaert, Edgard R. 1990. "Marcel Jousse: The Oral Style and the Anthropology of Gesture." *Oral Tradition* 5 (1): 91–106.

Sivan, Emmanuel. 1990. "The Islamic Resurgence: Civil Society Strikes Back." *Journal of Contemporary History* 25 (3): 353–64.

——. 1995. "Eavesdropping on Radical Islam." *Middle East Quarterly* 2 (1): 13–24.

Skinner, Quentin. 1997. *Liberty Before Liberalism.* Cambridge: Cambridge University Press.

Skovgaard-Petersen, Jakob. 1997. *Defining Islam for the Egyptian State: Muftis and Fatwas of the Dar al-Ifta.* Leiden: Brill.

Smith, Bruce. 1999. *The Acoustic World of Early Modern England: Attending to the O-Factor.* Chicago: Chicago University Press.

Smith, Jane I. 1979. "The Understanding of Nafs and Ruh in Contemporary Muslim Considerations of the Nature of Sleep and Death." *The Muslim World* 69 (3): 151–61.

——. 1980. "Concourse Between the Living and the Dead in Islamic Eschatological Literature." *History of Religions* 19 (3): 224–236.

Smith, Jane I., and Yvonne Y. Haddad. 1979. "Afterlife Themes in Modern Quranic Commentary." *Journal of the American Academy of Religion* 47 (4): 699–720.

———. 1981. *The Islamic Understanding of Death and Resurrection.* Albany: State University of New York Press.

Smith, Sylvia. 2005. "Cairo Dilemma Over Calls to Prayer." *BBC News*, April 29, Internet edition.

Smith, Wilfred Cantwell. 1981. *On Understanding Islam.* The Hague: Mouton Publishers.

Smyth, William. 1992. "Rhetoric and ʿIlm al-Balagha: Christianity and Islam." *The Muslim World* 82 (3/4): 242–55.

Starrett, Gregory. 1995a. "The Hexis of Interpretation: Islam and the Body in the Egyptian Popular School." *American Ethnologist* 22 (4): 953–69.

———. 1995b. "The Political Economy of Religious Commodities in Cairo." *American Anthropologist* 97 (1): 51–68.

———. 1998. *Putting Islam to Work: Education, Politics, and Religious Transformation in Egypt.* Berkeley: University of California Press.

Stein, Alexander. 1999. "Well-Tempered Bagatelles—a Mediation on Listening in Psychoanalysis and Music." *American Imago* 56 (4): 387–416.

St. John, James Augustus. 1845. *Egypt and Nubia.* London: Chapman and Hall.

Stokes, Martin. In press. "Abd al-Halim's Microphone." In *Music and the Play of Power: Music, Politics, and Ideology in the Middle East, North Africa, and Central Asia*, ed. Laudan Nooshin. London: Ashgate Press.

Stoller, Paul. 1997. *Sensuous Scholarship.* Philadelphia: University of Pennsylvania Press.

Stout, Jeffrey. 2004. *Democracy and Tradition.* Princeton, N.J.: Princeton University Press.

Street, Brian. 1993. *Cross-Cultural Approaches to Literacy.* Cambridge: Cambridge University Press.

Tahtawi, Ahmad. n.d. *al-Qabr: ʿAzabuhu wa naʿimuhu.* Cairo: Maktaba al- Qurʾan.

Taylor, Jeremy. [1651] 1989. *The Rule and Exercises of Holy Dying.* Ed. P. G. Stanwood. Oxford: Clarendon Press.

Taussig, Michael. 1993. *Mimesis and Alterity: A Particular History of the Senses.* London: Routledge.

Tedlock, Dennis. 1983. *The Spoken Word and the Work of Interpretation.* Philadelphia: University of Pennsylvania Press.

Todorov, Tzvetan. 1982. *Theories of the Symbol.* Trans. Catherine Porter. Ithaca, N.Y.: Cornell University Press.

Tritton, A. S. 1971. "Man, Nafs, Ruh, ʾAql." *Bulletin of the School of Oriental and African Studies*, 34:491–95.

Turner, Bryan. 1994. *Orientalism, Postmodernism, and Globalism.* London: Routledge.

Voll, John. 1983. "Renewal and Reform in Islamic History: Tajdid and Islah." In *Voices of Resurgent Islam*, ed. John L. Esposito, 32–47. Oxford: Oxford University Press.

———. 1991. "Fundamentalism in the Sunni Arab World: Egypt and the Sudan." In *Fundamentalisms Observed*, ed. Martin Marty and Scott Appleby, 345–402. Chicago: University of Chicago Press.

Waardenburg, Jacques. 1995. "The Da'wa of Islamic Movements." In *Actas, XVI Congreso Union Européenne d'arabisants et d'islamisants*. Salamanca, AECI/CSIC/ UEAI, 539–49.

Wagdi, Muhammad. 1995. "Mu'jizat al-Quran: lafziyya aydan!" *al-Sha'b*. Februrary 21.

Wainwright, William. 1995. *Reason and the Heart: A Prolegomenon to a Critique of Passional Reason*. Ithaca, N.Y.: Cornell University Press.

Warner, Michael. 1990. *The Letters of the Republic: Publication and the Public Sermon in Eighteenth-Century America*. Cambridge, Mass.: Harvard University Press.

——. 2002. *Publics and Counterpublics*. New York: Zone Books.

Wensinck, A. J. 1979. "Khutba." In *Encyclopedia of Islam*. Leiden: E. J. Brill.

Wicks, Jared. 1998. "Applied Theology at the Deathbed: Luther and the Late-Medieval Tradition of the Ars Moriendi." *Gregorianum* 79 (2): 345–68.

Wilberg, Peter. 2004. "Charging the Question: Listening, Questioning, and the Counseling Dialogue." http://www.meaningofdepression.com/Charging%20The%20Question.doc.

Williams, Bernard. 1985. *Ethics and the Limits of Philosophy*. London: Fontana.

Winter, T. J. 1989. Introduction to *The Remembrance of Death and the Afterlife (kitab dhikr al-mawt wa ma ba'dahu): Book Forty of the Revival of the Religious Sciences (ihya' 'ulum al-din)*, by Abu Hamid al-Ghazali, trans. T. J. Winter, xiii–xxx. Cambridge, U.K.: Islamic Texts Society.

Wittgenstein, Ludwig. 1958. *Philosophical Investigations*. Vol. 3. Trans. G. E. M. Anscombe. New York: Macmillan.

Wockner, Cindy. 2004. "Converting Good Men into Killers." *Daily Telegraph* (Sydney), October 9

Wolin, Sheldon. 1996. "Fugitive Democracy." In *Democracy and Difference: Contesting the Boundaries of the Political*, ed. Seyla Benhabib, 31–45. Princeton, N.J.: Princeton University Press.

Zeghal, Malika. 1996. *Gardiens de l'Islam: Les oulémas d'al Azhar dans l'Égypte contemporaine*. Paris: Presses de Sciences Politiques.

——. 1999. "Religion and Politics in Egypt: The Ulema of al-Azhar, Radical Islam, and the State (1952–1994)." *International Journal of Middle East Studies* 31 (3): 371–99.

Zbikowski, Lawrence M. 1998. "Metaphor and Music Theory: Reflections from Cognitive Science." *Music Theory Online* 4 (1).

Zulick, Margaret. 1992. "The Active Force of Hearing: The Ancient Hebrew Language of Persuasion." *Rhetorica* 10 (4): 367–380.

Zumthor, Paul. 1990. *Oral Poetry: An Introduction*. Trans. Kathryn Murphy-Judy. Minneapolis: University of Minnesota Press.

INDEX

relations with the press, 11; use of sermons, 42–46, 49–50

El-Saadawi, Nawal, 125

eschatology. *See* death

ethical listening, 32–39, 75, 103; and cassette sermons, 10, 22–3, 69–74, 89–92, 95–96, 100–101; Islamic traditions of, 37, 63; and the public sphere, 107, 121; and the Quran, 37; techniques of, 69–71, 75, 80–87, 90–92, 100–101

ethical affects: *inshirah* (opening of the heart), 68, 72, 76, 92, 96, 194; *khawf* (virtuous fear), 68, 73–74, 90, 94–96, 132, 149, 181, 193–94; *khushu'* (humility), 42, 68, 70, 74, 82, 90, 149–50; 194; *nadam* (repentance), 68, 74, 194; *sakina* (tranquility), 72, 74, 92; *taqwa* (virtuous fear), 42, 70, 73–74, 82, 90, 95–96, 132, 134, 165, 182

Feld, Steven, 30

Foucault, Michel, 5, 39, 83, 139, 177, 202, 215n.1

Fraser, Nancy, 232n.3

Freud, Sigmund, 22

fundamentalism, 3–4, 108, 205–7; 209, 244–45n.1

funeral rites, 181–82, 195–96

Gaffney, Patrick, 216n.9, 237n.1

al-Ghazali, Abu Hamid, 35, 80–81, 100, 173, 201–2

al-Ghazali, Muhammad, 58, 61

gender: and the *da'wa* movement, 110–11; as sermon topic, 111

Ghunaim, Wagdi, 59, 132, 147, 191–92

governmentality, 5, 137, 139, 237n.46

hadith, 69; meaning of, 143, 223n.27; use in sermons, 145–47, 165; use in daily conversation, 109, 111, 119–20

Hadot, Pierre, 201

Hafiz, Abd al-Halim, 52, 122

al-Haqq, Ali Jad, 31

Hassan, Muhammad, 92–94, 122, 144–47, 169–70, 193; analysis of sermons of, 93–94, 127, 146–47, 170–72, 230n.23

Humaydi, Isma'il, analysis of sermons of, 197–200, 244n.27

Huwaidi, Fahmi, 209

i'jaz al-qur'an (inimitability of the Quran), 33–34, 152, 154–55, 219n.2

'ilm al-balagha (art of eloquence), 36, 40, 47

'ilm al-khataba (rhetoric), 219n.3

inshirah (opening of the heart), 68, 72, 76, 92, 96, 194

Islamic Revival, 2, 55, 205–7; and cassette sermons, 2–3, 6–7, 10, 59, 71; and Christianity, 207–11; critique of authority of, 59; and *da'wa*, 113, 207; democratic aspects of, 5–6, 117, 139–42, 209; economic aspects of, 94, 128–29; fundamentalism in relation to, 205–7; institutional basis, 56, 128; and modernity, 206; and nationalism, 113, 140–41; origins in Egypt, 56; political aspects of, 5–8, 56, 136–37, 140–41, 212; and popular media, 114, 127, 137–38, 193–94; and social class, 6, 71, 206; women in, 111; and youth culture, 7, 67–68, 111. *See also under* cassette sermons

Jousse, Marcel, 67, 76–79, 82, 84, 87, 97, 101–3, 124, 227n.5, 231n.33

al-Jurjani, Abd al-Qahir, 33–34

Kant, Immanuel, 13–14

Keane, Webb, 226n.51

khatib (preacher), (*khutaba'*, pl), 12; accessibility, 146–47; bureaucratization, 43–47, 50, 58; and ethical preaching, 47–48; historical role, 39, 43–47, 222–23n.26; as media figure, 138, 145–46; as mediator of God,